W9-AZX-066

Mack

Elusive Equity

Elusive Equity

Education Reform in Post-Apartheid South Africa

Edward B. Fiske   **Helen F. Ladd**

BROOKINGS INSTITUTION PRESS
Washington, D.C.

ABOUT BROOKINGS

The Brookings Institution is a private nonprofit organization devoted to research, education, and publication on important issues of domestic and foreign policy. Its principal purpose is to bring knowledge to bear on current and emerging policy problems. The Institution maintains a position of neutrality on issues of public policy. Interpretations or conclusions in Brookings publications should be understood to be solely those of the authors.

Copyright © 2004 Edward B. Fiske and Helen F. Ladd

All rights reserved. No part of this publication may be reproduced or transmitted in any form or by any means without permission in writing from the Brookings Institution Press, 1775 Massachusetts Avenue, N.W., Washington, D.C. 20036 (fax: 202/797-6195 or e-mail: permissions@brookings.edu).

Library of Congress Cataloging-in-Publication data

Fiske, Edward B.
    Elusive equity : education reform in post-apartheid South Africa / Edward B. Fiske and Helen F. Ladd.
        p.   cm.
    Includes bibliographical references and index.
    ISBN 0-8157-2840-9 (cloth : alk. paper)
    1. Educational equalization—South Africa.   2. Education and state—South Africa.
3. Educational change—South Africa.   4. Discrimination in education—South Africa—Prevention.   I. Ladd, Helen F.   II. Title.
    LC213.3.S6F57   2004
    379.2'6'0968—dc22   2004011355

9 8 7 6 5 4 3 2 1

The paper used in this publication meets minimum requirements of the American National Standard for Information Sciences—Permanence of Paper for Printed Library Materials: ANSI Z39.48-1992.

Typeset in Sabon

Composition by Betsy Kulamer
Washington, D.C.

Printed by R. R. Donnelley
Harrisonburg, Virginia

To Connor, Elijah, Devin, Myah,
Jude, Margaret, and Lilly with love

Contents

Preface

This book tells the story of South Africa's efforts to fashion a racially equitable state education system out of the ashes of apartheid—a story that is both significant and compelling. South Africa captured the imagination of the world when it succeeded, in 1994, in transferring political power from the white minority to the black majority without massive bloodshed. In part because of the heroic figure of Nelson Mandela, who emerged from twenty-seven years as a political prisoner to become the first president of the new democracy, South Africa became a global symbol of the struggle for human rights and racial equity.

Remarkable as it was, the successful transfer of political power from white to black hands was only a first step toward the construction of a strong, multiracial, and sustainable social order. South Africa's fledgling democracy also required new institutional structures built on the values embodied in the country's progressive new constitution, which guarantees equal rights for all South Africans.

Reform of the state education system exemplifies this broader transformation process under way in South Africa in the post-1994 period. The new government inherited a system designed to further the goals of apartheid, one that lavished human and financial resources on schools serving white students while systematically starving those with African, coloured, and Indian learners. Its task was to transform this system into one that reflected the values of the new democracy and to do so in a political and social context shaped by the historical legacy of apartheid, the nature of the power sharing that emerged from the negotiated settlement, and severe limitations on financial and human resources.

The story of education reform in post-apartheid South Africa is also important because it was driven by a quest for equity and fairness. The concept of educational equity is attracting growing attention in political debates around the globe. Equity is the underlying basis for the Education for All movement, coordinated by the United Nations Educational, Scientific, and Cultural Organization (UNESCO), that was initiated with a major world conference in Jomtien, Thailand, in 1990 and that held a ten-year follow-up conference in Dakar, Senegal, in 2000.

Finally, South Africa's experience is compelling because of the magnitude and starkness of the initial disparities and of the changes required. Few, if any, new democratic governments have had to work with an education system as egregiously—and intentionally—inequitable as the one that the apartheid regime bequeathed to the new black-run government in 1994. Thanks to the apartheid system, the socially constructed racial classifications were so clearly delineated that they can provide a firm basis for evaluating movement toward racial equity. Moreover, few governments have ever assumed power with as strong a mandate to work for racial justice. Thus the South African experience offers an opportunity to examine in bold relief the possibilities and limitations of achieving a racially equitable education system in a context where such equity is a prime objective.

We conclude that South Africa has made significant progress toward equity in education defined as equal treatment of persons of all races— an achievement for which it deserves great praise. For reasons that we explore, however, the country has been less successful in promoting equity, defined either as equal educational opportunity for students of all races or as educational adequacy. Thus educational equity has, to date, been elusive.

Our research examines education reform efforts through 2002, which is eight years after the end of the apartheid system. Since this is a very short period, far too short for a thorough overhaul of the system, education reform in South Africa is still very much a work in progress. Nonetheless, much has already been changed and much accomplished. If only because South Africans are in a hurry to make things work, it is reasonable to take stock of the country's progress at this time.

The Nature of Our Research

Education policy in post-apartheid South Africa has been the topic of numerous excellent articles and books, many of them published by researchers and organizations deeply involved in the struggle against apartheid and in the post-1994 education reform process. Among these organizations are the Center for Education Policy Development, Evaluation and Management in Johannesburg; Education Policy Units at various South African universities; the Education Foundation; and the Joint Education Trust. In addition, academics at universities throughout the country have contributed significantly to the literature on education reform in South Africa.

As a husband-wife team who spent the first six months of 2002 in South Africa, we have benefited greatly both from the published work of the analysts associated with these and other organizations and from the time that many of them have spent sharing their views with us in person. Though we cannot claim to have the insight that many of them possess from their years of direct experience in South Africa, we bring the independence and objectivity of informed outsiders and, we hope, the skills required to do justice to the complex story of educational transformation in South Africa.

One of us is an academic economist and policy analyst who has written widely on education reform in the United States. Her statistical skills are in evidence throughout the book in the analysis of trends and patterns across South Africa as well as in more detailed analysis of school-level data within provinces. The other is an education journalist who covered education reform in the United States in his capacity as education editor of the *New York Times* through 1991 and who since then has written extensively about education reform in developing countries. His observational and reporting skills are reflected in insights from principals and other school personnel as well as from his accounts of how various reform measures played out in schools. Together we perused policy documents, surveyed the academic literature, and interviewed academic experts and policymakers. These unstructured interviews, conducted between February and July 2002, were designed to broaden our understanding of the purposes of various policies as well as of the challenges that arose in their implementation.

For the benefit of international readers, we have included a chapter on the country's complex racial history and one on the role of education during apartheid. This history is essential as context for understanding the legacy of apartheid and how it shaped the country's efforts to transform its education system. For both international and South African readers, our primary contribution is to structure the discussion and detailed empirical analysis of the post-apartheid education reforms around three concepts of educational equity: equal treatment, equal educational opportunity, and educational adequacy. Although South African policy documents and discussions do not always refer to equity in these specific terms, they provide a powerful and useful analytical framework for understanding both the ways in which educational equity has been furthered and the ways in which it has remained elusive.

Acknowledgments

We express our deep appreciation to the institutions and people who made it possible for us to live in South Africa from January to July 2002 and who made that time so rewarding and productive. We are particularly grateful to the Fulbright Association, which provided a lecturing and research grant to Helen Ladd. We were based in the School of Economics of the University of Cape Town (UCT), and we are grateful to the faculty and administrators who became our friends and colleagues and who did so much to facilitate our work. Special thanks are due to Murray Leibbrandt, director of the School of Economics. We are also grateful to the Spencer Foundation, which provided additional research support. We thank participants in seminars that we presented at UCT and the University of Stellenbosch for their valuable feedback on early versions of our research. In addition, we benefited from comments on an earlier version of chapter 6 that we presented at an international education conference in Johannesburg in the summer of 2002 and on an earlier version of chapter 7 on school fees that will appear in a volume edited by Linda Chisholm and published by the Human Sciences Research Council.

We were fortunate to have access to policymakers throughout the state education system. We are particularly grateful to Peter Present, director of research at the Western Cape Education Department, who provided us with extensive school-level data from the Western Cape and was generous with his time and wisdom. We are also indebted to Riaan van Rensburg of the Eastern Cape Education Department, who provided the EMIS data for that province. At the national level, we met with Minister of Education Kader Asmal, who in addition to giving us time from his busy schedule was instrumental in arranging conversations with some of his top advisers. In addition, we appreciate the time and feedback from education and social policy experts at the Treasury, including John Kruger and Andrew Donaldson.

We are deeply indebted to the scores of South Africans, including researchers, policymakers, school principals, and vice chancellors of universities and technikons, who shared their time, data, and experiences with us. Among this group a few should be singled out: John Pampallis for his wisdom, contacts, and advice and for reviewing the draft manuscript; Linda Chisholm for her help with the curriculum chapter and comments on the fees chapter; Ian Bunting of UCT for sharing his data and expertise on higher education; Johan Muller, Nick Taylor, and Penny Vinjevold for their willingness to discuss the findings and conclusions of their own extensive education research; and Servaas van der Berg from Stellenbosch University, whose empirical research inspired some of our work. We are indebted to Tania Ajam, Luis Crouch, Brahm Fleisch, Jonathan Jansen, Lorraine Lawrence, Brian O'Connell, Bobby Soobrayan, and Derrick Swartz, among many others too numerous to mention. To all of them we offer our thanks.

No project of this scale can ever be completed without the help of dedicated research assistants. We are particularly grateful to our two South African assistants: Steven Kent, who did much of the school-level analysis, and Richard Walker, who helped with the provincial and higher-education data. At Duke University, we benefited from the assistance of Karin Ward, Sandeep Bhattacharya, and Alicia Groh. In addition, we are grateful to two Duke colleagues, William Darity and Allen Buchanan, both of whom read and critiqued the full manuscript. Their contributions are larger than they know.

Finally, we offer our thanks to Christopher Kelaher, Robert Faherty, Janet Walker, and others at Brookings Institution Press who shepherded this book through to publication. These include Vicky Macintyre, who edited this volume; Carlotta Ribar, who provided proofreading services; and Robert Elwood, who indexed the pages.

Elusive Equity

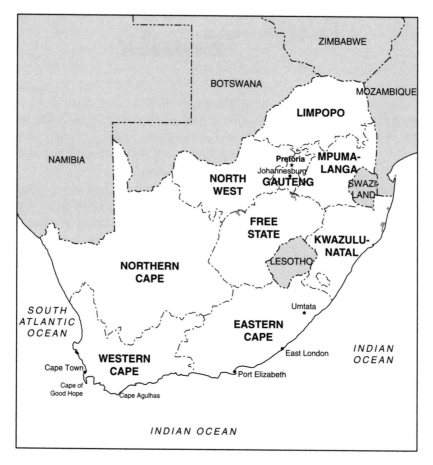

South Africa

one   Introduction

In 1953 the South African minister of native affairs, Hendrik Verwoerd, took the floor of Parliament in Cape Town to make the case for legislation restricting the quality of schools serving Africans. "Racial relations cannot improve if the wrong type of education is given to Natives," he declared. "They cannot improve if the result of Native education is the creation of frustrated people who, as a result of the education they received, have expectations in life which circumstances in South Africa do not allow to be fulfilled immediately."[1] The Afrikaner-dominated Parliament accepted Verwoerd's arguments and approved the Bantu Education Act of 1953, which asserted government control of church-run schools and forbade African teachers from criticizing the government or school authorities.

Fast forward to May 10, 1994. In a dramatic ceremony witnessed by an estimated 1 billion television viewers around the world, an African, Nelson Mandela, stood outside the Union Buildings in Pretoria and took the oath of office as the first president of a democratic South Africa. Marking as it did the orderly transfer of political power from white to black control, Mandela's inauguration was an extraordinary moment in modern history. In his address Mandela laid out a vision of a new South Africa that would "reinforce humanity's belief in justice, strengthen its confidence in the nobility of the human soul and sustain all our hopes

1. Sparks (1990, p. 196).

1

for a glorious life for all."[2] Significantly, the constitution of the new nation, adopted on an interim basis in 1993 and given final approval in 1996, guaranteed to South Africans of all races "the right to a basic education, including adult education."

The contrast between the repressive educational vision of Verwoerd and the idealism of Mandela and the new constitution could not be more striking. The approach articulated by Verwoerd, who would go on to serve as prime minister from 1958 to 1966 and become a personal symbol of apartheid, was a cornerstone of the apartheid era, which started when the National Party took power in 1948 and lasted more than four decades. The social, economic, and political system of apartheid was self-consciously racist and unequal. Starting from the tradition of racial segregation present in South Africa throughout the colonial period, apartheid systematically expanded and enforced the privileges of white South Africans, who in 1993 accounted for less than 12 percent of the population, at the expense of the black majority. Under apartheid, white people enjoyed good education, ready employment, and, through racially exclusive democratic structures, a sense of control of their individual and collective destinies. In contrast, black people—a group that included Africans, coloureds, and Indians—lived in an essentially totalitarian and dehumanizing environment in which their every move was restricted, education and vocational opportunities were severely circumscribed, and they were reminded daily, in big ways and little, of their relative powerlessness.[3]

The apartheid system began to crumble in the mid-1980s because of increasingly effective mass resistance within South Africa, economic circumstances, and international pressure, including the imposition of economic sanctions. In January 1994, after several years of protracted negotiations between the government and leaders of the black liberation movement, South African voters of all races went to the polls in the country's first truly democratic elections. Thus began the ambitious task of transforming the rigid and inequitable political, economic, and social structures fashioned during the apartheid era into a democratic society offering South Africans of all races the opportunity to participate as citi-

2. Sampson (1999, pp. 485–86).

3. In keeping with general practice, we use the term "black" to refer collectively to Africans, coloureds, and Indians. We discuss these groups later in the chapter and examine their origins in chapter 2.

zens, workers, and fulfilled individuals. Crucial to this task was major reform of the education system.

Purpose of This Book

During its more than four decades in power, the National Party relied heavily on the state education system to promote and sustain the values of apartheid and to keep the black population in check. Under apartheid, all aspects of education—governance, funding, professional training, and curriculum—were defined and operated along racial lines in an egregiously unequal manner.

The system was run by fifteen separate departments of education, some of which served African, coloured, Indian, or white students in the country's urban areas; others served Africans in the homelands and self-governing territories.[4] Schools for white students were funded generously, while those for black students were systematically denied adequate facilities, textbooks, and quality teachers. At the height of apartheid, per pupil spending in white schools was ten times that in the African schools. Even after a significant increase in spending on behalf of black students during the waning years of apartheid, spending on white students remained two and a half times that of African students in urban areas and three and a half that of African students in most of the homelands.[5] Education was compulsory only for white students, and the education for blacks was designed to reflect the view, as Verwoerd put it in his 1953 address to Parliament, that blacks should not rise "above the level of certain forms of labour."[6]

Just as a racially delineated education system had been central to the maintenance of apartheid, a completely new education system that eliminated all vestiges of racial inequity would be essential for the creation and functioning of a democratic South Africa. The purpose of this book is to describe the country's post-apartheid strategies for transforming its education system in the context of the nation's history and to evaluate their success in promoting a more racially equitable system. We focus mainly on the school sector and examine policies related to governance, funding,

4. Some people refer to nineteen separate education departments. See footnote 11 in chapter 3 for an explanation of the discrepancy.
5. Hunter Report (1995, p. 15).
6. Mandela (1994, p. 167).

and curriculum. These strategies included the establishment of a single national department of education, efforts to equalize resources across provinces and schools, and the introduction of a new curriculum. In addition, we devote one chapter to the transformation of higher education.

Our focus on the racial dimension of educational equity reflects the country's long history of racial segregation and inequity not only during the apartheid era but also in the colonial period that preceded it. To be sure, other dimensions of educational equity, most notably gender equity, are also of current policy concern in South Africa, but they are not the subject of this book. From a policy perspective, racial equity is the overriding issue, given the racial structure of South Africa's education system during apartheid.

The most natural racial categories to employ for such analysis are the four used by the apartheid system—African, coloured, Indian, and white—and those are the ones appearing most frequently in this book. We understand, however, that not everyone is comfortable with these categories.[7] Some would prefer to eschew all racial classification for fear their use, even by researchers, may lend legitimacy to racial labels that for many purposes are and should be irrelevant. Others would prefer an inclusive category for the three nonwhite groups. We agree that such a category can be useful and, consistent with common practice, adopt the term "blacks" to describe them. The term "whites" refers collectively to English and Afrikaners.

Terminology aside, it is important to remember that the four categories are socially constructed and thus are not meaningful in any fundamental sense. As we show in chapter 2, the various ethnic and racial groups are by no means culturally or politically homogeneous. Coloureds can be Muslims or Christians. Whites include both the Afrikaners of Dutch ancestry and the English—two groups that have very different cultural heritages and speak different languages. Africans come from a wide variety of geographic and tribal backgrounds and speak dozens of languages. The only reason that these entities became distinct racial groups was that the apartheid system treated them as such.[8] But it is exactly the social construction of race that is relevant for

7. See, for example, the discussion of racial terminology in Vally and Dalamba (1999, sec. 2).

8. See chapters 2 and 3 for descriptions of efforts during apartheid to differentiate the groups into smaller ethnolinguistic groups by moving large numbers of Africans with similar tribal or other backgrounds into "homelands" and through language policies in the schools.

the analysis in this book. It is because the apartheid system classified South Africans into four distinct racial categories and used these distinctions to differentiate the rights and opportunities of various individuals and groups that the four categories are so relevant for our analysis of the extent to which the country has moved toward a more racially equitable system.

We undertake our evaluation with a sense of awe at the progress that South Africa has made, tempered by recognition that the country still has a long way to go to create a racially equitable education system consistent with the goals and values of its new democracy. Our research covers the period of the early 1990s through 2002. In that year South Africa was only eight years into its new democracy (or six years if one dates it from the final approval of the constitution). This is a very short period—much too short for a fundamental transformation of the system. Nonetheless, because much has been changed and much has been accomplished—and because South Africa is in a hurry to make things work—it is reasonable to take stock of the country's progress at this time. The reader should be aware, however, that education reform is still very much a work in progress. Policy debates are ongoing over fundamental issues relating to school finance and the high cost of schooling to parents, school governance, the relationship of education and poverty, and the restructuring of tertiary education.

Racial Equity in Education

We evaluate South Africa's reform strategies using three standards of racial equity: equal treatment, equal educational opportunity, and educational adequacy. These concepts come from a rich philosophical tradition as well as the international literature on education reform. Although South African policy documents and discussions do not always refer to equity in these specific terms, they provide a useful framework for analyzing the country's progress toward a more racially equitable system.

Equal Treatment

Equal treatment, which can also be described as "race-blindness," means that no one should be treated differently simply because of his or her race. A racially equitable education system would be one in which race played no explicit role in the decisions made by any of its officials.

Thus equal treatment would rule out racially discriminatory school admissions policies, and it would require that school funding formulas not make distinctions between schools on the basis of their learners' race.[9] Such an approach is generally consistent with philosopher John Rawls's first principle of justice: namely, that each person has an equal right to a fully adequate scheme of equal basic liberties where basic liberty in this context includes the right to be treated as an individual rather than as a member of a racial group.[10]

In a country such as South Africa, with its long history of discrimination against blacks, one can understand the appeal of race-blind treatment as an equity standard for education. The new constitution, adopted in interim form in 1993 and in final form in 1996, rests on principles of equality. According to its bill of rights, "Everyone is equal before the law and has the right to equal protection and benefit of the law."[11] Further, equality includes "the full and equal enjoyment of all rights and freedoms."[12] Basic education is explicitly included among those rights, and the adoption of race-blind policies in the delivery of education would send a clear signal that the racial differentiation that had been the centerpiece of the apartheid system and that had had such devastating consequences for blacks was no longer acceptable.[13] At the societal level, race-blind policies would promote universal human dignity, one of the fundamental values mentioned in the first section of the constitution.

From other perspectives, however, this procedural principle may be deemed morally insufficient. When racial groups start out on an uneven playing field, as they certainly did in South Africa in 1994, equal treatment does not, in and of itself, go far enough.[14] Hampered by decades of underinvestment in school facilities and in the quality of teachers serving black students, uniform funding formulas for current operating spending will not provide the same educational opportunity to black students as to white students. Even if admissions policies no longer

9. South Africans use the terms "learners" and "educators" to refer, respectively, to students and to teachers and school administrators. We will use these terms interchangeably.

10. Rawls (2001, pp. 42–50).

11. South African Constitution, chap. 2, sec. 9 (1).

12. South African Constitution, chap. 2, sec. 9 (2).

13. South African Constitution, chap. 2, sec. 29 (1).

14. A similar argument is made by Glenn Loury (2002) in his discussion of affirmative action in the U.S. context.

explicitly discriminate against students on the basis of their race, black students in South Africa may be differentially excluded from some schools because of the language they speak, their family's poverty and inability to afford school fees, or prohibitive transportation costs. Thus equity defined as equal treatment, important though it may be for symbolic reasons in South Africa, would not move the country very far in terms of the other two standards.

Equal Educational Opportunity

Equal educational opportunity is a broader standard that expands the concept of equal treatment to include the potential for attainment. This concept of equity is consistent with Rawls's second principle of justice, namely, that there should be "fair equality of opportunity" for social and economic advancement.[15] This principle ensures not only that the possibility for such change exists, but also that all persons have a fair chance to attain it.

Given the historical disparities in educational investments by race in South Africa, this equity standard would require, at a minimum, that educational policies be "race aware." Thus a uniform curriculum for all schools would be inequitable if educators in schools serving black students were less qualified to implement it effectively than were educators in white schools. More generally, this standard calls for some affirmative or positive action—or, in the parlance of South African policymakers, "redress"—to counter past educational disadvantage. Such an approach would seem to find support in the constitution, which specifically states that "to promote the achievement of equality, legislative and other measures designed to protect or advance persons, or categories of persons, disadvantaged by unfair discrimination may be taken."[16]

To this end, policies might explicitly target schools or universities on the basis of their racial composition under apartheid. For example, capital funds could be provided for historically impoverished schools in the former homelands, or differentially high funding could be directed to historically black universities. Similar effects might be achieved without specifying racial criteria, perhaps by considering factors related to both race and educational disadvantage, such as poverty. The appeal of such an approach in South Africa is that it would not violate the standard of race-blindness.

15. Rawls (2001, p. 43).
16. South African Constitution, sec. 9 (2).

If defined narrowly as the opportunity to attend a particular school or to receive a certain quality of instruction, equal educational opportunity might be achievable in South Africa, albeit not without large additional expenditure and not within a short period of time. If interpreted more broadly, in the sense of a student's life chances, this equity standard is far too demanding.[17] It would require South African schools to offset all the family, individual, and societal problems that make it more difficult for black than for white students to succeed in school.[18] As we describe in chapters 2 and 3, the racial disparities in family income and educational attainment bequeathed by colonialism and apartheid are huge. It would seem unreasonable to expect the education sector alone to address them. A variety of noneducation policy initiatives would also be needed.

In practice, the test for equal educational opportunity is not a matter of whether the system produces equal educational *outcomes* for students of all races, but whether it eliminates differences in the educational opportunities for students of different races, where opportunities are defined by the quality of the schooling received. Like equal treatment, equal educational opportunity is a distributional standard that judges equity by comparing the opportunities available to members of different groups. It disregards whether educational opportunities provide some threshold level of desirable outcomes. This limitation does not apply to the concept of educational adequacy.

Educational Adequacy

The criterion of adequacy shifts attention to educational outcomes and attention to the minimum acceptable—or *adequate*—level of education. As long as all schools are providing such an education, under this standard it would not be inequitable for some schools to surpass this level.[19]

17. The philosopher Amy Gutmann highlights this criticism of equal opportunity as a prelude to the development of her democratic threshold principle of educational equity. Gutmann (1987, pp. 131–32).

18. Not only would it be costly and difficult, but it could also be undesirable in some situations. In the extreme, such an approach would inject the state education system so far into family matters related to the education of children that it could violate the liberal ideal of family autonomy. Gutmann (1987, p. 132).

19. This concept of educational adequacy forms the basis for many of the recent school finance cases in the United States. For a discussion of the concept as used in those cases and in associated legislation, see Ladd and Hansen (1999), Ladd, Chalk, and Hansen (1999), and Minorini and Sugarman (1999).

The challenge, of course, is to define the threshold level of adequate education. Here the central question becomes: adequate for what? One answer might lie in the Rawlsian concept of primary goods and the notion that every student should attain a minimum set of educational outcomes connected to his or her long-term life chances.[20] Another might draw on philosopher Amy Gutmann's concept of a democratic threshold. In her view, the primary role of education is to promote a democratic society, characterized by deliberative and collective decision-making, and hence the threshold is the level at which a person has the ability to participate effectively in the democratic process.[21]

Combining these two views, we conceive of educational adequacy in the South African context as the education level needed for someone to participate fully in both the political and economic life of the country. Though by no means simple to measure in practice, adequacy so defined takes note of the fact that threshold levels are specific to a given institutional and political context. During apartheid, Africans were not represented in Parliament and, as Verwoerd emphasized in his 1953 speech to this body, were not expected to advance beyond the level of laborer. By this standard, the white rulers concluded that a low level of education for Africans was adequate. However, standards of adequacy are very different in the post-apartheid period. For one thing, all citizens are entitled to participate fully in the new democracy and are thus in need of the skills required for critical and independent thinking. Moreover, because the country's economic vitality depends crucially on its ability to compete in the global knowledge-based economy, a typical worker must have a much higher level of education than in the past. Although the term "educational adequacy" is not normally used in South African discussion, the constitutional guarantee of a basic education is fully consistent with this notion of equity.

Though adequacy may be difficult to measure, educational outcomes declared acceptable for blacks in the past are clearly inadequate by today's standards. Trends in outcome measures for historically disadvantaged racial groups could shed light on the progress South Africa is making in this regard. The trend in school inputs, such as school facilities and quality of teachers in the schools serving previously disadvantaged students, would provide further insight into the current situation.

20. Rawls (2001, pp. 57–61).
21. Gutmann (1997). See also the discussion in Ladd and Hanson (1999, pp. 102–06).

Of course, the adequacy of educational outcomes depends not only on the quantity, nature, and quality of the available resources (such as teachers and textbooks) but also on the efficiency with which those inputs are used and hence on organizational and other factors.

Education Reform in Context

Under South Africa's new constitution, a person has an unqualified right to a basic education. By contrast, rights to other public services, such as health care and welfare, are linked to the availability of resources.[22]

This unconditional right to education in the constitution reflects in part the role that education played in sustaining the apartheid system as well as the importance of students and schools to the internal struggle against that system (see chapter 3). Emphasis on education reform also demonstrates the official commitment to securing basic rights for black students and lends legitimacy to the new government. In addition, a reformed education system would help the government carry out three of its primary social, political, and economic agendas: to meet the basic needs of all citizens, ensure that all citizens can participate fully in the political life of the country, and develop the human resources required to compete effectively in the global economy.

We write this book out of a conviction that education reform is a necessary element of South Africa's transformation into a racially equitable society. That said, education reform has not been its sole concern. Because the apartheid system permeated so thoroughly all aspects of South African life, the new black-run government has faced the simultaneous challenges of forging national unity in Pretoria, mounting a completely new federal system with nine provinces, improving the quality of life for the vast majority of a population that had been systematically impoverished during the colonial and apartheid periods, and positioning the country for full participation in the global economy.

As a result, education has had to compete for resources and attention with these other reform priorities. At the same time, education clearly forms an integral part of these other agendas.

The Social Agenda

When the new government took office, it faced huge social problems. As of 1993, the poverty rate was between 35 and 55 percent, a strik-

22. South African Constitution, secs. 27 and 29.

ingly high rate considering that South Africa's average income placed it among the world's "upper-middle-income countries."[23] Its poor were disproportionately living in rural areas, comprised female-headed households, and were almost 95 percent African. Contributing to the high poverty rates were high rates of unemployment: as of 1998 overall unemployment surpassed 25 percent and jumped to 37.5 percent if those too discouraged to look for work were included. The comparable rates for Africans were 32 and 46 percent, respectively.[24]

As of 1996, almost 40 percent of all households in South Africa had no access to running water, and a similar proportion had no electricity.[25] Even as late as 1999, only 17 percent of African households had flush toilets in their homes. Other problems associated with poverty included family breakdown and migration in search of employment, malnutrition (particularly among children), and the growing devastation caused by HIV/AIDS. According to one estimate, South Africa already had 100,000 AIDS orphans in 1999, and the numbers were expected to grow exponentially. By 2000 one of nine South Africans was infected with the virus. Understandably, the new government had a vast array of urgent social issues on its agenda, ranging from the building of new housing, the extension of electricity, and the development of water policies to the provision of job training and dealing with the HIV/AIDS pandemic.

An improved education system can play an instrumental role in addressing such issues. As attested by economic and sociological research worldwide, educated persons, on average, tend to have higher earnings than persons with less education.[26] Studies in South Africa confirm these patterns. A 1995 national household survey showed, for example, that mean monthly earnings of both African and white males aged thirty to forty-nine were highly positively correlated with years of schooling. The mean monthly earnings of African males who graduated from secondary school were more than twice as high as those of males who only completed primary school.[27] Even the very low levels of skills imparted to African children appear to translate into higher wages when

23. This classification comes from the *World Bank Development Report*, as cited in Wilson (2001, p. 3).
24. South African Institute of Race Relations (2001, p. 217).
25. Except where otherwise noted, the figures in the next two paragraphs are from the South African Institute of Race Relations (2001, pp. 37–41).
26. Hannum and Buchman (2003, p. 8).
27. Anderson, Case, and Lam (2001, p. 53).

they enter the labor force.[28] Moreover, education typically has a generational echo effect in that the children of more educated individuals, especially mothers, tend to be more educated than those with less well-educated parents.

Thus any long-term social strategy to improve the welfare of black South Africans will undoubtedly have to include a strategy for improving the quality of their education. The household survey data just cited also indicate that for any level of schooling, African prime-age males have much lower monthly earnings than white prime-age males and that a major contributor to the differential is far higher rates of unemployment among Africans. This observation highlights the fact that the ability of education policies to raise family income depends crucially on the country's success in reducing the extremely high rates of unemployment, particularly among Africans.

Political Participation

The South African constitution emphasizes that all citizens should be able to participate fully in democracy. Because Africans had been given little real political power under apartheid, the new government needed not only to set up provincial legislatures, municipal governments, and other new structures that would enable participation, but also to ensure that all citizens, including Africans, have the knowledge, ability, and inclination to assume their new roles as active citizens.

After the 1994 election, significant energy was devoted to setting up such institutional structures, as we describe in chapter 4. The country established nine new provinces and set up a complex system of cooperative federalism designed to provide an appropriate balance between provincial and national input into the policymaking process. The provincial legislatures were empowered to make decisions about education, health, and welfare, and the entire system of municipal and local governments had to be restructured, a process that is only now under way.

Education, especially the curriculum, is important for the success of the new political structures. Since the substance of the curriculum imparts the knowledge and skills necessary for participation, it needed to be revised to reflect the new values that define South Africa: it required a nonauthoritarian tone and an emphasis on democratic delivery, critical thinking, and critical inquiry rather than the rote learning of the apartheid era. As we describe in chapter 8, the resultant new cur-

28. Moll (1998).

riculum also promoted democracy by giving individual teachers more responsibility to design their own curriculum.

Economic Development

After a long period of being shunned by much of the international economic community through sanctions and other means, South Africa emerged from the apartheid period wanting to participate as fully as possible in that community. Much has been written about the role of human capital in promoting economic development and growth, especially in the context of an increasingly global economy. Developing countries with ample human capital tend to be in a better position than those without to innovate or to adapt technology from other counties. In addition, a more educated population enables a country to adjust more readily to a world economic system increasingly characterized by rapid flows of international capital. Thus the demands of the global economy put further pressure on South Africa to improve its education system.

Compounding the challenge of improving the quality of education for the existing cohort of school age children was the reality that a large proportion of the adult population was poorly educated. Demands for adult education and training thus competed with demands for investments in the schooling sector. Further, the prediction of economists that more spending on education will increase the productivity of the work force and thereby promote economic development assumes that the formal sector of the economy in question is sufficiently dynamic to expand and thus to absorb additional semi-skilled or skilled workers. If the newly educated are the rural poor with little access to wage employment, however, economic development and greater employment are not assured.[29] At a minimum, a country such as South Africa must combine education with other strategies for expanding the labor market. Even with a dynamic labor market, any benefits in the form of economic growth from investments in additional years of schooling are likely to take many years to emerge.[30]

The Relevance of South Africa's Experience

South Africa's national effort to build an equitable education system is, in and of itself, an inherently interesting and important story. In many

29. Hannum and Buchman (2003) and sources cited therein.
30. Krueger and Lindahl (2001, p. 25). See also Appiah and McMahon (2002).

respects, it is also unique. No other country in modern times has experienced racial segregation and racial inequity in the extreme form known as apartheid. Thus the question arises whether the South African situation is qualitatively different from that of other countries or whether it is simply an extreme example of forces that exist elsewhere.

The South African experience with education reform is of interest to other countries precisely because of the magnitude of the apartheid-era disparities and the resulting need for bold policy strategies. Bold strategies facilitate the social scientist's task of observing and analyzing inevitable tensions and trade-offs. Moreover, as in other areas of modern life, the urgent issues confronting educators today transcend national borders, as do possible solutions.

Indeed, the South African experience is relevant to other countries for a number of reasons:

—Educational equity is a topic of widespread political concern internationally. Post-apartheid school reform in South Africa serves as a natural experiment in which equity is a primary goal—a priority that stands in refreshing contrast to market-driven models that dominate so much of the educational discourse around the world.

—The distinction between race-blind policies and more interventionist policies designed to promote equality of educational opportunity by race is central to policy debates about racial equity in all countries. Seeing how this distinction plays out in terms of education reform in South Africa helps to clarify and inform the situation in other countries where the historical legacy may be less clear.

—South Africa's efforts to promote equity are taking place in the context of a restrictive economic policy dictated in part by global pressures, international institutions, and international comparisons. This case study illustrates how global pressures can restrict the actions of a developing country. Moreover, because of those constraints, South Africa's experience demonstrates the limits of what can be done without additional resources.

—Like many other countries, South Africa was forced to make difficult decisions about the relative roles of public and private resources in the funding of its schools. The path it chose—the use of school fees in public schools to keep parents from exiting to the private sector—is of potential interest to other countries.

—The South African experience illustrates the tension between the political need for quick results and the reality that education is a process that plays itself out over time. Although one can understand the country's preoccupation with the matriculation pass rate or with the rapid introduction of a new curriculum, for example, true progress toward racial equity requires attention to more fundamental aspects of the education system that may not generate returns for many years.

Our Analysis

Crucial to any analysis of education reform in the post-apartheid period is an understanding of South Africa's history and of the role of education during apartheid. In chapter 2, we briefly review the country's complicated colonial and apartheid history, particularly its racial dimensions. Readers who are familiar with South African history may want to skip this summary, but for others it provides essential background on the racial context of the post-apartheid period. Chapters 3 and 4 set the stage for the recent education reforms. In chapter 3, we describe the central role of education in supporting both the apartheid system and the struggle against it, and we spell out apartheid's legacy for education. In chapter 4, we describe the educational aspirations of the African National Congress on the eve of the election and the major constraints facing the new government as it sought to attain them.

The heart of the book, chapters 5 to 9, presents our detailed analysis of efforts to reform the school sector. This analysis is based on information from government documents and articles, our interviews with policymakers and school principals during the first six months of 2002, and our examination of provincial, school, and teacher data. The data come from all nine of the country's provinces and thus offer a picture of how the reforms played out throughout the country. Given that national education policies are implemented at the provincial level, however, it is useful to look below provincial averages to examine patterns across and within schools in particular provinces.

A major contribution of this study is our use of administrative data for two of the country's nine provinces. The availability of a complete census of schools and teachers within the impoverished and predominantly rural Eastern Cape and the relatively wealthy and more urban Western Cape makes possible a rich and comprehensive analysis of the course of reforms in those two provinces. To be sure, every province has distinctive characteristics, and no two of them could ever fully represent all nine. At the same time, our detailed analysis of patterns within two considerably different provinces represents an important tool for under-standing what the national reforms meant for previously disadvantaged schools and students.

Chapter 10 evaluates the progress toward racial equity at the level of higher education. In chapter 11, we summarize why equity has been elu-sive in South African education, consider prospects for future progress, and offer insights for other countries based on South Africa's experience.

two   The Racial Context
of South Africa

The apartheid era dawned in 1948 when the Afrikaner-dominated National Party won narrow control of the South African parliament and imposed race-conscious structures on every aspect of life, including education. Behind these structures lay a long history of complex relations both between and within the major racial groups in the country. As mentioned earlier, there are four such groups—Africans, coloureds, Indians, and whites—and conflicts between whites and blacks were part of the social fabric of South Africa from the early colonial period. Those tensions mounted during the many years of segregation that preceded apartheid, providing fertile ground for the political struggle that ultimately succeeded in bringing an end to the apartheid era in 1994.

Leading the struggle was the African National Congress (ANC), but it represented only one of numerous organizations and movements pursuing this objective—often as adversaries rather than allies. Hence the political settlement that paved the way for the birth of a democratic South Africa cannot be considered a total victory of one group over another. Rather, it was a carefully constructed compromise that left all of the major players with a stake in building a strong new multiracial society, as this chapter makes clear.[1]

1. The content of this chapter relies heavily on Beinart (2001); Beinart and Dubow (1995); Lodge and others (1991); Maylam (2001); and Seekings (2000).

The Peoples of South Africa

The original inhabitants of the southern tip of Africa were the pastoral Khoikhoi and the hunter-gatherer San peoples. Other major African groups were the Zulus in the northeast, the Xhosa in the southeast, and the Sotho, Pedi, and Tswana groups in the interior. There was no single African political or economic system, nor a common language. Instead, powerful chiefdoms, such as that of the Zulus, had emerged, each with its own cultural, economic, and political traditions.

Throughout the colonial period, from the seventeenth through the early twentieth century, Africans were the major source of labor in the white economy, first on farms, then in the gold and diamond mines, and eventually in factories. Although many of the original inhabitants did not survive beyond the mid-eighteenth century, in part because of white men's diseases, the African population showed considerable resilience in the face of European settlement. By 1910 Europeans constituted only about 20 percent of the population of South Africa and remained at that level for about half a century, until rapid African population growth in the 1960s brought them down to 14 percent. Race relations thus developed in a context in which Europeans were able to conquer the indigenous peoples but not displace them.[2]

The first white people to set foot in South Africa were the Dutch. In 1652 the Dutch East India Company sent Jan van Riebeeck out to set up a provisioning station for ships rounding the Cape of Good Hope. Van Riebeeck showed no interest in the native inhabitants other than as trading partners, and remnants of a bitter-almond tree fence that he erected to keep them at a distance can still be seen at the botanical garden in Cape Town. However, economic necessity prompted some Dutch to move out of the enclave and to begin cultivating adjacent land. The Dutch settlers were soon joined by French Huguenots and some Germans, and together they evolved into a community that described itself as Afrikaners, or "people of Africa." As the influence of Holland waned, the settlers developed a simplified form of the Dutch language that came to be known as Afrikaans. In keeping with their pastoral habits, they called themselves Boers, which means "farmers."[3]

The British had been sailing around the Cape since the sixteenth century without much inclination to challenge the Dutch presence. In 1795,

2. Beinart and Dubow (1995, p. 2).
3. Woods and Bostock (1986, p. 17).

however, as tensions with France mounted, Britain annexed the Cape Colony. The English were merchants rather than farmers and soon achieved economic hegemony over the agrarian Afrikaners, who began moving further inland, where they established the Orange Free State and Transvaal republics. English economic power was solidified in the 1870s when diamonds were discovered in Kimberly and gold in Witwatersrand. Entrepreneurs such as Cecil Rhodes wasted little time moving in to exploit these riches. Tensions between the Afrikaners and the British over the control of land intensified and eventually led to the South African War of 1899–1902, also known as the Anglo-Boer War, or simply the Boer War. The conflict pitted Boer settlers in the Free State and Transvaal against the British and their allies from Australia, Canada, and New Zealand, but it was by no means only a "white man's war." Hundreds of thousands of Africans played supportive roles on both sides.

Although the British won the war on the battlefield, their political leaders strived for cooperation among the dominant white groups and agreed to recognize the independence of the two Afrikaner provinces. In 1910 whites established the Union of South Africa as a new state that, like Australia and Canada, enjoyed status as a dominion under the crown. Under the leadership of the South African Party, which included both anglophone and Afrikaans-speaking members but was dominated by Afrikaners, the state began laying the foundations of apartheid. In a joint decision endorsed by the British government, the English and Afrikaners moved to place the interests of the country's African majority in the hands of the white minority and excluded Africans from the ballot.

The third racial group in South Africa is the coloured population. This community had its origin in the mixed-race offspring of African and European parents, but it was augmented by the descendants of slaves imported by the Dutch from various areas of their far-flung empire, including Indonesia, Malaya, and Indo-China, as well as from elsewhere in Africa. Many of the newcomers brought Islam with them, and its tradition has survived in the face of a dominant Christianity. Coloured people have had an enormous impact on South African life and culture, particularly in the areas around Cape Town, where they are most numerous. As construction workers and cooks, they shaped the architecture and the cuisine of the region and helped make the Afrikaans language the lingua franca by which the various racial groups could communicate.[4]

4. Sparks (1990, pp. 72–73).

Coloureds have led an ambiguous existence over the years, largely because of their close ties to Afrikaner language and culture. The apartheid-era government did not consider them white, yet they had no identity as a distinct community rooted in a specific geographical area of South Africa. At the same time, Cape employers could give coloured workers formal preference over Africans, and a tricameral legislative structure established in the 1980s, from which Africans were excluded, brought them symbolic political power. Although they too suffered mightily under apartheid, they enjoyed some privileges that were denied to Africans. This ambiguity has persisted in the post-apartheid era and has complicated relations between coloureds and the new black-run government.

The fourth and smallest racial group in South Africa comprises Indians. Initially brought in as indentured servants in the 1860s to work on British sugar plantations, they subsequently became traders. The Indian population was concentrated in Natal and Transvaal, and, like Africans and coloureds, faced restrictions on their ability to own land and vote. Mohandas Gandhi, who lived in South Africa from 1893 to 1914, was active in resisting government oppression of Indians. It was there that he first mobilized thousands of workers to engage in passive resistance, a method of struggle that he later used in India.

The Tradition of Segregation

Although strongly associated with the culture and character of Afrikaners, apartheid is deeply rooted in a colonial tradition of racial segregation that assumed formal status well before 1948. By the late nineteenth century, African and coloured persons had already been relegated to townships adjacent to white towns, a move calculated to separate black "slumyards" from white residential areas and also keep the black poor away from the white poor.[5]

Union in 1910 brought formal political segregation, with the exclusion of Africans from the ballot box. Over the next two decades, the white-controlled government enacted a series of laws imposing increasingly restrictive rules on where black persons could live and work. The Mines and Works Act of 1911 formalized segregation in employment, while the Natives Land Act of 1913 created a system of "reserves" giving white people control of 87 percent of the land and black people only

5. Aliber (2003, p. 474).

13 percent. These restrictions were not fully realized until the Native Trust and Land Act of 1936.[6] The Native Urban Areas Act of 1923 empowered local municipal authorities to segregate urban settlements according to race and to control movement by requiring the use of passes.

The rise of racial segregation prior to apartheid has been attributed to various factors.[7] The initial thrust, some say, came not from the Boers but from British colonial administrators in Natal, who devolved substantial local control to African chiefs with the twin aims of guaranteeing a stable political order and ensuring access to African labor. Migrant labor is also said to have played a significant role. In the late nineteenth century, African males leaving their villages to work in distant mines provided a ready supply of cheap labor essential to the mining industry, which was able to pay these workers "bachelor" wages while their families survived on subsistence agriculture in the reserves.[8]

Since migrant labor and reserve lands also served the needs of tribal societies, it can be argued too that segregation was heavily influenced by those on whom it was imposed. Chiefs sent out workers to earn money to buy firearms to defend the independence of their kingdoms, and the availability of land in the reserve was an incentive for migrant workers to return. As historians point out, "Attempts by the rurally based African population to defend their old ways of life were not segregationist in the sense that whites understood the term. But these could be compatible with elements of segregation in certain respects—as an expression of their own separate African identity, as a means to retain some control over their residual land, or as an expression of popular support for chiefs."[9]

Culture and Character of Afrikaners

Segregationist practices in South Africa up through the middle of the twentieth century were apparently not all that different from those in other colonial situations or, for that matter, in the United States.

6. See Beinart (2001, p. 10).
7. For a helpful discussion of this debate, see Beinart and Dubow (1995).
8. By 1910 the gold mining industry needed to recruit as many as 200,000 black workers each year, and an important consequence of the Natives Land Act of 1913 was to reinforce the migrant labor system by ensuring the survival of the reserves. Wolpe (1995).
9. Beinart and Dubow (1995, p. 10).

Apartheid, however, was quite a different matter. Not only did it elevate the previous segregationist policies to a new level of intensity but it ran counter to the political tide of democratic self-determination that swept across the world in the postcolonial era. This movement from segregation to apartheid was far from inevitable, however. South Africa's conspicuous defiance of the trends of the day must be seen against the backdrop of the particular history of the Afrikaans-speaking whites.[10]

Throughout the nineteenth century, Afrikaner farmers, driven by scorn for the English and a desire to be independent and self-sufficient, moved further and further into the interior of the country. As their contact with the rest of European civilization dwindled, these staunch Calvinists, known as Voortrekkers, came to see their situation through a biblical prism: "Afrikaner history became a search, sanctioned by God, for independence and identity against the combined forces of Mammon and Ham."[11] In the course of their expansion, they met resistance from the Africans who occupied the land they sought. Their victory over a Zulu army at the Battle of Blood River on December 16, 1838, achieved after swearing a covenant with God, became the stuff of Afrikaner legend. The legend was solidified in 1938 when Afrikaners celebrated the hundredth anniversary of what had come to be known as the Great Trek inland and built a large symmetrical monument to Afrikaner expansion on a hill outside Pretoria. A small oil lamp still burns there as a symbol of the "Light of Civilization."[12]

The Afrikaner emerged as a proud, stubborn, and self-sufficient loner who had little respect for authority—even within the Afrikaner fold.[13] With the arrival of the British, the Afrikaner sense of identity came under threat:

Having missed the eighteenth century, [Afrikaners] had the nineteenth century burst in on them. Having lived as free men with almost no administrative restraints, the rule of law and pervasive orderliness of a major imperial power arrived to entangle them.

---

10. Beinart and Dubow (1995, p. 6) note that an alternative to segregation had seemed possible in the Cape in the nineteenth century when the British developed a form of colonial self-government that was potentially nonracial in character.

11. Beinart (2001, p. 65).

12. Sparks (1990, p. 110).

13. The isolation of the Voortrekkers may be overstated. As some historians point out, even trekkers in the interior continued trading relationships with the outside world, as well as commercial, military, and even sexual relations with Africans.

The intrusion at first irked then angered the Afrikaners, and over time it produced a legacy of grievance that fired their nationalism and turned a community of undisciplined individualists into a cohesive national unit that baffled the world with its obduracy.[14]

Although Afrikaners became part of the governing process following the South African War, they continued to experience hard times in the early decades of the twentieth century. Many Afrikaner men returned from the war to find their farms scorched and no longer viable. Unable to survive on the land, they migrated into the cities but lacked the skills to cope with life there. The ultimate humiliation was having to compete for jobs with African workers, whose numbers in the cities were soaring. The problem of the "white poor" came to dominate Afrikaner politics, and for a time their cause was even taken up by the Communist Party. A 1930–32 report of the Native Economic Commission explicitly linked the poor-white problem to African urbanization and the breaking down of the reserves.[15]

Inspired in part by the rise of fascism in Europe during the 1930s, young Afrikaner intellectuals began arguing for a long-term survival strategy built around racial separation, purity, and guarantees of a white-led homeland. Afrikaner journalist Schalk Pienaar offered the following "sophisticated defense" of apartheid based on the Afrikaner's right to survive:

It was but yesterday that the Afrikaners wrested from British imperial occupation the right to be a nation, to be independent in partnerships with their countrymen of British stock. And today, with this battle that is all of Afrikaner history hardly fought, the demand comes that they submit to a new imperialism, not this time to the weapons of Europe, but to the numbers of Africa. The answer, not unnaturally, is no. Unlike the English in India and the Dutch in Indonesia, the Afrikaner has nowhere else to go. For him there is no Britain and no Holland to return to; for him no central shrine of national existence to survive the death of the outposts. On the soil of Africa he, and with him his history, culture and language, stay or perish.[16]

14. Sparks (1990, p. 46).
15. Beinart (2001, p. 122).
16. Quoted in Sparks (1990, pp. 208–09).

The political arm of Afrikaners was the National Party, founded in 1914 by General J. B. M. Hertzog, a former member of the South African Party, which had taken power after union. Though the National Party included anglophone politicians, it was dominated by Afrikaners and cast itself as a predominantly lower-middle-class movement championing Afrikaner cultural rights and economic advancement. By 1920 it had become the largest in the country, and in 1924 it was able to form a coalition government closely identified with Afrikaner farmers and small business. Over the years, the party broadened its mission to embrace the interests of white South Africans in general.

The Afrikaners' political unity broke down amid the economic turmoil of the 1930s, and from 1934 to 1948 the South African Party, led by another former general, Jan Smuts, ruled South Africa. In the elections of 1948, however, the National Party, taking advantage of white economic anxieties and concerns that Smuts was becoming uncertain in his policies and too concerned with international issues, won a thin parliamentary majority. Over the next five years, the Nationalists invested heavily in strengthening the party organization—an effort that paid off when the 1953 election gave them a comfortable working majority.

How Apartheid Maintained White Supremacy

The Nationalist victory in 1948 ushered in a forty-six-year period in which the government dedicated itself to securing the social, economic, and political privileges of the white minority at the expense of Africans, coloureds, and Indians. The operative concept was "apartheid"—a new term, coined for the 1948 election campaign, meaning "separateness."[17]

Apartheid as a political and social ideology was built on four basic premises. First, to preserve the national identity of South Africa's four ethnic groups, or "nations"—each of which has its own language, culture, history, and social traditions—they must live and develop independently of each other. As racial theorist Geoff Cronje of Pretoria University explained, "The Afrikaner believes that it is the will of God that there should be a diversity of races and nations and that obedience to the will of God therefore requires the acknowledgment and maintenance of that diversity."[18] Second, white people are the custodians of civilization and therefore have an obligation to lead other groups toward civi-

17. Woods and Bostock (1986, p. 72).
18. Sparks (1990, p. 149).

lization at their own pace. Third, in order to carry out this role, whites must have their privileges protected. Fourth, according to apartheid apologists, black persons may be divided into many nations, but white people, of whatever background—most notably British and Afrikaners—constitute a single nation.

While the broad lines of its principles were clear, apartheid was by no means a single, coherent ideology, much less a detailed blueprint for social policy. For one thing, its architects were torn between their desire for racial exclusion in the political and social spheres and pressures for integration in the economic sphere. Hard-line "visionaries" pushed for "total apartheid," which meant African land reserves would be viable and self-sufficient states and white South Africans would no longer be dependent on black labor. "Pragmatists" in the opposing camp, which included Hendrik Verwoerd, prime minister from 1958 to 1966 and minister of native affairs before that, believed economic segregation was impractical. This faction pushed for "grand apartheid," which would limit black presence in white areas as much as possible without suffering the economic sacrifices implicit in full economic segregation, most notably the loss of black labor. On this issue, by and large, the pragmatists had their way.[19]

How much of a "grand plan" was in place when the National Party came to power in 1948 is debatable. The new government certainly moved quickly to enact a series of restrictive laws, starting with the Prohibition of Mixed Marriages Act of 1949. Recent scholarship suggests, however, that its social engineering in the 1950s was simply a way of addressing particular issues, such as the growing black urbanization that threatened white jobs. Clearly, Afrikaner businessmen saw the situation quite differently from theologians and other intellectuals enamored of racial purity. Further tensions existed between Afrikaner ethnic nationalism and the broader goal of white solidarity, and between hard-line Boer racism in the north and the more liberal traditions of the Cape.

Once they assumed and consolidated political power, the Nationalists began the systematic construction of elaborate political, social, and economic systems aimed at furthering racial separation and white supremacy. Apartheid was fundamentally about white control of space and land, and the desire for control drove ideology, not the other way around. Building on earlier legislation, the Group Areas Act of 1950 and the Prevention of Illegal Squatting Act of 1951 designated every res-

19. Maylam (2001, p. 202).

idential area for occupation by a particular racial group. Nonwhites living in areas designated white were forcibly removed, even if their families had been there for generations. Moving people around became a major governmental activity, one that opened up enormous economic opportunities for developers and builders who could purchase expropriated houses, fix them up, and resell them to whites. The Group Areas Act has its greatest impact on coloured and Indian families: over three decades, about 600,000 of them were removed from Cape Town, Durban, and other urban areas.[20]

In order to accommodate both the large number of blacks who were being uprooted and the substantial flow of new arrivals from the countryside, the government established "townships" on the edges of major cities. For security purposes, these townships were separated by major roads, rivers, and railroad lines, which made it difficult for unrest in one area to leapfrog to another. Blacks were allowed to commute to the cities to work but had to return to their assigned township at night, and whites were restricted from entering the townships. The quality of housing in the townships was generally poor, ranging from small blocklike units constructed at government expense to makeshift shelters built by residents out of whatever materials they could find.

In pursuing grand apartheid, the Nationalists also created the fiction of independent "homelands," which some critics preferred to call "Bantustans."[21] The theory was that every African was linked by ancestry to a particular geographical area and that he or she should be a citizen of that homeland rather than of South Africa. Economically "superfluous" Africans—those not needed by white employers for work in urban areas—were expected to move physically to their designated homeland, while "useful" ones were allowed to remain close to urban centers, albeit without political rights and under conditions of poverty. The Bantu Self-Government Act of 1959 established ten homelands, four of which were actually given "independence," starting with Transkei in 1963 and subsequently Bophuthatswana, Ciskei, and Venda. The act ceded leadership to a network of local authorities, mainly tribal chiefs, co-opted into the process. Though referred to as independent republics, no foreign country recognized them as such. The other six ostensible

20. See Beinart (2001, p. 153).
21. Although this term originated with the government, officials later dropped it in favor of "homelands," which sounded better. Anti-apartheid supporters continued to use "Bantustans" so as not to go along with the government's euphemisms.

homelands successfully resisted the fiction of independence and came to be known as "self-governing territories."[22]

The system of herding blacks into their own geographic areas left 70 percent of the South African population with access to only 13 percent of the land, and most of that land was economically nonviable. This contrived social system required an elaborate set of laws that needed constant revision as opponents of apartheid discovered and exploited loopholes. The most hated regulations were the so-called pass laws, which required blacks to carry personal reference books, or passes, documenting their racial identity at all times and to present them to authorities on demand.[23]

The apartheid system was enforced by state security forces, which took advantage of the poverty of most blacks to recruit informers and did not hesitate to use lethal force, including torture, to maintain order. The brutality of the era—including retaliatory violence by opponents of apartheid—was subsequently documented by the Truth and Reconciliation Commission set up in the late 1990s. The Nationalist government did all it could to shackle the white press and to keep whites—both Afrikaners and English—ignorant of what was being done in the homelands and townships to maintain their privileged way of life.

The Breakdown of Apartheid

The apartheid system in its heyday was ruthlessly effective in maintaining white privilege. Among other things, it assured all qualified Afrikaners of access to higher education and government employment. Indeed, it has sometimes been described as the world's most successful affirmative action program.

That said, apartheid was never able to function smoothly. As already noted, Parliament was constantly closing loopholes discovered by opponents, and not all government policies were upheld by the courts. To solidify control, the state began strengthening its security forces and

22. These six territories are Gazanulu, Lebowa, KaNgwane, KwaNdebele, KwaZulu, and QwaQwa.

23. Key pieces of legislation aimed at keeping the races separate and blacks under control were the Job Reservation Act, the Group Areas Act, the Prohibition of Mixed Marriages Act, the Bantu Education Act, and the Reservation of Separate Amenities Act. Many of these laws were given names that would have seemed comical had the intent not been so perverse. The 1952 legislation requiring blacks to carry passes, for example, was named the Abolition of Passes and Coordination of Documents Act.

allowed them to become increasingly repressive and violent, especially after March 1960, when sixty-nine antipass protesters were killed by nervous policemen in what came to be known as the Sharpeville Massacre. Apartheid also required an elaborate and costly bureaucracy and an even stronger military force as black-run governments hostile to apartheid replaced sympathetic white ones in neighboring countries. Apartheid's hold on the population of South Africa peaked in the late 1970s and early 1980s, when various forces, including mass resistance among blacks, began to take their toll. This movement—known to South Africans today as "the struggle"—led to a genuine crisis of political legitimacy that in turn set the stage for the historic compromise of 1994 transferring political power in South Africa from white to black hands.

The struggle had roots in the segregation era that preceded formal apartheid. An important milestone came on January 8, 1912, when several hundred of the country's most prominent African citizens—professional men, chieftains, clergy, businessmen, teachers, and others—assembled in Bloemfontein to form the South African Native National Congress, subsequently renamed the African National Congress (ANC). Bitterly disappointed that the Act of Union of 1910 had excluded rather than extended African political participation and angry at subsequent actions limiting the rights of African workers, this group resolved to promote African interests not through sympathetic intermediaries but through the action of Africans themselves.[24]

Dominated by a mission-educated and anglophile elite, the early ANC sought not to protest the existence of a colonial society but to achieve full political and economic assimilation into it. A point of protest, for example, was the barring of Africans from first-class compartments on trains. The ANC also supported strikes by municipal workers on behalf of better wages, and by the early 1920s it was joined by two other organizations with roots in labor and committed to a more radical agenda: the Industrial and Commercial Workers' Union (ICU), whose activities extended to rural areas, and the South African Communist Party (SACP), which was predominantly white but committed to class struggle. However, the ICU was fragmented and the SACP weakened by governmental harassment and internal purges. As a result, the

24. Lodge (1983, p. 1).

ANC failed to achieve broad support in either urban or rural areas and was still relatively small by the 1930s.[25]

In 1935 more than 400 delegates from a wide range of black organizations met at an All African Convention (AAC) to protest further restrictions on black rights, and the late 1930s brought an increase in trade union activities. In the early 1940s a resurgent ANC worked closely with the SACP and various unions on behalf of black economic and political rights and with the South African Indian Congress (SAIC) to protest government efforts to restrict Indians' rights to acquire property. The protest movement was weakened, however, by the government's successful crushing of a miners' strike in 1946. By the time apartheid replaced segregation as the dominant organizing principle for South African society, the organized protest aimed at expanding black economic and political involvement had become a succession of failed efforts to resist the further erosion of such rights.

The victory of the National Party in the 1948 elections substantially raised the stakes of political activity in South Africa for both sides. In 1952 the ANC led what became known as a defiance campaign against unjust laws that may not have succeeded in filling the country's jails with protesters but certainly helped establish it as a mass organization. In 1955 an Assembly of the People met in Johannesburg to adopt a Freedom Charter, a blueprint for a democratic and multiracial South Africa, and about this time individuals such as Nelson Mandela, Walter Sisulu, Govan Mbeki, and Oliver Tambo took on prominent roles and matured as political leaders. Nevertheless, by the mid-1960s overt political activity inside the country had been virtually eliminated. Leaders of the ANC and other opposition organizations were either in jail or in exile, and liberation movements were "reduced to obscure passivity."[26]

Having failed at peaceful forms of protest, the ANC weighed whether the time had come to wage an armed struggle against the seemingly overwhelming forces of the state. In June 1961 the ANC national executive committee approved a proposal from Nelson Mandela to maintain the organization's official nonviolent position but also to establish a separate organization, Umkonto we Sizwe (Spear of the Nation), that would be open to whites, Indians, and coloureds, as well

25. For a description of protests before 1950, see Lodge (1983, pp. 1–3) and Seekings (2000, pp. 1–28).
26. Seekings (2000, p. 5). See also Pampallis (1991).

as Africans and that would pursue sabotage and other militant forms of protest.

By the mid-1970s black South Africans were again thinking about organized political activity. Though legally banned, the ANC began establishing underground structures inside the country and forming links with a new generation of increasingly restive students, and by the early 1980s it had reemerged as a major opposition force. Outside South Africa, the ANC represented an estimated 10,000 to 15,000 persons scattered throughout as many as twenty-five countries, most notably Angola, Tanzania, and Zambia. The most substantial numbers were members of Umkonto we Sizwe, which until 1989 used camps in Angola as a basis for guerrilla activities against police, military, and other targets in South Africa.[27]

This renewed opposition to apartheid was fueled by a set of ideas spawned by churches and educational institutions in the 1960s and known as "black consciousness." Years of subjugation to whites, it was argued, had caused blacks to lose confidence in themselves, and the only way for them to build a nonracial society was to develop their own political, social, and cultural organizations without the assistance of whites. The term "black," embracing not only Africans but coloureds and Indians, was itself a challenge to the prevailing racial categories of apartheid, which used negative terms such as "nonwhite" or "non-European." Black consciousness drew not only on local traditions of ethnic pride but also on contemporary movements outside of South Africa, notably Black Power in the United States, liberation theology, and the writings of Frantz Fanon.

In his autobiography, Nelson Mandela characterizes black consciousness as "less a movement than a philosophy" emphasizing ethnic pride and racial consciousness, concepts that had led him to push for the foundation of an ANC Youth League in 1944. The arrival of militant black consciousness advocates in the prison on Robben Island where he was confined moved Mandela to write,

> [Just] as we had outgrown our Youth League outlook, I was confident that these young men would transcend some of the strictures of Black Consciousness. While I was encouraged by their militancy, I thought that their philosophy, in its concentration on

27. For a discussion of the ANC in exile, see Lodge and others (1991, pp. 173–84).

blackness, was exclusionary and represented an intermediate view that was not fully mature. I saw my role as an elder statesman who might help them move on to the more inclusive ideas of the Congress movement. I knew also that these young men would eventually become frustrated because Black Consciousness offered no program of action, no outlet for their protest.[28]

In 1969 black students broke with the National Union of South African Students, an organization dominated by white liberals in English-speaking universities, and set up the South African Students Organization (SASO) to assert the importance of unity for all blacks in the struggle against white domination. The most prominent exponent of black consciousness was Steve Biko, the charismatic president of SASO whose presence dominated black politics for much of the next decade. His death in 1977 while in police detention was pivotal in arousing public opinion against apartheid both in South Africa and abroad.[29]

Black consciousness had its most important political impact in the schools, where numerous black university graduates steeped in this philosophy took up teaching posts. The South African Students Movement (SASM), based in the heart of Soweto, organized protests against practices such as interschool music competitions, which leaders charged were disruptive of educational activities, and against the general inadequacy of what the government called "Bantu education." The uprisings, which involved attacks on administrative buildings, vehicles, beerhalls, and liquor stores, continued through the end of 1977 and led to the loss of more than 1,000 lives.[30]

As Mandela had predicted, militant African students eventually moved their political strategy away from black consciousness, establishing connections both with well-resourced white student organizations and with Indian activists. Another wave of student protests in 1979 and 1980 involved burnings and consumer boycotts targeted at white businesses. Soon the forces unleashed by students spread well beyond their own ranks.

On the afternoon of August 2, 1983, 10,000 persons attended a mass rally in Mitchell's Plain, a new coloured township on the Cape Flats of

28. Mandela (1994, p. 486).
29. Beinart (2001, pp. 232–33); Lodge (1983, pp. 6–7); Pampallis (1991, pp. 240–42).
30. Beinart (2001, pp. 236–38); Pampallis (1991, p. 256).

Cape Town, and formed the United Democratic Front (UDF).[31] Consistent with tradition of the ANC, the UDF was explicitly nonracial and drew the support of church leaders such as Bishop Desmond Tutu, the Reverend Frank Chikane, and the Reverend Allan Boesak, who told the crowd, "We have arrived at a historic moment." Indeed, the UDF had brought together more than 500 anti-apartheid organizations as well as individuals from around the country.

A particular target of the UDF was the so-called tricameral parliament approved in 1983 in a whites-only referendum to defuse mounting political opposition. It established two new parliaments—a House of Representatives for coloureds and a House of Delegates for Indians—that would sit separately from the white-run House of Assembly but whose executives would be allowed to participate in a President's Council dominated by the National Party. The country's African majority was excluded from the new structure, though they were granted greater representation in segregated local councils in the homelands and townships. Blacks perceived the new structures not as a move toward inclusiveness and a break with any key principles of apartheid but as a crude attempt to pit the three groups against one another and to co-opt non-African black leaders. The UDF campaign against the first elections in August 1984 was largely successful, with only 17.5 percent of coloureds and 16.6 percent of Indians voting.[32]

By 1985 the popular struggle that had begun in the schools in 1976 had risen to a crescendo nationwide. Scores of UDF affiliates took up the ANC's call to make South Africa ungovernable by destroying much of the administrative apparatus in the townships. Police stations and shops in the townships were burned, and "people's courts" sprang up, as did the practice of "necklacing" those identified as informers by placing tires doused with petrol around victims' necks and lighting them. Banners sporting the colors of the banned ANC—green, black, and gold—appeared, and funerals became political events.

The National government responded by moving large numbers of troops into the townships, and in July 1985 the prime minister, P. W. Botha, declared a state of emergency, thereby introducing even more formidable policing powers, but in the process, undermining support in segments of the white community, especially the business sector. The government persisted with mass detentions and in 1988 banned the

31. See Seekings (2000) for a thorough history of the UDF.
32. Pampallis (1991, p. 276).

UDF. The organization continued, however, under the guise of the Mass Democratic Movement and in 1989 unilaterally declared itself unbanned and resumed public activity.

Complexity of the Struggle against Apartheid

Despite the success of the UDF, opposition to apartheid was never monolithic. Even the ANC, the largest black political movement, was but one of various voices that rose in protest from both the left and the right. As one historian put it, "The fact of oppression did not necessarily determine the trajectory of responses."[33]

In 1959 militant blacks impatient with the willingness of ANC leaders to work with whites and with communists formed the Pan Africanist Congress (PAC) under the leadership of Robert Sobukwe. The PAC campaigned against the ANC's endorsement of the Freedom Charter and the following year put its weight behind the antipass campaign that led to the Sharpeville Massacre. Lacking a strong base in traditional ANC areas, however, the PAC did not last long as a viable political structure. Sobukwe was imprisoned, then released and banned, and he died in 1978 while still under government restrictions. The PAC enjoyed a modest resurgence in the late 1980s when it mounted guerrilla operations against state security forces.

A significant challenge from the left came in the early 1980s with the formation of the Azanian People's Organization (AZAPO), a black consciousness group that was instrumental in assembling a loose association known as the National Forum Committee (NFC), which challenged ANC and UDF nonracialism. The forum adopted the Azanian Manifesto, calling for socialism in South Africa and denouncing a system that made all blacks oppressed members of the working class and all whites members of the capitalist class. Affiliates of the NFC, however, never gained the widespread support enjoyed by the UDF.[34]

The most significant divisions within black politics in South Africa in the 1980s and early 1990s came not from the left but from conservative forces rooted in the traditional values of rural and tribal cultures. The most powerful exponent of these was Chief Mangosuthu Gatsha Buthelezi, head of Inkatha Yenkululeke ye Sizwe (Freedom of the Nation). Inkatha had been established by King Solomon Dinuzulu in

33. Beinart (2001, p. 96).
34. Pampallis (1991, p. 277).

1928 as a means of arousing enthusiasm for the Zulu monarchy, but it soon foundered. In 1975 Chief Buthelezi, Solomon's nephew, revived it as a mass organization emphasizing Zulu cultural renewal, and it quickly evolved into a powerful political force. Buthelezi was installed as a chief in 1957, serving as head adviser to the king, and in 1970 he took charge of the newly established KwaZulu Territorial Authority. Professing opposition to apartheid, he refused to accept full independence for the Zulu "homeland"—a move that gave him considerable leverage with the National government, which wanted to push him in that direction.

Although Buthelezi had been a member of the ANC Youth League for a short time, his views evolved in quite different directions from the black mainstream. Inkatha emphasized ethnicity and respect for traditional authority, and it was the only black political organization that wholeheartedly embraced capitalist rather than socialist values. In the 1980s Buthelezi became a vocal critic of ANC guerrilla activities, not out of any philosophical opposition to violence but because he thought that it was tactically futile to go up against such superior state forces. His strategy was to seek power through territorial hegemony and economic strength.

When the most powerful black trade unions formed the Congress of South African Trade Unions (COSATU) in 1985, Buthelezi countered by organizing a rival Zulu-dominated trade union, the United Workers' Union of South Africa, as a pro-capitalist force. Buthelezi's group won support among political conservatives in Britain, the United States, and elsewhere as a safer alternative to the ANC, which was seen in such circles as sympathetic to communism. Inkatha used armed force against its black political rivals, including the leaders of COSATU and UDF, and much of the violence that preceded the country's first democratic elections in 1994 was ascribed to Inkatha. During negotiations for a new constitutional framework, Buthelezi waged a partly successful battle for a federalist system of government that would enhance regional Zulu influence.

The National Party on the Defensive

Throughout the 1980s the National government also faced mounting economic pressures. The tide of urbanization among nonwhites could no longer be stemmed for it was now evident that South Africa's relatively sophisticated economy needed skilled black workers to compete in the emerging global economy. Recognizing that whites could not have it both ways—forcing blacks to live in isolation while contributing to the growing economy—the government began investing heavily in education for blacks in the 1980s, and by 1988 a larger number of black students were graduating from high school than white students.[35]

The National Party, under the leadership of P. W. Botha, sought to alter the former "terms of domination," meaning coercion, by relying more on co-option.[36] Legal recognition was granted to black trade unions, and pass laws were eased in 1986 after successful legal challenges. The Mixed Marriages Act and racial sections of the Immorality Act were abolished in 1986, and freehold property rights for Africans in towns were extended, as was the state pension system. Such reforms prompted a backlash within the National Party, whose right wing became convinced that the government was selling out white workers. In 1982 a group of ultraright members of Parliament who had opposed Botha's new policies was expelled from the party and formed the new Conservative Party.

A central part of Botha's strategy was to build up a black middle class—Africans, coloureds, and Indians—whose members would be favorable to capitalism and whose higher standard of living would have a moderating influence on the liberation movement. Large companies such as Anglo American Corporation began promoting black workers into lower- or middle-level management positions, and an Urban Foundation was formed in 1979 to give small business loans to blacks and help them purchase their own homes. In 1985 black businesses were permitted to trade in some formerly white business districts. Despite these and other measures, the black middle class remained small, and, more important, continued to identify with the oppressed rather than allow itself to be co-opted.[37]

The apartheid government was also operating in a changing, and increasingly hostile, international environment. For the first quarter century of the apartheid regime, white rule in South Africa was buffered by a circle of sympathetic colonial states to the north. In 1974, however, a coup in Lisbon led Portugal to withdraw from Angola and Mozambique, and in 1979 white rule in Zimbabwe collapsed. In the wake of these events, South Africa mounted commando raids to kill ANC and other

35. Sparks (1990, p. 376).
36. Lodge and others (1991, p. 200).
37. Pampallis (1991, p. 282).

refugees in Mozambique and Zimbabwe and to occupy large sections of southern Angola. Such activities were both expensive and unpopular among whites, who were reluctant to send their sons to fight against the military wing of the ANC in hostile environments. Furthermore, economic setbacks following the oil crisis of 1974 increased public awareness of the huge domestic costs of maintaining apartheid and made corporate and business interests more open to Thatcherite and Reaganite concepts of free-market economic policy—concepts not necessarily consistent with South Africa's racially constrained economic system.[38]

By the late 1980s the moral authority of the Nationalists had been irredeemably compromised around the world. Starting in 1957, the ANC campaigned for trade and other sanctions against South Africa. In 1963 the United Nations Security Council imposed a ban on weapon exports to South Africa, and in 1985 Western bankers refused to roll over South African loans. The following year intensifying contacts between the ANC and Western governments and business leaders paid off when the country's major trading partners, including a reluctant United States and Britain, adopted sanctions. As anti-apartheid movements thrived on campuses throughout the world, many universities and local governments withdrew investments from South Africa, and the campaign for Nelson Mandela's release from prison caught the public imagination.

The National government responded to its global public relations problem by toning down its racist rhetoric and arguing that it was defending capitalist principles and Western democratic ideals against the forces of international communism that were the backbone of the ANC, the SACP, and other liberation organizations. The abrupt collapse of the Soviet Union, however, seriously undermined this particular pretext for the apartheid system.

A Negotiated Settlement

By the early 1990s it was abundantly clear that neither side could win. As Mandela told a group of Afrikaner generals,

> If you want to go to war . . . I must be honest and admit that we cannot stand up to you on the battlefield. We don't have the resources. . . . But you must remember two things. You cannot win

38. Beinart and Dubow (1995, p. 19).

because of our numbers; you cannot kill us all. And you cannot win because of the international community. They will rally to our support and they will stand with us.[39]

Some form of cooperation and political power sharing was obviously in the interest of both sides.

In 1985 Botha had offered to release Nelson Mandela and other political prisoners on the condition that they renounce armed conflict. Mandela declined the offer, but shortly afterward secret conversations began between him and government officials, and he was permitted to communicate with ANC leaders in exile. In February 1990, F. W. de Klerk, who had become prime minister in 1989 after Botha had suffered a stroke, made a dramatic speech to Parliament in which he announced the unbanning of the ANC and other proscribed organizations, the imminent release of Mandela and other political prisoners, and the government's intention to enter into formal talks aimed at transforming South Africa into a nonracial democracy in which South Africans of all races would participate fully.

By then the National Party had shed much of its right wing to the Conservatives and begun to revoke racist laws such as those limiting where blacks could live. Meanwhile, ANC leaders, unnerved by the collapse of communism, were backing away from radical economic ideas such as nationalization of mines and banks, and, against some internal opposition, the ANC suspended military operations. As Mandela also understood, post-apartheid South Africa would need the skills of the white minority. Since human capital is a highly mobile resource, it was in the ANC's interest to find ways to placate the white minority and to avoid accelerating emigration.

Formal negotiations to design a future South Africa began in 1991 at the World Trade Center in Kempton Park through the mechanism of the Convention for a Democratic South Africa (CODESA). The talks took place in an unusual roundtable setting that brought together a wide range of political groups, including homeland governments. Considerable agreement was reached on the need for an undivided country, a multiparty democracy, separation of powers and a bill of rights that would guarantee the rights of minorities and protect private property.

In May 1992, however, CODESA broke down over the issue of a uni-

39. Sparks (1996, p. 204).

tary state. While accepting the inevitability of a new shared-power arrangement, the Nationalists were eager to avoid putting into black hands the sort of centralized governance system that had served the cause of Afrikaner self-advancement so well over the previous four decades. De Klerk and his fellow negotiators thus sought some sort of federalized or regionalized governance structure that would allow the National Party to exercise regional or local influence, and they proposed a system of "consociational democracy" that included minority-group veto and a rotating presidency. This thinking had the support of Inkatha, which sought a federalist system in order to preserve its power in KwaZulu-Natal. The ANC, not wanting its capacity as a future ruling party shackled by veto powers of smaller parties and the need to work for consensus, pushed instead for a system of majority rule.

When negotiations resumed, any optimism that South Africans might just succeed in finding a peaceful way out of apartheid was soon tempered by an outbreak of violence. Groups from both ends of the political spectrum staged attacks to undermine the talks and to promote their own vision of a future South Africa. Between 1990 and 1994 an estimated 14,000 persons died in the resulting political violence, often carried out at crucial points in the negotiating process. Much of the violence was mounted by right-wing Afrikaners and by members of the state security apparatus. Followers of Inkatha, secretly funded by the semiofficial "third force" closely tied to the security forces, battled ANC adherents not only in Natal but in the Rand, while the Azanian People's Liberation Army, the armed wing of the Pan Africanist Congress, sought to embarrass the ANC by staging attacks against whites. "Politicized security forces and a Kalashnikov culture threatened to engulf the country," noted one observer. "A Lebanese or Yugoslavian future was involved. Violence was becoming an unpredictable and fragmenting force for all parties, raising the spectre of civil disintegration."[40]

Undeterred by such developments, the ANC and the government persisted in their negotiations, and by November 1993 agreement had been reached on the design of an interim constitution. The Nationalists agreed to compromise on the issue of a unitary state once they had secured the more important objectives of entrenching private property and a capitalist economic system. The agreed framework included an interim constitution, elections open to participation by citizens of all

40. Beinart (2001, pp. 277–79).

races, and the formation of a government of national unity.[41] Buthelezi remained obstinate to the very end—even threatening to mobilize a guerrilla force in the manner of Jonas Savimbi in Angola. Under the pressure of his allies in the business community and in the West, however, he eventually decided that the financial and other rewards of being part of the new black-run government outweighed his reservations. He did manage to win vaguely defined recognition for the Zulu king and traditional authorities, and barely a week before the election Inkatha's name was added to the ballots.[42]

The "historic compromise" devised by South Africans thus achieved the seemingly impossible: the orderly transfer of political power from the white minority to the black majority. Moreover, it headed off what one prime minister had described as "a future too ghastly to contemplate."[43]

41. Spitz and Chaskalson (2000, p. 16).
42. Beinart (2001, p. 284).
43. Davenport (1998, p. vii).

three   Education
and Apartheid

June 16, 1976, was a fateful day in the history of South Africa. On that date an estimated 15,000 schoolchildren took to the streets of Soweto, the sprawling and densely populated African township on the outskirts of Johannesburg, to protest a more aggressive government policy requiring that half of all classes in secondary schools be taught in Afrikaans. The students, who viewed Afrikaans as the language of their oppressors, launched the demonstrations over the admonitions of parents and teachers. When a small detachment of armed white policemen ordered a group of protesters to halt, the students responded with jeers and waved fists. Tear gas was fired; rocks and sticks were thrown.

Suddenly, the police opened fire with live ammunition, and a thirteen-year-old boy, Hector Peterson, was killed instantly by a shot in the back.[1] The young man marching next to him picked him up and, with the victim's sister running alongside in tears, carried him to a parked car. A news photograph of the three demonstrators became a lasting visual symbol of the struggle against apartheid, and the image can now be seen engraved on a marble monument at the site with an inscription that reads, "In memory of Hector Peterson and all other young heroes and heroines of our struggle who laid down their lives for freedom, peace and democracy."

The Soweto uprising triggered riots and violence in black residential areas across South Africa. The fact that such a pivotal event in the mod-

1. Sparks (1990, p. 302).

ern history of the country was initiated by students upset with a government education policy indicates how important schools and students were to the apartheid system and the struggle against it. As Nelson Mandela, who did not learn about the unrest in Soweto until later when new political prisoners began arriving at his prison on Robben Island, noted in his autobiography, "The consequences of Bantu Education came back to haunt the government in unforeseen ways. For it was Bantu Education that produced in the 1970s the angriest, most rebellious generation of black youth the country had ever seen. When these children of Bantu Education entered their late teens and early twenties, they rose up with a vehemence."[2]

The Soweto uprising was a culminating point in South Africa's long history of segregated and unequal education, which was the norm from the earliest days of British rule. Before 1948, Africans who did manage to receive an education owed the opportunity primarily to foreign churches and missions that took up the cause of tutoring them in the English language and in Western ways. Mandela, for example, was educated at Methodist schools before going on to a college founded by Scottish missionaries. Even before the Nationalists came to power, states Mandela, the government was spending six times as much on every white child as on their African counterparts. Fewer than half of all African children were in school, with only a "tiny number" graduating from high school. "We were limited by lesser facilities," he commented, "but not by what we could read or write or dream."[3]

Education under Apartheid

The National Party government understood the importance of state education as a vehicle for dealing with the "native problem." Although they lacked a detailed plan at first, the Nationalists wasted little time converting the already inequitable education system of the segregation era into a powerful means of maintaining order and socializing various elements of the population to their appropriate roles in society. Schools for Africans became "part of a broader network of control agencies, including the pass office and police station."[4]

The basis for that strategy emerged in the *Report of the Commission*

2. Mandela (1994, p. 170).
3. Mandela (1994, p. 166).
4. Asmal and James (2001, pp. 197–98).

of Enquiry into Native Education 1949–51, referred to as the *Eiselen Commission Report* (1951), after its chair, W. W. M. Eiselen.[5] Citing inefficiencies and wastage associated with missionary education of Africans, the commission called for a bureaucratic structure based on rational planning and technical efficiency run by white professionals. The commission articulated a vision of education "as a vital social service concerned not only with the intellectual, moral and emotional development of the individual but also with the socio-economic development of the Bantu as a people."[6]

Consistent with this vision, Parliament in 1953 passed the Bantu Education Act, giving churches and mission groups, which at the time provided more than two-thirds of schooling for Africans, the choice of surrendering control of their schools to the government or accepting gradually diminished state subsidies. Most Anglican churches transferred their schools to the government, but Roman Catholics kept theirs going with diminished state assistance. The African National Congress (ANC) organized a school boycott to protest these transfers, but it was unsuccessful, leaving the Nationalists with systematic and comprehensive control over every aspect of education for Africans.[7]

The education Africans received was poor in quality and designed to keep them out of the modern sector of the economy—thus ensuring a steady supply of cheap labor, particularly for the agricultural, mining, and domestic service sectors. "What is the use of teaching a Bantu child mathematics," asked Minister of Native Affairs Hendrik Verwoerd, "when it cannot use it in practice?"[8] On the positive side, the new arrangement provided for greater state involvement in education for the first time and established a system of mass education for Africans, something that the ANC had been advocating for two decades.[9] The importance of this educational base became evident in the 1980s when, as described in chapter 2, the National government, realizing that it was losing the battle against black urbanization and needed more workers,

5. Kros (2002) refers to Eiselen as the architect of apartheid education. For a historical analysis of the commission, see Fleisch (2002b).
6. Such a structure would require the joint planning of social services such as housing, recreation, health, and planning. It also called for the coordination of agricultural education in the schools with state agricultural projects in the rural areas for linkages between training programs and employment opportunities. See Fleisch (2002b, p. 44).
7. Fleisch (2002b, p. 39).
8. Jansen (1990, p. 200).
9. Kallaway (2002, pp. 11–12).

began to invest heavily in black secondary schools and to reduce restrictions on black enrollment in white universities and technikons, or polytechnic institutions.

The organizational structures of the education system under apartheid reflected Nationalist theory that South Africa's four ethnic groups, or "nations," should live and develop independently of each other. Thus separate education systems were established for each racial group.[10] Further administrative changes followed in 1984, when the tricameral parliament was created to give coloureds and Indians—but not Africans—a limited political voice. Each of the three chambers was empowered to run its own schools through its own department of education.

Thus in the final years of apartheid, white students attended schools under the control of the House of Assembly (HOA); coloured students were in schools run by the House of Representatives (HOR); and Indian students attended those run by the House of Delegates (HOD). Education for Africans living in townships remained under the control of the Department of Education and Training (DET). Four additional departments of education ran schools in the "independent" homelands of Bophuthatswana, Ciskei, Transkei, and Venda, and separate departments were set up in the six "self-governing" territories that had resisted designation as independent states. A national department with no operating authority brought the total number of separate education departments to fifteen.[11]

Language-in-Education Policy

Like all other aspects of schooling, language policy in education was used for political purposes: to control black students by separating them into multiple ethnolinguistic groups, and also to separate Afrikaner from English students.[12] Prior to 1948 white schools offered instruction

10. See chapter 1. The Coloured Person's Education Act of 1963 set up a separate department for coloured students, while the Indian Education Act of 1965 did likewise for Indians. The National Education Policy Act of 1967 superseded the Bantu Education Act and placed African schools outside homelands under the control of the Department of Education and Training.

11. Some publications refer to nineteen separate departments rather then the fifteen mentioned here. The discrepancy arises because the white (HOA) schools were operated by provincial departments of education serving the four large provinces that existed prior to 1994: Cape, Natal, Orange Free State, and Transvaal. These four provincial departments are sometimes included in the total.

12. This short history of language-in-education policy is based primarily on Heugh (1995). See also Reagan (1987).

in both Afrikaans and English, but the apartheid government separated these schools, offering English instruction in some and Akrikaans in others so as to reinforce and preserve Afrikaner culture and identity.[13]

Consistent with the government's goal of maintaining separate cultures, identified through language, the National government also required mother-tongue instruction in the African schools. Conveniently for the Nationalists, in 1953, the same year that Parliament passed the Bantu Education Act, UNESCO published a major report recommending international support for using the mother tongue as the initial medium of instruction. Until then mother-tongue instruction had been the norm in African schools for the first four years of schooling. The new legislation extended this period to eight years, which subsequent research found preferable to the shorter period. Because the extended period was introduced alongside apartheid's impoverished program for Africans, however, its potential benefits could not be fully realized. Once they became operative, however, the four "independent" homelands rejected the National policy of eight years of mother-tongue instruction and opted for teaching in English after four years.

After the first eight years of school, African students would no longer be instructed in their mother tongue. Instead, they were expected to take half their courses in Afrikaans and half in English.[14] By that time students should have had enough exposure to those languages to be able to make the shift. As already mentioned, it was the more aggressive effort by the National Party to make Afrikaans compulsory that led to the Soweto student uprising in 1976.

Funding and Curriculum

Not surprisingly, the apartheid government allocated resources to schools on the basis of race. As late as 1994, after the National government had significantly increased spending on black students, the amount spent per pupil in white schools was more than two and a half times that spent on behalf of black students in the urban townships. Even

13. Afrikaners were not the first group in South Africa to use language policies in schools to pursue ethnic objectives. Immediately after the South African War of 1899–1902, Lord Alfred Milner, the British High Commissioner, had pursued an education policy providing for English as the medium of instruction in all public schools. The aim was to anglicize Afrikaners, and it resulted in strong opposition from Afrikaners and the establishment of many private schools.

14. The education system for Africans offered eight years of primary school rather than the seven years in the systems run by other departments.

greater disparity existed between white schools and schools in the African homelands.[15] As the minister of education stated in a 2000 report for an international assessment, "The aim was to perpetuate white supremacy by giving whites a better quality education than that given to other races."[16]

This aim was also promoted through the curriculum, as spelled out in the so-called Christian National Education Policy of 1948, which "explicitly and implicitly placed different values on children of different colors and genders."[17] Whereas mission schools had emphasized cultivating the individual, apartheid schools extolled ethnic pride, racial identity, and "separateness."[18] Curricula were written with white learners in mind and little effort was made to consider the needs of nonwhite learners. Instruction for the latter was designed to reinforce their lesser social status. Advanced vocational and technical subjects were available only to whites, as were higher-level math and science.[19]

Apartheid also greatly affected history instruction, which sought to legitimize the prevailing social order and to teach students from the various racial groups about their proper place in that order. The role of Afrikaners in South African history was glorified while other groups, especially Africans, received little mention. When they were mentioned, Africans tended to be described in terms of physical or other stereotypes, such as "fearsome Zulus." Indeed, schools promulgated "a system of values which amongst other things promoted racial fears, hatred and conflict."[20] These values were enforced through an inspectorate system that kept classroom teachers in line. The typical black learner, writes journalist Allister Sparks, faced a system "designed to stifle ambition and train a working class":

Our young black boy or girl will be going to a school in a dilapidated building with filthy and inadequate toilet facilities, broken windows, too few desks, not enough books, and a hundred or

15. Hunter Report (1995, p. 15).
16. Ministry of Education (2000, sec. 2.1.2, p. 6).
17. Chisholm (2001, p. 2).
18. Jansen (1990, pp. 200–01).
19. Jansen (1990, pp. 201–02) argues that the Nationalists had no need to provide separate curricula for black schools because the purposes of any such curricula were already achieved by the "institutionalized inequality built into Black schools as a result of racially discriminatory funding, overcrowded classrooms, dilapidated buildings, inadequate facilities, and unqualified teachers."
20. Chisholm (2001, p. 3).

more to a class. The teachers, likely as not, will have no more than an elementary-school education and will be tired and uninspired by the hopeless task. The school may have police and soldiers on the premises to keep an eye on the students and spot "agitators." They may even be in the classrooms during classes, in their uniforms and with their guns, and in their strutting arrogance strip the headmaster and staff of any dignity or authority. There will be informers in the school, too, black kids desperate for food, security, and the little prestige that money can buy.[21]

Higher Education

Race guided practices in higher education as well. Like primary and secondary schools, those institutions providing higher education for Africans were started by churches. Fort Hare, the first college for Africans on the continent and the alma mater of Nelson Mandela and many other African leaders, was established in 1916 as the South African Native College. Before World War II, it was the only option available to Africans seeking higher education. With the advent of apartheid, the National government saw the need to provide some university training to Africans, if only to perpetuate the notion that Africans were citizens of distinct nations that required trained leaders, teachers, and civil servants.

Contrary to what its name suggests, the Extension of University Education Act of 1959 barred Africans from attending the previously "open" English universities of Cape Town, Witwatersrand, and Natal without ministerial permission, but it also laid the groundwork for a new system of black higher education. Fort Hare was transformed into an Afrikaner-operated university for "Xhosa and South Sotho groups," and a number of other "tribal colleges" were established for different ethnic groups. Included were the Universities of Western Cape in Cape Town for coloured students and Durban-Westville for Indian students. Subsequently, in the late 1970s, universities were set up for African students in the self-governing territories and homelands. These institutions were managed as extensions of the civil service and used to train needed government workers and teachers. All in all, ten new universities for black students were set up between 1959 and 1982.[22]

21. Sparks (1990, p. 224–25).
22. Cooper and Subotzky (2001, pp. 2, 3, and 7).

Another form of higher education began as colleges of advanced technical education (CATEs) in the late 1960s and evolved into "technikons" in the late 1970s.[23] Offering a three-year degree, the technikons represented a new level between matriculation and the university bachelor degree. By 1980 there were seven technikons serving white students and one for distance learners. Seven technikons were also opened for black students between the late 1970s and the late 1980s, five of them in the homelands. The main function of all technikons was to provide vocational training programs rather than research or postgraduate training.[24]

While white students had access to quality universities, some of them among the best in Africa, black students were relegated to institutions with inferior facilities, instructors, and course offerings. Moreover, because most of the universities for Africans were located in rural areas, their students and faculty members—whites as well as Africans—were cut off geographically and intellectually from other races and from the influence of English liberal traditions.

The Role of Education in the Struggle against Apartheid

Although most black students received an authoritarian education designed to discourage critical thinking, there were some notable exceptions. One such school was Livingstone High School, which served coloured students in Cape Town and over the years became a center of critical thinking and opposition to government policy. Teachers invited speakers to talk about world politics, encouraged students to read critical exposés about South Africa, and provided films and panels about colonialism, capitalism, and apartheid. Not surprisingly, the government responded by banning, firing, and sometimes arresting teachers.

A major figure at Livingstone was Richard Dudley, who taught there from 1945 to 1984 and was the de facto head of the school despite the fact that the government would not approve him as principal.[25] "It was Mr. Dudley who took us under his wing and politicized us," recalled

23. The CATEs originated as technical institutes serving the needs of the mining and advanced manufacturing sectors of the economy (Cooper and Subotsky, 2001, pp. 3–5).
24. Cloete and others (2002, p. 79).
25. The following discussion is based on an interview with the authors and on Wieder (2002, pp. 199–204).

Shafiek Abrahams, a Livingstone graduate who is now principal of Phoenix Secondary School in the Manenberg township of Cape Town. In pressing students to become more militant in the struggle against apartheid, Dudley and his fellow educators also stressed the importance of quality education, both academically and politically, and the need to remain in school and obtain the education they would ultimately need to be effective. "The government sought to destroy the intellectual life of non-whites, but we put ideas in students' heads," Dudley commented in an interview with the authors. "We formed literary and debating societies and reached out to other schools. We used the growing numbers of youth in the country to create social pressure to drive the government to release Mandela and to make concessions. It was a tremendous battle to do this while maintaining education."

But schools like Livingstone were unusual, and during the late 1970s and early 1980s disrupting the functioning of state-run schools became an important tactic of resistance to government policies, with students providing most of the shock troops for this effort. They were certainly not in short supply. Between 1950 and 1975 the number of African children in school rose from 1 to 3.5 million, with secondary-level enrollment increasing fivefold between 1965 and 1975, to 280,000. Particularly significant was the emergence of a new generation of African youth, born or socialized in urban areas with radically different political identities from those of previous rural-oriented generations. Despite enormous class sizes, poorly trained teachers, and inadequate instructional and physical resources, schools in townships such as Soweto educated large numbers of literate, inquisitive, and activist-minded youths and readily facilitated the building of networks and associations. Such schools became "sites of expansion, of expectation, of deprivation and of explosive political potential."[26]

Though Soweto was the epicenter of student resistance, the unrest spread to other locations in 1976 and 1977: Natal (now KwaZulu-Natal), the Northern Transvaal (now Limpopo), and other townships of the Southern Transvaal (now Gauteng). Despite the government's efforts to crush the student movement, its supporters successfully organized large-scale school boycotts in 1980 and even tried to replace apartheid education in the Cape with their own program. A major uprising in 1984 culminated in the educational crisis of 1985 and 1986, which brought black schooling to a virtual standstill.

26. Beinart (2001, p. 236).

For their part, state security forces did all in their power to keep the schools open and functioning. During the 1985–86 revolts in the Cape, the South African Defense Force helped ensure that students wrote their exams: "There were reports of students being forced to write at gunpoint, of exam rooms being tear gassed, of students and teachers being arrested," and at one school "a whole class of hysterical pupils, their teacher and a group of anxious parents were arrested and detained for two hours because pupils had laughed at a policeman during the exams."[27]

During the 1980s a major debate developed within the anti-apartheid movement over the issue of "liberation before education" versus "education for liberation." Since schools were instruments of white control, some felt it important to boycott them and in effect shut them down. Others, including the teachers at Livingstone, feared such action would create a generation of illiterates. Meager though it might be, they argued, blacks needed whatever formal education they could get to ensure the long-run success of the struggle against apartheid.

Those taking the "education" position pressed their views through the National Educational Crisis Committee (NECC), founded in March 1986 at a conference attended by 1,500 delegates representing civic, youth, student, and labor organizations linked to the United Democratic Front. The NECC slogan was "people's education," in keeping with its vision that education should serve the interests of all the people of South Africa and promote democratic values and a wider social consciousness, not elitism.[28] The slogan was specifically designed to link the education movement with the broader political struggle, the goal of which was to get black students back in school and let them take control of their own education. They would then substitute the authoritarian and rote learning methods of apartheid-era schools with critical thinking and creativity.[29] To this end, NECC developed revised English and history curricula, and by May 1986 many schools in Soweto and Eastern Cape were introducing some of these new elements. Such efforts faltered, however, when the government imposed a state of emergency in June 1986.[30]

For a variety of reasons, "people's education" failed to garner universal support. Realistically, its promise could only be realized after

27. Weber (1992, p. 105).
28. Motala and Vally (2002, p. 180).
29. Soobrayan (1998, pp. 32–33).
30. For a concise account of the NECC and "people's education," see Price (1991, pp. 211–15).

apartheid ended. Furthermore, it represented more of a vision than a clear initiative. Unhappy with their school materials, school fees, and suppression of their leadership, students were also slow to respond to the call to return to school, and tensions between students and teachers remained unresolved. Ongoing repression within the schools was not the only problem. Many students were further radicalized by the high unemployment rates that restricted their opportunities once they left school.

Despite severe government repression throughout the late 1980s and the banning of the NECC and other organizations, the "people's education" movement had an ongoing impact. It inspired schools to establish democratic structures such as student representative councils and parent-teacher-student associations. Though rudimentary in form because of government repression, these bodies provided a foundation for future democratic structures. Another outgrowth of the movement was the establishment of Education Policy Units at a number of research universities and the widespread encouragement of nongovernmental education organizations, which were supported financially by Scandinavian and other Western donors, including the U.S. Agency for International Development.

The Beginnings of Education Reform

As apartheid's hold on the country weakened in the late 1980s, conditions in black schools began to improve. Recognizing that the economy required more black workers above the level of menial labor, the government increased its investment in these schools. The children of the black majority enrolled and persisted in school in increasing numbers, and by 1988 the number of black high school graduates exceeded that of whites for the first time (though the participation rates of black students still remained far below those of white students). Total spending on education as a share of gross domestic product increased from 5.5 to 5.8 percent in the late 1980s to 7.3 percent in 1993–94, and as a share of total government expenditure, from about 22 percent to about 24 percent.[31]

Simultaneously, the government was finding it difficult to enforce its policy of complete racial segregation in the schools. Many schools serving white students, including the most selective and prestigious in the

31. Financial and Fiscal Commission (1998, table 3.5).

country, quietly began accepting African, coloured, and Indian learners, primarily from the small emergent black middle class. In 1991 the government was forced to make some adjustments to accommodate the policy breakdown. Initially, the white schools were told they could choose one of four models—labeled Models A to D—that differed in the size of their state subsidies and the limits on the proportion of black students permitted.[32] In 1992, however, the government decided to convert virtually all the former white schools to Model C schools. Such schools were eligible for state subsidies but had to raise the rest of their budgets through fees and donations. Parents in each school were to elect a governing body that would impose and collect school fees and assume ownership of the fixed property and equipment of the school. Until the new government assumed power in 1994, the percentage of black students in each Model C school was capped at 50 percent.

Official recognition of the need to accept the racial integration, or "transformation," of white schools reflected the erosion of a basic tenet of apartheid. Whites acquiesced to protect their interests in anticipation of what now seemed an inevitable post-apartheid era. Model C schools entrenched the principles of decentralized school governance, gave the nonpublic sector a role in the ownership of school property, and, through the imposition of school fees, encouraged the use of a mixture of public and private funds to finance current operations.

At the level of higher education, the long-established English-medium universities of Cape Town, Natal, Rhodes, and Witswatersrand led the way in defying apartheid policies in the early 1980s by quietly accepting black students. By the 1990s the almost all-white Afrikaans-medium universities and technikons were also beginning to integrate their student bodies.[33] This racial transformation of higher education occurred at the same time that the system as a whole was undergoing major expansion, and the black proportion of enrollment increased dramatically (see chapter 10). Surprisingly, however, this enrollment growth did not continue into the post-apartheid period.

32. Often referred to as the Clasé models, after Piet Clasé, the minister responsible for white education, the models were as follows: Model A schools would become private schools and would be able to admit black students like any other private school; Model B schools would remain as state schools and could admit up to 50 percent black learners; Model C schools are described in the text; Model D schools, which were added to the options later than the others, were allowed to admit an unlimited number of black students. This model was added because of the declining white enrollment in some state schools. Pampallis (2003, p. 145).

33. Wilson (2001, p. 4).

The Educational Legacy of Apartheid

Although apartheid came to a formal end with the country's first truly democratic elections in 1994, its negative effects persist in all aspects of South African society, including education. In a recent essay on the legacy of apartheid, economist Francis Wilson observed:

> The destructive impact of the "Bantu Education" system wrought damage that will take decades if not generations to repair. The old pre-apartheid education system, despite its many faults, had the potential for ensuring a decent education for all South Africans during the second half of the 20th century. But the mean-spiritedness which underlay the philosophy of "Bantu education"; the inadequacy of the funds made available throughout most of the apartheid years; and the crippling effect of job-reservation and the color-bar on the acquisition of skills and experience by the majority of workers could almost have been designed to prevent them from being adequately prepared for the challenges of globalization in the 21st century.[34]

This legacy lay behind the challenges that South Africa faced in designing an education system that would meet the needs of its new democracy in an increasingly global economic environment. Four aspects of the apartheid legacy are particularly pertinent for education: residential segregation and persistent poverty among Africans, inadequate resources and low-quality instruction for black children, low levels of educational attainment among black adults and low student achievement, and the absence of an adequate "culture of learning."

Residential Segregation, Poverty, and Inequality

Visitors to South Africa are immediately struck by apartheid's success in segregating different races by residential area. In urban locations, large tracts of township housing for black families, both formal and informal, are physically separated from the cities themselves or from previously all-white suburbs. In many cases, the separation is achieved by distance. In other cases, townships are adjacent to formerly white residential areas but separated by major highways, rivers, or railroad tracks that make it difficult to move from one area to another.

34. Wilson (2001, p. 3).

To be sure, thousands of families from the emerging black middle class have now moved into previously all-white areas. However, there is virtually no movement the other way, and the overwhelming majority of both white and black South Africans, even those in urban areas, continue to live entirely among members of their own race. The best schools tend to be located in the formerly white residential areas and are in a position to draw middle-class blacks, who commute daily from nearby townships. But they are barely accessible to the masses of low-income black families residing in such areas.

Of even greater significance for the majority of Africans is their segregation into the territories and homelands established during the apartheid era and the high incidence of poverty in those areas. These areas were, by design, rural, impoverished, and economically and politically dysfunctional. The land is infertile and jobs scarce. Historically, most black males had to go outside these areas to find work in the gold mines around Johannesburg or in other urban areas, leaving behind many women and children. Even though a 1993 World Bank assessment ranked South Africa as an "upper-middle-income" country, poverty was endemic. Depending on the definition used, the proportion of the population classified as poor ranged from 35 to 55 percent. Poverty was especially common among Africans and was located largely in rural areas.[35] As of 1999, over half of the rural African work force was unemployed, 900,000 African households living in former homelands had no access to arable land, and two-thirds of that number also had no livestock other than chickens.[36]

South Africa as a nation is notable for its huge overall inequality in the distribution of income compared with other countries. A direct legacy of apartheid, the differences between racial groups are particularly large. Africans are significantly overrepresented among poor households and underrepresented among wealthy ones. Although estimates of the proportion of overall inequality attributable to differences between racial groups vary depending on the methodology used, the best estimate, based on 1995 data, appears to be about 45 percent.[37]

Interestingly, by 1996 inequality *within* racial groups, even within African households, is also significant, as indicated by the Gini coefficient (a common measure of inequality based on a scale of 0 for no

35. Wilson (2001, p. 3).
36. Aliber (2003, p. 480).
37. Liebbrandt and Woolard (2001, p. 674).

TABLE 3-1. Inequality in Income, as Measured by the Gini Coefficient, by Racial Group, 1975, 1991, and 1996[a]

	1975	1991	1996
African	0.47	0.62	0.66
Coloured	0.51	0.52	0.56
Indian	0.45	0.49	0.52
White	0.36	0.46	0.50
All	0.68	0.68	0.69

Source: Whiteford and van Seventer (2000, pp. 7–30).
a. The Gini coefficient ranges from 0 for complete equality to 1 for complete inequality.

inequality to 1 for complete inequality). Whereas overall inequality across households remained essentially constant between 1975 and 1996 (at the very high level of 0.68), inequality within each racial group increased substantially (table 3-1), implying a decline in the inequality *between* racial groups. Among Africans, the poor got poorer over the twenty-one-year period while the rich got richer. As a result, the share of African households in the highest-income decile increased from only 2 percent in 1975 to 22 percent in 1996.[38] These figures are consistent with the trends discussed in chapter 2: although most black households were, and continue to be, very poor, even before the end of the apartheid era a new group of black middle- and upper-income households was clearly emerging.

These patterns have important consequences for education policy. First, the educational preferences of middle-class African households are likely to be closer to those of their white middle-class counterparts than to those of impoverished Africans in the townships or former homelands. Thus the danger arises that in the post-apartheid period, middle-class blacks will be more concerned with ensuring that their educational needs are met than in promoting the interests of poor and marginalized blacks. Second, children from poor households are typically more educationally challenging, and thus more costly to educate, than those from more affluent households, yet their families are in no position to supplement public funding for education with private contributions. An abundance of such children poses a significant educational funding challenge for the government. Finally, the low income of many Africans combined with their residential segregation is likely to significantly limit their access to the better schools.

38. Whiteford and van Seventer (2000), as reported in Leibbrandt and Woolard (2001, table 2, p. 673).

Poor Quality of Schooling for Black Learners

Apartheid's second legacy to education is the poor quality of schools. Its educational policies systematically deprived black schools of resources in virtually all areas, from textbooks to toilets. Hardest hit were two fundamental prerequisites for quality education: school facilities and qualified teachers.

As of 1991, the shortfall in classrooms surpassed 29,000 in black primary schools and 14,000 in black secondary schools.[39] Whereas black students, particularly African students, were crowded into classrooms holding as many as 50 or more, other racial groups enjoyed much smaller classes. Unfortunately, residential segregation—particularly the segregation of Africans in rural homelands—made it impossible simply to transfer learners from areas where classrooms were not available to schools with "excess" classroom space.

The shortage of classrooms was only part of the facilities problem. As of 1996, the majority of primary and combined schools had no electricity, 25 percent had no access to water within walking distance, and 15 percent had essentially no sanitation facilities.[40] Another issue was the physical security of schools, which persists even today. Many schools in the townships look like armed camps, with barbed wire around the perimeter and locks everywhere, sometimes even on the doors of classrooms, in an effort to keep the school safe from vandals and the children safe from local gangs.

Teachers and other personnel are of equally serious concern. In the mid-1990s, a person was deemed qualified to teach if she or he had a senior certificate plus three years of additional training. According to a teacher audit in 1995, however, almost a quarter (24.3 percent) of all teachers were underqualified to teach on the basis of this criterion. Even that figure understates the magnitude of the problem because many teachers received very poor training at teachers' colleges under the control of the homeland governments. Some were so bad that all such institutions have since been shut down. The leadership within many of the black schools was also poor. The only requirement for becoming a school principal was seven years of teaching experience. As a result,

39. The estimates are based on classroom sizes of forty students for primary schools and thirty-five for secondary schools. For further discussion, see chapter 6. The classroom shortages were estimated by Taylor and Smoor, as reported in Nicolaou (2001, tables 4.1 and 4.2).

40. Ministry of Education (2000, tables 14, 15, and 16).

FIGURE 3-1. Educational Attainment of South African Adults over Fifteen Years of Age, by Race, 1996

Percent

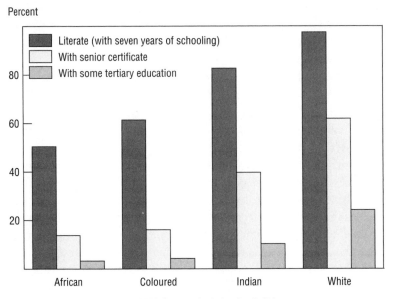

Source: Based on data from 1996 Census, Statistics South Africa.

many principals in rural areas lack the training and skills needed to improve the schools they run.

In short, a long period of underinvestment in the schools serving black learners left them in a poor condition that was not conducive to teaching and learning. The magnitude of the shortfalls and the extent to which they have been addressed in the post-apartheid period are explored in chapter 6.

Low Educational Attainment and Achievement

According to the 1996 census, almost one out of five (19 percent) South Africans aged twenty or older have never been to school.[41] Ninety-two percent of these formally uneducated persons were black, 61 percent were women, and many lived in poor rural areas.[42] As figure 3-1 shows, only one of two Africans fifteen years and older was literate (as defined by having at least seven years of formal schooling) and only

41. Reported in Ministry of Education (2000, p. 7). The original source is Statistics South Africa.
42. Asmal and James (2001, pp. 187–88).

one in seven had passed the grade 12 senior certificate examination known as "matric" (short for "matriculation"), which is the equivalent of graduating from secondary school. Only one in thirty-three had any tertiary education. The comparable rates for coloured persons were somewhat higher but still low, while those for Indians were considerably higher. Highest of all were the rates for whites: more than 97 percent were literate, almost 62 percent had earned a senior certificate, and 24 percent had some tertiary education. The low rates of educational attainment for nonwhite adults complicated the educational challenge facing the new government. Policymakers in the post-apartheid era not only had to improve the quality of education for school-age blacks but also had to find ways of providing education for those who, through no fault of their own, had been unable to receive an adequate education during the apartheid period.

Two post-apartheid surveys show that achievement levels were low not only by international standards but, in one case, by those of other countries in sub-Saharan Africa.[43] The Third International Mathematics and Science Study, carried out in 1995, tested more than 500,000 school pupils in forty-five countries in these two subjects. Results showed that South African learners had the lowest average scores of any participating country in both mathematics and science at the two levels in which South Africa participated, the last years of middle school (grades 7 and 8) and the final year of secondary school.[44] Unfortunately, no other sub-Saharan countries were included in the study.

The Monitoring Learning Achievement Study carried out by South Africa's Ministry of Education in 1999 in cooperation with UNESCO reported even more discouraging results. The larger international study tested a representative sample of grade 4 students in 400 primary schools in eighteen African countries in literacy, numeracy, and life skills. With reference to South African learners, the ministry concluded: "Generally, the performance of Grade 4 learners in all the three tasks is poor. The average task scores are all below 50 percent, which one could consider an average."[45] Among the more than 10,000 South African students tested, the average literacy score was 48 percent and the

43. Ideally, we would cite data from international comparisons of test scores during the apartheid era. Since South Africa did not participate in international comparisons until after apartheid ended, though, such comparisons are not available.

44. Howie (1997). South Africa did not participate in the grade 4 tests because of complications related to language.

45. Ministry of Education (2000, sec. 5.3.4, pp. 40-41).

numeracy score a dismal 30 percent. These results compared unfavorably with those of eleven other African countries. South African students scored at the very bottom by a substantial margin on the numeracy test, shared the bottom position with Senegal in the life skills section, and outscored only three countries on the literacy test. In some rural provinces, nearly a third of South African learners scored below 25 percent on the various tests.[46]

As might be expected from the low numeracy scores, black students at all levels tend to receive minimal training in math and science and relatively more in the humanities and social sciences. At the tertiary level, for example, black students were disproportionately enrolled in technikons rather than universities, were in lower-level tracks rather than in upper undergraduate and graduate ones, and in humanities and social science courses of study.[47] Such patterns reflected both the poor mathematics and science training under apartheid education and labor policies that assigned most Africans to semiskilled or unskilled jobs. The exceptions, as already noted, related to the need for black teachers and civil servants. Somewhat ironically, the restructuring of the overall governmental system (see chapter 4) produced the greatest loss in jobs in the very areas in which educated Africans were overrepresented.

The "Culture of Learning"

Because of apartheid and the struggle against it, black schools also lack a "culture of learning." Even today, South African educators in township and former homeland schools complain that students see little economic or other payoffs in academic achievement. Teachers trying to battle such attitudes get little support from parents or other caregivers, most of whom are struggling with a host of poverty-related issues, ranging from safety to psychological depression. Cynthia Mafuya, principal of the Lukhanyisweni Senior Primary School, a rural English-medium school in Eastern Cape, talked of the difficulty of getting parents, almost none of whom have jobs, to come to school to discuss problems: "Schools are seen as a place where students go to meet educators. Parents don't see it as their business. Teachers know best."

Theta Suthole, principal of the Nomlinganiselo Primary School in the Crossroads township of Cape Town, placed part of the blame on the

46. No significant gender differences emerged. See Ministry of Education (2000, pp. 39–40).
47. Cooper and Subotzky (2001, chap. 5).

sense of dependence imposed on Africans by the apartheid system: "We need to educate parents to move beyond a culture of handouts and to start taking ownership. The majority of our parents never went to school, and none of the members of the governing body have done matric. But some parents are learning. Vandalism has been a problem, and we talked to them about the importance of having a school in the community. After those meetings parents volunteered to come and spend a night at the school."

Mobilizing active support for education among low-income families has been made all the more difficult by a lingering fear of education as an instrument of political subjugation. As discussed earlier, the Soweto uprisings were driven in part by a conviction that schools were "the enemy" and by proponents of "liberation before education." Such attitudes were common within the South African Democratic Teachers Union, which by the early 1990s was winning the allegiance of large numbers of young teachers who had participated in the campaigns against apartheid as high school and college students and who entered the profession committed to democracy and social change. Many of these young teachers chafed at the authoritarianism still evident among school administrators and department officials, and they launched a defiance campaign that succeeded in undermining teacher accountability systems. "In the period 1992–1993, it was common to hear of principals in places like Soweto being forced out of their schools. With the paralysis that gripped the apartheid department, nothing prevented the slide of many secondary schools."[48]

Such attitudes die hard. One of the lingering adverse effects of apartheid cited by the Ministry of Education was "the total collapse of the teaching and learning culture as people resisted subjugation of the so-called Bantu education."[49] The problem led the department in the mid-1990s to launch a formal culture of learning, teaching, and service campaign designed to rebuild a positive perception of education.[50]

Conclusion

Policymakers in the government that assumed power in 1994 were confronted with the momentous task of undoing the race-based structures

48. Fleisch (2002a, p. 89).
49. Ministry of Education (2000, sec. 2.1.2).
50. Fleisch (2002a, p. 91).

of apartheid-era education and introducing a system more consistent with its democratic values. As explained in chapter 4, they approached this task with high aspirations for all levels of education. Although the challenge they faced would have been daunting under any circumstances, it was made more so by the continuing legacy of apartheid and by various constraints beyond the control of educators, including features of the negotiated political settlement that guided the transition from apartheid to democracy.

four   Educational Aspirations
and Political Realities

The journey we are embarking on is long and hard. The educational problems of our country run deep, and there are no easy or quick-fix solutions.
But this framework maps a way toward the transformation and reconstruction of the education and training system and the opening of access
to lifelong learning for all South Africans. We need to walk this path
together in confidence and hope.   —*African National Congress, 1994*

The architects of post-apartheid South Africa understood that a restructured state education system would be critical to the building of a new
and democratic social order. Universal education would be a principal
means by which the long-oppressed black majority would be equipped
to function as skilled workers and active citizens. The educational aspirations of the African National Congress (ANC) were embodied in section 29 of the new constitution: "Everyone has the right to a basic education, including adult basic education, and to further education, which
the state, through reasonable measures, must make progressively available and accessible." The right to a basic education applies to all persons, children and adults alike, and, in contrast to other rights such as
health care, is not qualified.

Transforming this right into a practical reality was easier said than
done, however. Policy had to be developed and implemented within the
framework of the negotiated settlement that permitted the peaceful
transfer of political power. Since the settlement was designed both to

promote the interests of the newly empowered black majority and to protect the educational interests of the white minority, power was more dispersed than the ANC and its allies would have preferred. To complicate matters, a large share of the country's limited resources were already being spent on education and would be difficult to increase further. Finally, the country's capacity to develop policy far exceeded its capacity to implement it.

Aspirations for the New Education System

In the early 1990s, as it became clear that apartheid was faltering, the ANC and its political allies such as the Congress of South African Trade Unions (COSATU) began mapping out a new education system. Many of the policy documents circulated for debate borrowed heavily from the experience of other countries, notably Australia, the United States, England, and New Zealand. At this stage, the ANC emphasized objectives and values denied by apartheid—such as equality, participation, and democracy—rather than issues relating to the quality of teaching and learning.[1]

A draft *Policy Framework for Education and Training* issued in January 1994 spelled out the principles that would guide an ANC government if it were to take over power in the upcoming election.[2] This document reflects the consensus reached by the ANC and its partners in the democratic alliance. In it they sought to counteract three key features of education under apartheid: fragmentation along racial and ethnic lines, unequal access to education and training by race, and lack of democracy. Another primary concern was the breakdown of the culture of learning within schools and the "conditions of anarchy in relations between students, teachers, principals and the education authorities" that had emerged during the struggle against apartheid. The policy initiatives—a wish list as it were—proposed for the following five years were expected to correct these features and create a new system that would allow all South Africans to "participate fully in all facets of the life of their communities and the nation at large."[3]

A first step would be to integrate education and training. As the document stated, their separation under the old system left most people

---

1. For more about these discussions see de Clercq (1997) and Chisholm (2002).
2. African National Congress (1994).
3. African National Congress (1994, pt. I, sec. 1).

"under-educated, under-skilled and under-prepared for full participation in social, economic and civic life." Linking the two was a way of enabling workers who had historically been denied access to social or vocational mobility to gain new skills and formal recognition of the knowledge they possess. Hence the document proposed to establish a single national ministry of education and training along with a national South African Qualifications Authority (SAQA) to help learners "progress to higher levels from any starting point in the education and training system."[4]

The policy framework urged that "absolute priority" be given to introducing ten years of free and compulsory general education, and to ensuring that this new compulsory education be of high quality, especially in "disadvantaged townships, farms, villages, informal settlements and rural areas."[5] The compulsory stage would be followed by three years of a variety of tracks leading to credentials consistent with the integration of education and training. Measures to improve quality would include a "reception class" for beginning students and smaller class sizes (not to exceed 40 learners).

Another critical step would be to replace the fifteen racially defined education systems with a single national system that would operate in cooperation with departments in each of the nine new provinces. The national ministry would be responsible for formulating overall policy, setting norms and standards, providing the necessary financial resources, and overseeing higher education. The provincial departments would be responsible for "planning and managing all aspects of education and training provision other than higher education." The governance of each school would be in the hands of a locally elected board made up of parents, teachers, and, at the secondary level, students.

The ANC document acknowledged that achieving ten years of compulsory quality education would require major investments in education. In particular, the system would be pressed to invest in preparing and developing teachers and improving school buildings. New schools would also be needed to "remove the backlog of school classrooms, to enroll the 15–20 percent of children who are not currently at primary

4. This concept of integrating formal and nonformal education draws heavily on international concepts promulgated by the World Bank and UNESCO in the 1970s–90s. For a discussion of South African policy in a comparative context, see Chisholm (1997).
5. African National Congress (1994, pt. III, sec. 7).

school . . . and to cater [to] the needs of the growing population."[6] Although it called for some of the improvements to be financed out of efficiency savings elsewhere in the system, the document recognized that public sector investment spending would increase "considerably in real terms over the first few years of the new administration."[7]

The framework also called for major changes in curriculum and language policy to rectify apartheid's shortcomings: it had perpetuated divisions by race, class, and gender; denied common citizenship and a national identity; was unresponsive to changing labor market needs; and was irrelevant to current needs. Moreover, teaching practices were racist, dogmatic, and outmoded. To make the curriculum more relevant, parents, teachers, students, and the private sector would have to become involved in its development. Thus the ANC called for a new national core curriculum specifically designed to "prepare individuals for the world of work and social and political participation in the context of a rapidly changing and dynamic global economy and society," with associated procedures for assessment of student progress and certification, the production of textbooks, and the development of libraries.[8]

Another ANC criticism was that language policies had been used as a mechanism for "the control of Black people, for reinforcing their exclusion from full social and economic participation and from political power, and for enforcing the cultural agenda of the ruling white groups."[9] Hence African languages were undervalued and underdeveloped, and Africans had little choice over the language in which they would be instructed. In support of multilingualism, the document proposed a democratic consultative process for determining the language or languages of learning based on three principles: the right of the individual to choose the language of learning; the right to develop the linguistic skills necessary for full participation in national, provincial, and local life; and the need to promote and develop South African languages neglected under apartheid.

In the ANC's view, institutions of higher education ought to be representative of the South African population, and higher education needed to be transformed for the benefit of the economic, political, cultural, and intellectual life of society.[10] The system would be structured around

6. African National Congress (1994, pt. III, sec. 6).
7. African National Congress (1994, pt. III, sec. 6).
8. African National Congress (1994, pt. V, sec. 3).
9. African National Congress (1994, pt. V, sec. 12).
10. African National Congress (1994, pt. VI, sec. 24).

universities and technikons (which would provide undergraduate and graduate degrees) and colleges (which would grant professional diplomas and certificates). Flexible access into and between the institutions would be facilitated by a single national qualifications structure. The system would be expanded, especially in the college and technikon sectors and in the areas of science, technology, and economics. A central concern was that disadvantaged students gain greater access to institutions of higher education.

In addition, the document called for new programs in strategic areas, such as early childhood education, a national system of adult basic education, and appropriate services for special education at the national and provincial levels. However, the document mentioned no specific priorities in this regard.

These aspirations reflected decades of frustration at the educational injustices imposed on South Africa's black majority under apartheid. Although progress has been made, most of the aspirations relating to access, funding, and curriculum are still far from being fully realized. The reasons for that are largely attributable to a political and economic context that required significant compromises by the ANC, most notably regarding the negotiated arrangements for power sharing, the lack of new revenue for education, and limited managerial capacity.

The Negotiated Settlement and the Sharing of Power

The ANC-led Government of National Unity headed by Nelson Mandela was a constitutionally defined multiparty assembly consisting of seven political parties that won seats in South Africa's first democratic elections in April 1994.[11] Initially the ANC, the National Party, and the Inkatha Freedom Party shared executive powers, but on June 30, 1996, the Nationalists withdrew from the government to become part of the opposition. Closely allied with the ANC was the trade union group, COSATU, and the South African Communist Party.

The fact that the transformation involved negotiated change rather than a radical rupture with the past had important consequences for educational policy. As noted by Kader Asmal, the current minister of

11. The 1994 elections produced the following distribution of seats in the South African Parliament: ANC, 252; National Party, 82; Inkatha Freedom Party, 43; Freedom Front, 9; Democratic Party, 7; Pan Africanist Congress, 5; and African Christian Democratic Party, 2.

education, and Wilmot James, former dean of humanities at the University of Cape Town, "One consequence of a negotiated change is that reforms must proceed with inherited assets and liabilities. The deracialization of schooling had to be evolutionary, and every positive step toward this end required an act of political will."[12]

Cooperative Government

Particularly important were the form of the new governmental system and the division of responsibilities among its tiers (subsequently called spheres). During the negotiations described in chapter 2, the ANC and its allies had pushed for a centralized system in which the national government would have the power to ensure equality of social services throughout the country. The National Party and its allies, most notably Zulu Chief Buthelezi and his Inkatha Freedom Party, sought a more decentralized system through which they might retain power in some parts of the country. The compromise was to establish nine new provinces that would work cooperatively with the central government.

Section 4 of the constitution gave the national government and the nine new provinces joint responsibility for the provision of the major social services, including education, health, and welfare. Together the various levels of government constitute what the constitution calls "cooperative government," a uniquely South African arrangement designed to encourage the different levels of government to work together rather than compete. In consultation with various provincial representatives, the national government sets national norms and standards for each of the service areas, which the provinces are then expected to implement. The provincial governments have very limited authority to raise their own revenue; instead they rely primarily on revenue-sharing grants from the national government.[13]

The nine new provinces replaced four larger provinces plus the homelands and self-governing territories that had constituted the prior governmental system. Although all nine provinces were newly established, some—such as Western Cape, Gauteng and Free State—could draw directly on the administrative capacity of the former system. Western

12. Asmal and James (2001, p. 186).
13. For background on the political discussions that led to this cooperative arrangement, see Haysom (2001). Federal debates played a major role in the constitutional debates, but note that the term "federalism" does not appear in the constitution. This term was pejoratively associated with the apartheid era and became a byword for obstructing majoritarian democracy (p. 44). See also Pampallis (1991).

Cape, for example, benefited from the fact that its capital, Cape Town, had been the capital of the former Cape Province. Others—such as Eastern Cape, Limpopo, and KwaZulu-Natal—represented an amalgamation of former homelands or territories and pockets of white South Africa. The challenge for those provinces was far greater. Not only did they have to establish new governments essentially from scratch, but they also had to combine the cultures of a variety of administrative structures, some of which had been dysfunctional before. As a result, the new provinces differed significantly in their political and managerial capacity. There were also large differences in their wealth and education-related assets, such as the educational attainment of their populations and the quality of their school facilities.

A comparison of provinces by income, share of the population living in rural areas, poverty, and other factors (table 4-1) indicates that the two wealthiest are Gauteng in the north, which includes Johannesburg and the administrative capital Pretoria, and Western Cape in the south, which includes the city of Cape Town, the seat of Parliament. Among the poorest are Eastern Cape, KwaZulu-Natal, and Limpopo (formerly Northern Province) and North West, all of which were consolidated in part from former homelands.

This new arrangement forced policymakers at the national level to devote significant attention to developing functioning provincial legislatures. To that end, they provided each province with a single pot of money, called the equitable share grant (see chapter 6), and let each provincial legislature make its own decisions about how to allocate the funds among the functional areas of education, health, and social services. Despite any inclinations national policymakers might have had about directing how the money should be spent, they understood that this power should reside in the provincial legislatures in order to legitimate these bodies and to strengthen the local democratic process. During the transition period before 1996, education funding was still largely under national control, but once the provinces were up and running, education funding rested on budget negotiations between the various functional areas within each province.[14]

As explained in chapter 6, contradictions and tensions soon emerged between the equalizing pressures from the center and the realities of policymaking and implementation at the provincial level. A case in point

14. Chisholm and others (1999, p. 393).

TABLE 4-1. Demographic Characteristics of the Nine Provinces

Percent, except where noted

Province	Population (thousands)	White population	Income per capita (rand)	Rural population	Poverty rate[a]	Adults with senior certificate	Persons aged 5–17 years
Eastern Cape	6,302,524	5.2	2,401	64.9	63.9	13.7	31.4
Free State	2,633,503	12.0	4,958	46.5	50.0	17.2	25.6
Gauteng	7,348,425	23.2	15,094	6.62	19.9	31.1	23.1
KwaZulu-Natal	8,417,020	6.6	6,657	63.0	51.5	19.1	31.4
Limpopo	4,929,365	2.4	2,158	91.2	72.4	16.0	36.2
Mpumalanga	2,800,710	9.0	5,066	67.5	48.8	17.6	29.0
Northern Cape	840,323	13.3	7,092	26.7	37.8	16.5	26.0
North West	3,354,824	6.6	3,326	72.4	37.2	16.2	28.3
Western Cape	3,956,876	20.8	11,203	14.3	18.4	28.0	25.5
Total	40,583,570	10.9	3,524	51.3	45.7	20.8	29.0

Source: Data on income, rural population, and persons 5–17 are from Financial and Fiscal Commission (1995, table 1). Data on the general and white population, poverty rate, and adults with senior certificate are from the 1996 Census, Statistics South Africa.

a. Poverty rate as reported in source. Alternative estimates of the household poverty rate based on consumption expenditures of 800 rand or less per month generate lower poverty rates (Statistics South Africa, 2000). The discrepancy comes from serious underreporting of income in the census.

was the opposition to the national government's efforts to impose nationally uniform student-to-teacher ratios throughout the country.

School Governance

As part of the negotiated settlement, schools were to become self-governing. Eager to preserve as much of their former privilege as possible in the new social order, whites pressed for control over their schools. To Afrikaners, it was particularly important to control language, religious, and cultural instruction in order to maintain their nationalist tradition.

In the early 1990s whites had already begun restructuring their schools in anticipation of the transfer of considerable political control to the black majority (see chapter 3). Parents in the (formerly all-white) model C schools were given ownership of the physical property as well as significant control over hiring and admissions policies, and they were permitted to augment state resources with school fees. The question was whether those schools would be allowed to retain those powers after 1994. On the one hand, ANC-dominated policy groups urged greater state control, with school assets reverting to the state. On the other hand, Model C supporters argued that these schools were already educating a large number of disadvantaged students and could serve as an example for the development of other schools.

Schools that formerly served white students were allowed to maintain significant control over their schools through locally elected school governing bodies. That approach gained political acceptability because it was extended to all schools. As we described in chapter 3, many black Africans who had struggled against apartheid distrusted and scorned schools as instruments of the repression. The best course of action, many believed, was to turn ownership and control over to local school communities, which seemed a logical outgrowth of the parent-teacher-student associations promoted by the "people's education" movement. The political trade-off involved in this move was momentous. It gave Model C schools the power to set their own policy on admissions (albeit subject to a number of limitations, including no racial discrimination), school language, the hiring of teachers, and obligatory school fees. While former black schools also gained those powers, they were much less well equipped to use them in ways to enhance school quality. As we show in chapters 5 to 9, the differences in social and managerial capital in the various types of schools directly affected the country's efforts to promote a nonracial and equitable education system.

Lack of New Resources

South Africa emerged from the apartheid era at a time when the prevailing international economic wisdom focused on economic efficiency, cost cutting, market-led reform, and fiscal austerity.[15] Because South Africa was already spending more than 7 percent of its GNP on education, a share that was high by international standards, even the ANC agreed that there should be no increase. Thus any growth in spending on education would have to come from economic growth. At the same time, the new government accepted the prevailing view that called for an austere budget policy, which restricted economic growth. As a result, despite the country's pressing educational needs, inflation-adjusted spending on education declined somewhat during the late 1990s.

Education Spending in International Perspective

In the final years of apartheid, education spending in South Africa increased from 5.7 percent of the country's gross national product (GNP) in 1987–88 to 7.3 percent in 1993–94. In real terms, spending increased at the rate of 5.2 percent a year, far outpacing the annual population growth of 2.2 percent.[16] Even so, racial disparities in funding remained large.

Thus, when the new government took over in 1994, it inherited not only these disparities but also a high total amount of public spending by international standards. According to United Nations data for 1995–97, South Africa spent 7.6 percent of its GNP on education, which far exceeded the 4.7 percent average for the seventy-eight countries that the United Nations characterized, along with South Africa, as having medium human development.[17] Similarly, South Africa's commitment of 22 percent of its budget far exceeded the 16 percent average for the other countries. In fact, South Africa was among the top ten highest-spending countries in its comparable group.

15. See Chisholm (1997) for an insightful analysis of South African education in an international context. See Carnoy (1995) for an analysis of how the changing world economy has affected education policy in developing countries.
16. Buckland and Fielden (1994, p. iii).
17. The United Nations measures a country's level of human development by its life expectancy, per capita income, and level of education. The high development group consists of forty-eight developed countries of Europe and elsewhere. The bottom thirty-six include countries such as Gambia, Guinea, and Malawi. We calculated the averages from the UNDP Human Development Report (2001, table 9).

Although its spending was clearly high compared with that of many other countries, was it too high? This is a complex question. Other comparable African countries such as Namibia, Botswana, and Lesotho (and also Zimbabwe in an earlier year) were devoting even greater shares of their GNP to education, and some developed countries, most notably the Scandinavian countries, were also spending 7.5 percent or more of their GNP on education. In addition, South Africa was educating a larger proportion of its school-age population than was the case in many other developing countries (see chapter 7). One might also argue that, given its apartheid history and the important role that an educated citizenry would play in its new democracy, South Africa would have done well to put the international comparisons aside and instead to have viewed spending on education as an investment that would yield high returns in the future.[18]

Instead, concerns about being out of line with other countries as well as studies indicating waste within the education sector dominated the discussion and led even the ANC to be wary about expanding the education budget. Although it did acknowledge the need for an immediate injection of new funds for the construction of new schools, the ANC explicitly noted that "since education already accounts for more than one-fifth of public expenditures, the scope for additional recurrent financing . . . is likely to be limited."[19]

Thus the country would have to turn to efficiency gains to free up funds for the required improvements. According to the ANC policy framework, such gains might come from reducing the high repetition rates in many schools, economies of scale in administrative costs that would be captured by moving to a unified education system, and attention to class size and teacher-pupil ratios to ensure cost-effective use of teachers.[20] The ANC assumed that any costs associated with normal population growth would be "financed from increments to budgetary resources arising from economic growth."[21] Unfortunately for education, the new government then proceeded to adopt a macroeconomic strategy that restricted economic growth.

18. For example, see Colclough (1995, p. 14).
19. African National Congress (1994, pt. III, sec. 6).
20. African National Congress (1994, pt. III, sec. 6). In the same paragraph the document also referred to reducing dropout rates, a desirable goal but not one that is likely to free up educational resources.
21. African National Congress (1994, pt. III, sec. 6).

The Adoption of GEAR and a Neoliberal Economic Strategy

With the transfer of power to the new Government of National Unity in 1994, one of its initial priorities was to establish a comprehensive macroeconomic strategy. The ANC's platform had included a Reconstruction and Development Program (RDP) that sought to increase the rate of economic growth after the country's abysmal economic performance in the previous decade, increase investment to stimulate growth and modernize production, and promote greater equality in the distribution of income and wealth.[22] Nevertheless, the RDP was less a coherent macroeconomic plan and more a call for an expansionary monetary and fiscal policy designed to promote growth, reduce poverty, and redress past inequities. The RDP would have required large increases in state spending on social services, including education, especially in the form of capital spending.[23]

The RDP was for all practical purposes replaced, although never repudiated, in June 1996 with the adoption of a new macroeconomic strategy emphasizing Growth, Employment, and Redistribution (GEAR). Although proponents of GEAR claimed it shared many of the same goals as the RDP program, GEAR focused far more on reducing the deficit and limiting inflation than on expansionary policies. In the process, it played down the need to redress past inequities. Although GEAR included a public investment program designed to address backlogs and enhance the long-run competitive capacity of the country, these investments would only have been possible had the economy grown at the projected 6 percent rate, which did not happen.[24]

GEAR represented an orthodox or neoliberal macroeconomic strategy consistent with the "Washington consensus" then being promoted by international organizations such as the International Monetary Fund (IMF) and the World Bank. That view called for reducing fiscal deficits through expenditure restraint and a tight monetary policy along with rapid trade liberalization.[25] In contrast to an economic strategy explicitly designed to create jobs, the GEAR strategy was intended to promote the interests of capital by creating an environment friendly to domestic and international investors with the hope that the benefits would ulti-

22. Republic of South Africa (1994).
23. Nicolaou (2001).
24. Nicolaou (2001).
25. Weeks (1999, p. 795).

mately trickle down to the poor and the unemployed. A central goal of the program was to attract foreign capital.

The ANC leadership opted for what some have described as a policy retreat from its commitment to creating jobs, stimulating the economy, and reducing poverty for several reasons.[26] A primary concern was undoubtedly the weakness of the South African economy and the large debts it inherited from the apartheid government. To complicate matters, South Africa's large conglomerates were pressing for speedy abolition of exchange controls. The ANC also wanted to protect the interests of the newly emerging black business elite, and was convinced by the prevailing international wisdom of the IMF, the World Bank, Western governments, and many economists that the neoliberal approach was the only alternative for South Africa given the realities of the global economic environment. To be sure, the international organizations had no direct leverage in South Africa since the ANC chose not to accept loans to which conditions could be attached. More significant was the indirect lobbying in favor of the Washington consensus that getting "macro fundamentals right" was essential for the success of other policies. For implementing GEAR, South Africa received high praise from the IMF in its 1997 report.[27]

The shift toward an austere macro policy was also influenced by the fall of communism in the late 1980s and early 1990s, which dried up any assistance the ANC may have garnered from that direction. Furthermore, the economic failures of other African countries made it all the more imperative for the new black-controlled government to separate itself from the policies of those other countries and to send a strong signal to otherwise wary investors, both domestic and foreign, that it would be fiscally responsible.[28]

GEAR did succeed in reducing the budget deficit and lowering inflation. However, it failed to expand foreign investment as predicted or to generate economic growth. On the contrary, high interest rates attributed to GEAR restricted investment and reduced jobs. Economic growth failed to reach the predicted annual rate of 6 percent and instead stayed under 3 percent every year between 1997 and 2002.

26. The following discussion relies heavily on Michie and Padayachee (1998, pp. 632–34).
27. International Monetary Fund (1997).
28. Beinart (2001, pp. 274–75).

Although the sluggish growth in the world economy during the 1990s was in part responsible for the slowdown, GEAR apparently played a large hand in it.[29] Also during that period, both private sector and public sector employment declined each year, and unemployment increased significantly.

Economists differ on whether GEAR was an appropriate economic strategy for South Africa at that time. Critics point out that the economic conditions in South Africa differed greatly from those in Latin America and other sub-Saharan African countries where fiscal austerity programs may have been a reasonable response to extreme economic imbalances. Because South Africa was not suffering from the high rates of inflation and volatile exchange rates that were common in those countries, fiscal austerity may not have been the way to calm investors and to stabilize the economy.[30] Whatever its merits as economic policy, the politics of the situation are clear: South African policymakers determined they had little choice. It was either fiscal austerity or the possibility of being written off by the international investment community.

Implications for Education Spending

The sluggish economy combined with the perception that South Africa was already spending too great a share of its budget on education greatly restricted the revenue available for this sector in the late 1990s. As a result, inflation-adjusted spending remained essentially constant from 1997–98 through 2001–02.[31] Total spending on education by both national and provincial governments and spending by provincial governments alone were both lower in real terms in 2001–02 than they were four years earlier; spending on ordinary public schools was virtually the same in both years. Without a growing pot of money for education during the late 1990s, South Africa had great difficulty making its education system more equitable. Most of the increases in funding for previously disadvantaged provinces and schools had to come at the expense of those that previously had more support, yet any such moves were impeded by the decentralized governance system that was part of the negotiated settlement.

29. Weeks (1999, pp. 808–09).
30. Weeks (1999, p. 798).
31. Based on data from RSA National Treasury (2001), adjusted for inflation using the deflator for gross domestic product (GDP).

Limited Managerial Capacity

Unlike many other developing countries, some regions of South Africa boasted a high-quality governmental infrastructure and significant managerial capacity. That was particularly true in the provinces that had been carved out of well-functioning larger provinces from the apartheid period. At the other extreme were the ones amalgamated out of the former homelands and territories, with their dysfunctional and corrupt governments.

Nonetheless even the provinces with the strongest infrastructure faced significant managerial challenges. Gauteng, for example, not only had to forge a new department from four racially defined education departments but also had to make the managerial culture more consistent with the values of the new government. To that end, the new team in Gauteng relied on outside managers to confront recalcitrant bureaucrats carried over from the old system, moved the head office from Pretoria to Johannesburg to persuade many of the existing managers to leave, and rejected a hierarchical structure of organization in favor of a flat, two-tiered structure with eighteen semiautonomous district offices and a strong head office.[32] In addition, it favored a culture of "collective responsibility" and openness to stakeholders.

Though understandable and perhaps necessary to signal change, these efforts brought new problems that, according to an authoritative account by an insider, slowed the process of educational transformation.[33] Within months, executive managers were paralyzed by endless meetings with stakeholders, and a large number of experienced managers and educational specialists left the department. Although the concept of collective responsibility may have served organizations well during the struggle against apartheid, it was less well suited to an organization that would be judged by its ability to deliver education services to a constituency with raised expectations.

The situation differed in the Western Cape largely because, as one of only two provinces that were not dominated by the ANC, it remained under the political control of the National Party. Thus during the 1994–95 period, when the power and responsibilities of the provinces were still being worked out at the national level, the education bureau-

32. Fleisch (2002a, p. 23).
33. Fleisch (2002a, chap. 2).

cracy that had served white students in the former Cape Education Department was able to maintain significant power by providing much of the administrative expertise for the new department. In addition, the authorities that had gained control over the education of the coloured students in the 1980s through the House of Representatives continued to be influential and to exert a largely conservative force.[34] In contrast, education officials who had previously worked in the Department of Education and Training (DET) on behalf of black learners were in a difficult position, not knowing whether they were to report to the DET head office in Pretoria that was being shut down or the new Western Cape Ministry of Education. Although a new provincial department of education was up and running quite quickly in comparison with the departments in other provinces, it lacked legitimacy in the eyes of the ANC and its allies.

The managerial limitations in the wealthy provinces might have slowed the transformation in some ways, but they pale in comparison with the limitations in other provinces, where inefficiency, corruption, and poor leadership were rampant. The challenge of establishing new departments of education was immense in the Eastern Cape and other provinces amalgamated out of the former homelands, with their dysfunctional bureaucracies. Hence the process was far from complete even nine years later. Between 1995 and 2002, Eastern Cape was a revolving door for heads of education and spent most of 2002 trying to hire a new one. Charges of official corruption, mismanagement, and administrative chaos have plagued the department throughout its short history.

A team from the National Department of Public Service and Administration visited Eastern Cape in 1999 to assist the Department of Education in developing a strategic plan, a new organizational structure, a plan for improving service delivery, and a human resource plan.[35] The team concluded that the hierarchical and centralized structure set up in 1997 to include six regional offices and forty-one districts was obsolete and nonfunctional and needed to be replaced. The new plan was to have a central office that focused more on policy development, planning, and coordination and twenty-two new district offices that would be responsible for delivering education services.

34. Kruss (1997, p. 96).
35. Memorandum to the Member of the Executive Council from the Superintendent General, on the Report on the Recommended Organization and Establishment: Department of Education (n.d.).

Though much of the new structure had been implemented by 2002, serious problems remained. Five months into that school year, for example, school supplies that had been promised at the beginning of the year had still not arrived in one part of the province, prompting more than 60,000 pupils to boycott classes. A damning television report highlighted corruption, mismanagement, nonpayment of pensions to teachers, and the general collapse of the education system. In addition, payments to contractors building new schools were held up because the education budget had not been fully processed, and the school feeding program for young students, a program administered not by the national Department of Education but by the national Department of Health, had been suspended in that province because of corruption and mismanagement. Without a food program, many poor students in rural areas had little incentive to go to school and their ability to learn once they got there was impaired.[36]

The absence of managerial capacity in many provinces generated a huge gap between the policies developed at the national level and the ability of provincial departments to implement them. As will become clear in chapter 8, the national Department of Education also experienced serious limitations in its ability to roll out its new curriculum.

Methodology

It would be an unwieldy task to analyze policy outcomes at the national level and across all nine provinces in the space of this book, especially since provincial Departments of Education face very different racial contexts and challenges. Hence our analysis of learners, teachers, and schools concentrates on two provinces: Western Cape and Eastern Cape. We chose these two provinces largely because they represent two ends of the spectrum. Western Cape, one of the two wealthiest provinces, experienced the largest reduction in teachers of all the provinces as the country tried to equalize resources across provinces. At the other extreme, Eastern Cape, one of the poorest and most dysfunctional provinces, provides insight into the nature and magnitude of the problems that South Africa continues to face as it seeks to fashion a more equitable education system. At the same time, neither of these provinces—nor indeed

---

36. As of January 2004, that program was to be transferred to the national Department of Education and gradually expanded to secondary schools.

FIGURE 4-1. Racial Composition of Population, by Province, 1996

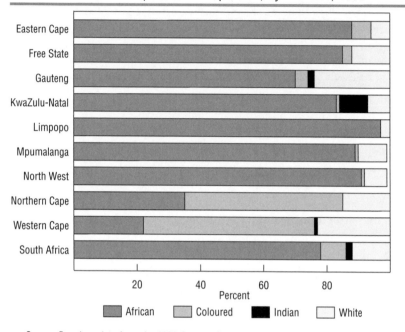

Source: Based on data from the 1996 Census, Statistics South Africa.

any of the others—can be deemed typical, since each is confronting education reform in the context of its own unique history.

In addition to being wealthy, Western Cape is one of the two most urban provinces and has one of the highest shares of white residents among its population. Particularly striking is its large proportion of coloured people in comparison with the other provinces (see figure 4-1). Under apartheid, the Cape area was designated a "coloured labor preference" area, which meant that employers were required to favor coloured workers and that the growth of the African population was strictly limited. For that reason, coloured persons currently account for more than 50 percent of the population in Western Cape and are the dominant racial group in the province. The remainder of the population is evenly divided between Africans and whites, with each accounting for about 21 percent of the population in 1996. About 60 percent of the 1996 population lived in the thriving Cape Town Uni-City area, with most Africans and coloureds still living in the racially segregated townships that had been designated for them under the apartheid system.

Having been part of the larger Cape Province (one of four provinces in the old system), Western Cape retained much of the administrative capacity of the larger province. With the support of many coloured voters who sided with the National Party in the 1994 election, Western Cape was one of only two provinces to emerge from the apartheid period with a government not controlled by the African National Congress. (The other province was KwaZulu-Natal, which elected a government controlled by the Inkatha Freedom Party.) Western Cape was controlled by an alliance of non-ANC parties until late 2001, at which time the ANC became part of the ruling alliance.

Eastern Cape, with its much larger, blacker, poorer, and more rural population, was formed by merging part of the former Cape Province with two former homelands, the Ciskei and the Transkei, as well as with other small territories. Ciskei and Transkei (which refer, respectively, to the near and far sides of the Kei River) have a history that is politically rich and of great significance to South Africa. Transkei was the birthplace of Nelson Mandela and many other leaders of the ANC who received their education in the area's mission schools before they were taken over by the apartheid government. Ciskei is the home of the University of Fort Hare, where Mandela and many other leaders throughout Africa received their university education.

Eastern Cape faced far greater challenges than Western Cape, both because of its extreme poverty and the difficult managerial task of merging homeland governments that had been administratively weak and corrupt during apartheid. That is why it has been slower to develop the managerial capacity to function effectively as a province. It continues to suffer from tremendous poverty, illiteracy, and unemployment. The primary industries are automobile production (in the metropolitan areas of Port Elizabeth and East London) and agriculture, textiles, tourism, wool, and timber (in the rest of the province). Although Eastern Cape boasts several universities and a number of technical colleges, its education system reflects years of neglect under apartheid.

We base much of our analysis on detailed information, including the characteristics of teachers, for every school in the two provinces. The data come mainly from the Education Management Information System (EMIS) and from the personnel and salary (PERSAL) files supported by the national Department of Education but provided to us by officials in the two provinces. The national data system was established in the mid-1990s as a way to ensure that national policymakers would have the information they needed to examine trends and to make national policy. School administrators are required to fill out an annual school survey, the results of which are compiled within each provincial EMIS office and are sent on to the national EMIS office. Though not complete, these data provide a wealth of information, much of which has never before been used by researchers for analysis at the provincial level.[37]

37. Various researchers have used the data for description and analysis at the national level. See, for example, the descriptive data presented quarterly in *Edu-Source*, the macro-indicator analysis in CEPD (2001), and the analytical work by van der Berg (2001). Much less research has been done using data at the provincial level, but see Crouch and Mabogoane (2001) for analysis of Gauteng and Northern Cape and van der Berg and Burger (2002) on Western Cape. For Western Cape, we have access to a large and almost complete data set for the year 2001 along with selected data, including data on matriculation results, for previous years. For Eastern Cape, we have complete EMIS and PERSAL data over the period 1996–2001 but no detailed data on matriculation results. Incomplete response rates in the early years in the Eastern Cape limit our ability to make good use of some of the data for the early years.

five   Governance and
Access to Schools

Pinelands is a comfortable middle-class suburb in Cape Town located near the city's spectacular Table Mountain. During the apartheid era, it was an all-white residential area. Although contiguous to coloured and African townships, Pinelands is bordered by railroad tracks, highways, and a river, all of which limit access to bridges. Since the repeal of the Group Areas Act in 1991, this suburb has experienced a gradual inflow of coloured, African, and Indian residents—almost all of them middle-class and many of them employed locally by Old Mutual, a major insurance company.

Pinelands' three primary schools, each with 400 to 450 students, are undergoing the changes experienced by formerly white schools during the 1990s. Local residents refer to them by the color of their learners' uniforms: the "Blue School," the "Red School," and the "Green School."[1] There is also a private school, Canons Creek, which serves mainly white students, and a single secondary school, Pinelands High School. Though the public schools enrolled only white students during the 1980s, the Blue School is now about 95 percent black and has a black principal, while the Red School is about half black, and the Green School is less than 30 percent black. The high school enrolls slightly more than 1,000 students, well over half of whom are now black

1. The Blue School is Pinelands Primary School, the Red School is Pinelands North Primary School, and the Green School is Pinehurst Primary School.

because many of the local white students have chosen to attend other more prestigious high schools "closer to the mountain."

The Blue School was the first to take advantage of the government's 1991 offer permitting white schools to accept black students. It welcomed the opportunity not only as the right thing to do but also as a way to bolster its enrollment, which was sagging because of the neighborhood's aging population. At first, the Blue School accepted only two or three black students in each grade, but gradually the numbers increased as more came in from nearby townships. Once blacks outnumbered white students, the latter began avoiding the school.

In contrast, the Green School, with its disproportionately white student body, markets itself as a school that serves the local Pinelands community. According to principal Alf Turner, the people in this community have "similar socioeconomic standing and values." The question is, "Does someone from a squatter settlement have the same values and life view as people in this school? If there is an overwhelming majority . . . with negative values, that will affect the majority. It's not a racial thing; it's a class thing. It's an issue of what is acceptable—the approach to sexual conduct, use of drugs, and that sort of thing."[2]

Only the Red School serves the "new South Africa" in the sense that it consciously strives for a mixed group of students. Most of its black students come from middle-class homes in Pinelands and elsewhere, although some come from nearby black townships. "People here are content with the racial mix," said Ann Morton, the school principal. "Whites want a higher white ratio than the average for the country as a whole, but they still want a mix. The reality of South Africa is that you must deal with a mix of people. Our kids accept each other as South Africans."

The situation in Pinelands reflects some of the issues connected with South Africa's efforts to achieve more racial equity in education. Is it acceptable for the Green School to discourage applications from black students who do not conform to its middle-class values, as long as the school does not specifically discriminate on the basis of race? Can racial equity be served if schools define their own school communities and exercise control over their admissions policies? Will the Red School be able to maintain its relatively even mix of white and black learners over time given that parents can choose the school their child attends, or will

2. All such quotations in this chapter are from interviews with the authors between February and July 2002.

it eventually become almost exclusively black, as the Blue School did? Perhaps most important of all, does what happens in the formerly white schools matter in any fundamental sense, except to white families and middle-class black families in the major urban areas? After all, the number of white schools is small and the apartheid policies separated blacks in townships and homelands, which means the vast majority of the black population throughout the country will remain in all-black schools.

The South African Schools Act of 1996

The main thrust of the new education system embodied in the South African Schools Act of 1996 (SASA) is to deracialize education and to promote race-blind policies throughout the system. At the same time, for reasons discussed in chapter 4, the act made all schools self-governing. This move opens the door to school practices that are not race-blind and that may limit the educational opportunities for historically disadvantaged students. Complicating the situation is the issue of language. With eleven official languages in South Africa—two white and nine African—educational opportunities, language, and race interact in complex ways.

A Deracialized Education System

The 1996 act opens with the following statement: "Whereas the achievement of democracy in South Africa has consigned to history the past system of education which was based on racial inequality and segregation," a new national system of schools is needed "to advance the democratic transformation of society, to combat racism and sexism and other forms of unfair discrimination and intolerance . . . and [to] uphold the rights of all learners, parents and educators."[3] To this end, it made nine years of education compulsory for all learners and established a single national system of public and independent schools to be guided by a uniform set of national norms and standards relating to governance, organization, and funding.[4] The separate racially defined departments of education that existed under apartheid were replaced with a

3. South African Schools Act, Preamble.
4. The nine years of compulsory education specified in SASA excluded the reception, or pre-school year, called for in the A1994 ANC Policy Framework and the government's subsequent 1995 White Paper on Education and Training. While recommending this reception year, the White Paper recognized that it could not be made compulsory until sufficient capacity was available within the education system. Department of Education (1995, Section 22).

single unified national system, and compulsory education was extended for the first time to all students regardless of their race.

The procedure for developing the national norms and standards that guide matters such as funding and teacher allocations are specified in the National Education Policy Act (NEP), also enacted in 1996. Under this legislation the national minister of education is charged with determining national policy after consulting with the appropriate consultative bodies, including the Council of Education Ministers, which is composed of education ministers from each of the nine provinces. This consultative procedure, which exemplifies the country's new system of cooperation between the spheres of government, is designed to ensure that national education policy takes into account the interests of the provinces.

Despite its primacy, the national government cannot implement uniform education policies throughout the country. As mentioned earlier, it gives each province a single pot of money for education, health, social services, and miscellaneous other functions. The provincial legislatures are then free to allocate those funds as they wish, with the result that education in some provinces is more generously supported than in others (see chapter 6). Furthermore, when national and provincial laws conflict, the constitution provides that the provincial law will take precedence except when the matter is best addressed by uniformity across the country or when national legislation is necessary to achieve various goals, including "the promotion of equal opportunity or equal access to government services."[5]

School Governing Bodies

SASA provides for two types of schools: public (state) schools and independent (private) schools. Independent schools are privately owned and employ their own educators. The proportion of South African students who attend such schools remains small (see chapter 7), and most South African learners are in public schools.

Consistent with the negotiated settlement designed to protect the interests of various class-based and ethnic communities, SASA directed that all public schools be self-governing. Each school is to be run by an elected school governing body (SGB) consisting of the school principal and elected representatives of parents (who must constitute the majority), teachers, other staff members, and, for secondary schools, students. SGBs are required to adopt a constitution and mission statement for the

5. South African Constitution, sec. 146, 2, c, v.

school, and they enjoy significant power, including the authority to administer and control the school's property and to recommend to the provincial department of education which teachers should be hired.

In recognition of the reality that not all schools have the capacity to manage their own finances, only schools capable of doing so are given control over certain additional financial matters. These are referred to as Section 21 schools after the section in the SASA that describes their powers. However, every SGB has certain other responsibilities with potentially significant implications for racial equity. These include the power to set admissions policy (subject to a variety of nondiscrimination provisions), to determine what language or languages will be used in the school, and to set school fees.

ADMISSIONS POLICY. To expand the opportunities for black students, parents were given the freedom to apply to any school they wished, and schools were no longer legally allowed to exclude students on the basis of race. At the same time, SASA specifically gives school governing bodies the authority to determine which students to admit, provided they "admit learners and serve their educational requirements without unfairly discriminating in any way."[6]

The act does not explicitly define discrimination other than to say the school may not base admissions decisions on test results and cannot refuse to admit a student because his or her parents cannot pay school fees, do not subscribe to the school's mission statement, or refuse to waive claims for damages to their child.[7] Parents of students who are not admitted to a school must be informed of the decision in writing, and they have the right to appeal the decision to the provincial minister of education. Despite these limitations on their authority—as other studies and our interviews with teachers and principals suggest—SGBs that want to discriminate can find many ways, not always legal, to pursue admissions policies that have an adverse impact on historically disadvantaged students.

6. SASA, sec. 5(1). In 1999 the national minister of education permitted provincial education departments to establish feeder zones for public schools in order to control the number of students in each school and to coordinate parental preferences, among other things. Under that new policy, students were still free to choose schools but first preference would have to be given to those who live in the feeder zone and second preference to those whose parents work in the zone. No province had delineated feeder zones by 2000. See Pampallis (2003, p. 149); also Department of Education, *Admission Policy for Ordinary Public Schools*, Government Gazette, 400 919347 (1999).

7. SASA (1996, sec. 5(3)).

LANGUAGE POLICY. One mechanism for discriminating is language policy. SASA gives governing bodies the authority to determine the language policy of each school, subject only to the constitution, any applicable provincial laws, and, in theory, the proviso that SGBs not use such policy to discriminate by race. But language and race are inextricably linked. The mother tongue for most Africans is one or more of the country's nine indigenous African languages; for most coloured people it is Afrikaans, and for whites it varies with their background and is typically either Afrikaans or English. Although some schools offer instruction in two languages, a good number rely on one, and the SGB's decision in this regard often makes the school more attractive to learners of one race than to those of another. Crude efforts to use language policy to exclude blacks have been ruled unconstitutional, but more subtle efforts are undoubtedly quite common.[8]

SCHOOL FEES. School governing bodies are encouraged to levy obligatory school fees to supplement revenues from the state. These fees are important for various reasons (see chapter 7), one being that high fees provide another means of discouraging blacks from applying to a school, since many black families are likely to have less disposable income than many white families. In 1998 the national government tried to reduce the adverse impact of high fees on black enrollment by providing full or partial fee waivers to low-income families. This change did not fully solve the problem, however, because it gives schools new incentives to try to restrict their applicant pool to those likely to be able to pay the full school fee.

Racial Integration of the Schools

The only national study of racial integration in South African schools of which we are aware was done by Servaas van der Berg using 1997 data.[9] The study excluded schools in the provinces of Eastern Cape and Mpumalanga. Van der Berg divided the others into racial types on the basis of the predominant race of their students, with 70 percent as the arbitrary cutoff of students being of one race.[10] Thus, for example,

8. Vally and Dalamba (1999, sec. 4.2.2).
9. Van der Berg (2001).
10. Although this is an arbitrary cutoff, whatever it is makes little difference since 88 percent of all pupils were in schools with more than 90 percent of the pupils from a single race group. Van der Berg (2001, p. 406).

"mainly African" or "mainly coloured" schools are those with more than 70 percent African or coloured students, respectively.[11] "Mixed schools" were those in which no racial group accounted for more than 70 percent of the students, and "other" schools were those that refused to provide information by race, many of which were in Western Cape.

According to van der Berg's calculations, 96 percent of the African learners were in "mainly African" schools and only 3.2 percent were in "mixed schools." Moreover, within the "mainly African" schools, 99.6 percent of learners were African. In other words, most African students are still in schools with other African students. This fact is not at all surprising given the racial dominance of the group and the racially distinct residential patterns entrenched during the apartheid period.

Likewise, white students still attended mainly white schools: 77 percent were in "mainly white" schools, and the average proportion of white students in those schools was 90 percent or more; 22 percent were in racially mixed schools; and virtually none attended the other types of schools. Thus as of 1997, more than three-quarters of South Africa's white learners still had very little exposure to African or coloured peers in school. Eighty-five percent of coloured students were in "mainly coloured" schools, while more than half of the Indian students were in racially mixed schools.

From these 1997 data one may conclude that the only way to improve educational opportunities for the vast majority of Africans in the country is to improve the schools they attend. While integrating the formerly white schools is certainly important to transforming the education system into a nonracial system, that integration will do little to enhance the educational opportunities of most African students.

Western Cape and Eastern Cape, 2001

Our own analysis of racial patterns across schools in Western Cape is limited by the fact that about half the white schools and about 30 percent of the coloured schools refused to provide student breakdowns by race on the argument that they are now race-blind and simply do not pay attention to race. Nonetheless, enough schools did provide the necessary information for us to estimate the racial breakdown for schools grouped by their former department.

11. In fact, he labeled the "mainly African" schools "mainly black" schools. We have replaced the term "black" with "African" to be consistent with the way in which we have used these terms throughout this book.

The results for primary and secondary schools in Western Cape appear in tables 5-1 and 5-2, respectively.[12] The Department of Education and Training (DET) served Africans in the townships, the House of Representatives (HOR) coloured students, the House of Delegates (HOD) Indian students, and the House of Assembly (HOA) white students.[13] For schools lacking racial data, we attributed the same distribution by race in comparable schools in that department at the same level of community poverty, on the assumption that the tendency for schools to admit black students would be influenced by the poverty level of the school's community.[14] Whether the resulting estimates of black shares are biased upward or downward is not clear. Although it is tempting to hypothesize that the schools not providing racial information are more likely to have something to hide—namely that they have lower black percentages than comparable reporting schools—that does not in general appear to be the case. Among the three schools in Pinelands described at the beginning of this chapter, for example, only the Green School, the one with the lowest share of black students, reported the racial breakdown of its students.

HOR schools that serve coloured students are the predominant institutions in this province. In 2001 more than 65 percent of students at the primary level (table 5-1) and more than 50 percent of those at the secondary level (table 5-2) were enrolled in HOR schools. At the other extreme, HOD (Indian) schools served less than 1 percent of the student population. The DET (African) schools served about 20 percent of the students at both levels, and the HOA (white) schools served about 16 percent of the primary students but 25 percent of the secondary school students.

Almost 100 percent of the primary students in the former DET schools are African, 93 percent in the former HOR schools are coloured, 91 percent in the former HOD schools are Indian, and 66 percent in the former HOA schools are white. Thus the former African

12. The total numbers of schools and students in these tables are slightly below the true totals because of insufficient data from a few schools. Nonetheless the patterns across former departments are generally accurate.

13. Only a few schools in 2001 did not exist under the old system. Two of those were established to serve primarily coloured students and four to serve black students in the townships. We have classified those new schools by the department they would have been in had they existed before 1996.

14. For more information on the poverty quintiles used for this calculation, see chap. 6, n. 43.

TABLE 5-1. Primary School Students, by Former Department and Race of Student, Western Cape, 2001[a]

Percent, except where noted

Students by race	DET (African)	HOR (coloured)	HOD (Indian)	HOA (white)	Total
All students					
Total	109,374	377,211	1,182	91,348	579,115
Percent of total	18.9	65.1	0.2	15.8	100.0
Estimated racial mix within former departments					
African	**99.7**	6.4	1.3	5.8	23.9
Coloured	0.3	**93.2**	7.7	25.3	64.8
Indian	0.0	0.2	**91.1**	2.1	0.6
White	0*	0*	0.0	**65.8**	10.4
Other	0*	0.2	0.0	0.7	0.2
Total	100.0	100.0	100.0	100.0	100.0
Estimated racial mix across former departments					
African	**78.7**	17.4	0*	3.9	100.0
Coloured	0.1	**93.7**	0*	6.2	100.0
Indian	0.0	15.5	30.1	**54.4**	100.0
White	0*	0.1	0.0	**99.9**	100.0
Other	0*	54.8	0.0	44.5	100.0

Source: Based on data from Western Cape Education Department.

a. Primary schools include intermediate schools. 0* = less than 0.1 percent. Numbers in bold italic denote highest percentage within columns for the within-department distributions and within rows for the across-department distributions.

A small number of schools had to be omitted from the analysis because of missing data. Estimates for schools that did not provide information on the racial mix of their students were made in line with the distributions of reported racial figures for schools within categories defined by their former department and poverty quintile.

Unclassified students in Indian schools in the next-to-poorest poverty quintile were assumed to be all Indian since there was no other basis on which to distribute them among racial categories.

township schools still serve only African students, the former coloured schools serve mainly coloured students along with some African students, the former Indian schools serve mainly Indian and some coloured students, and the formerly white schools are the most mixed, with 35 percent of their students being black. One must be careful in interpreting the figures for the formerly white schools because they represent the group average rather than the pattern in individual schools. Some formerly white schools are in fact now predominately black (as in the case

TABLE 5-2. Secondary School Students, by Former Department and
Race of Student, Western Cape, 2001[a]
Percent, except as noted

Students by race	DET (African)	HOR (coloured)	HOD (Indian)	HOA (whites)	Total
All students					
Total	62,419	160,732	2,823	73,269	299,243
Percent of total	20.9	53.7	0.9	24.5	100.0
Estimated racial mix within former departments					
African	*99.5*	8.9	1.2	4.2	26.6
Coloured	0.5	*90.9*	42.5	29.1	56.4
Indian	0.0	0.2	*49.0*	1.0	0.8
White	0.0	0*	0.0	*64.4*	15.8
Other	0*	0*	0.0	0.0	0.4
Total	100.0	100.0	100.0	100.0	100.0
Estimated racial mix across former departments					
African	*78.1*	18.0	0*	3.9	100.0
Coloured	0.2	*86.5*	7.1	12.6	100.0
Indian	0.0	10.2	*58.2*	31.7	100.0
White	0.0	0*	0.0	*100.0*	100.0
Other	0.3	8.9	17.3	73.6	100.0

Source: Based on data from Western Cape Education Department.
a. Secondary schools include combined schools. 0* = less than 0.1 percent. Numbers in bold italic denote highest percentage within columns for the within-department distributions and within rows for the across-department distributions.
Estimates for schools that did not provide information on the racial mix of their students were made in line with the distributions of reported racial figures for schools within categories defined by their former department and poverty quintile.

of the Blue School described earlier), and others are disproportionately white (as in the case of the nearby Green School). In the absence of accurate data for each school in the Western Cape, it is impossible to provide a complete picture of the nature of the racial integration.

The racial mix across the former departments was as follows: 79 percent of the African primary students were in former African schools, 94 percent of the coloured students were in former coloured schools, and essentially 100 percent of the white students were in the formerly white schools. Patterns at the secondary level are similar.

It thus appears that the race of students in schools served by the for-

TABLE 5-3. All Students, by Former Department and Race, Eastern Cape, 2001[a]

Percent, except where noted

Students by race	Transkei (Homeland)	Ciskei (Homeland)	DET (African urban)	HOR (coloured)	HOA (white)	Total
All students						
Total	1,281,482	221,267	336,338	124,966	72,090	2,103,913
Percent of total	60.9	10.5	16.0	5.9	3.4	100.0
Racial mix within department						
African	*99.94*	*99.99*	*98.46*	24.99	30.53	92.67
Coloured	0.06	0.01	0.55	*74.69*	11.24	5.10
Indian	0.00	0.00	0.02	0.10	2.39	0.13
White	0.00	0.00	0.98	0.22	*55.84*	2.09
Total	100.00	100.00	100.00	100.00	100.00	100.0
Racial mix across departments						
African	*65.68*	11.35	16.98	1.60	1.13	100.0
Coloured	0.69	0.01	1.72	*86.96*	7.55	100.0
Indian	2.00	0.00	1.97	4.54	*61.58*	100.0
White	0.01	0.01	7.47	0.62	*91.48*	100.0

Source: Based on data provided by Eastern Cape Department of Education.

a. Includes students in primary, combined, and secondary schools. Numbers in bold italic denote highest percentage within columns for the within-department distributions and within rows for the across-department distributions.

In addition to the students in the specified former departments, the total includes 2,797 students in four small territories, 3,703 students in former Indian schools, and 61,270 students in schools built since apartheid. Of the 61,270 students in new schools, 95.5 percent are African, 4.2 percent are coloured, and fewer than 0.3 percent are white.

mer departments still indicates the predominant race of the students, that some African secondary school students have moved to coloured schools, and that some coloureds and Africans have switched to formerly white schools. There has been virtually no movement of white students out of the formerly white schools.

The patterns for Eastern Cape are shown in table 5-3. Here the entries are based on reported figures, since the school principals in that province apparently had no qualms about disclosing racial breakdowns. We report patterns for the schools within the two former homelands, Transkei and Ciskei. We also provide data from the DET, which, as in the Western Cape, operated the African schools in the urban townships, as well as from the HOR for coloured schools and from the HOA for white schools. Also included in the totals are another 3.3 percent of all students. The biggest category of those students consists of the 61,270 mostly African learners in schools established since the end of apartheid.

Table 5-3 reports aggregate information on the three types of schools: primary, secondary, and combined primary-secondary. Aggregation was necessary because of the large number of combined schools in the Eastern Cape, most of which are located in the rural Transkei, which accounts for about 61 percent of all students in the province. Were we to report patterns separately by primary, secondary, and combined schools, the former two categories would underrepresent the Transkei and the latter would overrepresent it. Thus the combined table represents the most accurate overall picture of the racial patterns in the Eastern Cape. As table 5-3 shows, the province has more than 2 million learners, 93 percent of whom are African, about 5 percent coloured, a negligible proportion Indian, and only 2 percent white.

Furthermore, learners in schools from the three former African departments (the two homelands and DET) are still overwhelmingly African, a not surprising outcome given the racially demarcated residential patterns established under apartheid. The formerly coloured schools are still about 75 percent coloured, with the other 25 percent African. The formerly white schools are the most diversified. While close to 56 percent of the students are white, about 31 percent of the students are African and 11 percent coloured. About 94 percent of the African students are in schools run by the former Transkei, Ciskei, or DET, and only about 1.1 percent are in formerly white schools. The comparable share for coloured students is higher in that about 7.5 percent of them are in formerly white schools. More than 60 percent of the Indian students are in formerly white schools, but their overall numbers are minuscule.

Trends in Formerly White Schools in Eastern Cape

Although the formerly white schools in Eastern Cape serve only 3.4 percent of all students in that province, they are the most diversified and provide some insight into trends in racial integration over time. Indeed, the main story in the Eastern Cape is not the integration of the formerly white schools but, consistent with the national picture, the fact that most schools serve, and will continue to serve, a primarily African and very rural student population.

FIGURE 5-1. Black Students in Former White Schools, Eastern Cape, 1997 and 2001

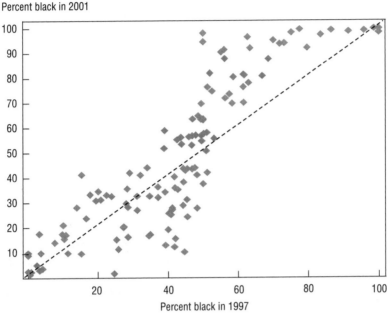

Percent black in 2001

Percent black in 1997

Source: Based on data from the Eastern Cape Department of Education.

Figure 5-1 displays the relationship between the percentage of black students in 1997 (on the horizontal axis) and in 2001 (on the vertical axis) for 128 of the 178 formerly white schools operating in 2001. The 128 schools are the set for which complete data are available for each year between 1997 and 2001.[15] Points along the dashed line indicate that the share of black learners was the same in both years. Points above the line indicate an increase in the black share over time; points below indicate a decline in the black share. Though the data for individual schools, particularly those for 1997, undoubtedly contain some errors, the overall picture is informative. The figure indicates that some for-

15. While schools are legally required to submit annual data to the government, the Eastern Cape Department of Education has not been able to collect data consistently over time. As of 2001, the data set appears to be complete, but not for earlier years.

merly white schools were essentially all black by 1997. Furthermore, the black share of enrollment rose substantially over time in any formerly white school that started with a black share of about 52–80 percent in 1997. Thus once black students became the majority in the school, the racial mix was likely to continue to change, with white students leaving the school and black students filling the empty spaces.

For schools that started with a black share of 35–50 percent in 1997, the picture is much more mixed. The black share rose in almost half of those schools and fell in more than half. This pattern might suggest that some schools in danger of becoming majority black made explicit efforts to keep the share well below the point at which the school might tip and become a primarily black school. Schools that had black shares below 30 percent in 1997 may also have a tipping point. Many of those schools experienced increases in their black shares but kept black enrollment well below 50 percent.

A study of language policy in some of these Eastern Cape schools by researcher Vivian de Klerk illustrates the close relationship between language and race in school admissions.[16] The first part of the study was based on survey responses from the middle-class parents of 194 Xhosa-speaking African children and on personal interviews with 26 of them. All of the children had been sent to English-medium schools in Grahamstown. The second part was based on personal interviews with the heads of the six primary schools, both public and independent, in which the children were enrolled. The parents' responses show a clear preference for an English-language school, even if their children stand to lose their Xhosa language and culture. These parents view English as the language that will open up the greatest financial and political rewards, and they actively promote the shift from Xhosa to English for their children.

The heads of school were careful to deny flouting outright the regulations against using language to deny admission and the prohibition against tests, including language tests, as the basis for admissions decisions. Nevertheless, they did acknowledge using various forms of informal screening in combination with records from previous schools to gauge a student's facility with English and to discourage applications from those whose English was inadequate.[17] They also seemed aware of a potential tipping point, noting that Xhosa parents would not be happy if the proportion of non-English speakers was too high, say, over 50 per-

16. De Klerk (2002).
17. De Klerk (2000, pp. 15–18).

cent. At that level, the school would no longer be sufficiently English to serve the language goals of the Xhosa parents. Nor would white parents accept these proportions. In formerly white areas such as Grahamstown, dissatisfied parents would have the option of sending their child to one of the private schools that typically tried to maintain the ratio of non-English speakers closer to 30 percent.[18] Thus in this case the preferences of the middle-class black parents reinforced those of the white parents in favor of restricting the proportion of Xhosa speakers in the school. (See chapter 9 for further discussion of language policy and its implications for racial equity.)

Race and Parental Choice in Pinelands

Although the fee and language policies of schools undoubtedly affect parental choices, neither of these was the differentiating factor among Pinelands' three primary schools. All charged relatively high fees. The Green School charged students the highest annual fee (4,500 rands), but it exceeded Red and Blue fees by only about 10 to 15 percent. In addition, all used English as the medium of instruction, although the Red School had at one point taught in Afrikaans. The principal difference between the three schools was the racial composition of their students.

The role of race in parental decisions emerges clearly at Pinelands High. In the late 1990s its student body was equally balanced between white and black, but the proportion of whites dropped to 35 percent by 2002 and appeared to be declining further. "There is a perception that the high school is becoming a 'black' school," said Ann Morton, principal of the Red School, which sent only half of its graduates on to the local high school in 2001. "One hears that there are almost no whites in grade eight." As David Arguile, the principal of Pinelands High, acknowledged, "Rumors are being floated that we will lose some whites next year."

Racial mix continues to be a factor in the choice of a primary school in Pinelands, though usually discussed obliquely, under the heading of educational quality. "There is a definite perception that the Green School is more white and thus more attractive," said Arguile, "but you'd have to have a lot of courage to say that in South Africa at the moment. So people find other explanations of their choices, and academic excellence is acceptable."

18. De Klerk (2002, p. 22).

Mervyn Counsell, the principal of the Blue School, acknowledges the complexity of parental motivation. On the one hand, "the issue wasn't necessarily race. Parents did not like the fact that their children's friends were no longer from Pinelands," he said. On the other hand, race has played a role in the fact that his school has virtually no white students: "People won't admit it, but it's a color issue. They say they want their child in a multiracial, multicultural environment, but it's a different story when they have to make adjustments." Emily Holmes, who has taught at the Blue School for thirty years and served as acting principal for a year, concedes that "lack of stimulation in the home" has been a concern among teachers of some black students and that this need has influenced some parental opinions about the school: "There was a lot of fear that standards would be lowered because teachers would have to spend time on kids from disadvantaged areas," she said.

The Green School clearly views—and promotes—itself as the strongest of the three primary schools academically. According to its principal, Alf Turner, "When I arrived in 1992 the Blue School had clearly been out of favor with the community, presumably because its academic standards had been slipping. Our school has now become the preferred school. People view us as the best option from an educational point of view."

In the absence of any objective measures of student achievement such as gains in test scores, it is difficult to say much about the relative quality of the three primary schools. Evidence from other countries suggests that parents often judge educational quality by the racial mix of students—particularly by the share of white students or of high-performing students.[19] Although the Green School would appear to be benefiting from this tendency, Alf Turner dismisses allegations of racism: "Parents are making educational choices. As long as educational standards are maintained and the school is desirable, no one has a problem." However, Turner added, "apartheid worked so well in keeping people apart that there is a lot of nervousness. People fear that black children are not up to dealing with the kind of education that whites got."

The enrollment trends in Pinelands are creating some tension among the three primary schools. At a meeting of the school principals in early 2002, the leaders of the Blue and Red Schools accused the Green School

19. Fiske and Ladd (2000). See also references to this issue in Plank and Sykes (2003).

of deliberately seeking to become a white enclave. Concerns were heightened by a rumor that about a dozen white parents at one of the pre-primary schools had conspired to enroll their children at the Green School. Ann Morton of the Red School heard about this after one child whom she had already accepted into grade 1 for the coming year was withdrawn and the parent of a second was considering doing likewise. With parents free to choose schools and governing bodies making decisions without regard to their impact on other schools, it is not surprising that the Red School was alarmed, since its ability to maintain a relatively even racial balance was fragile at best.

The dispute was fueled by the fact that in 2002 the Green School added a second section to its first grade. Principal Turner said this move was a one-time decision that came about not because of any agreement by parents to boycott the other schools but because of complaints from a number of parents who lived in the "outer limits" of Pinelands and would normally have been admitted to the Green School but whose applications were initially rejected because of space limitations. "All hell broke loose," Turner recounted. "These parents said that they would send their children out of Pinelands rather than go to either of the other two schools. So I went back to the governing board, and to accommodate them we started a new class. Next year will be different because there are fewer pre-primary students coming along."

David Arguile of the high school has been serving as a mediator between the Green School and its two accusers. He has proposed that the three schools issue a joint statement affirming that all three are committed to multiracialism. Although such an approach might make sense from a societal perspective, the fact that schools are self-governing means that individual ones are free to promote the interests of the parents they serve rather than the broader interest of society.

Several years earlier the Red and Blue schools floated the idea of reorganizing the three primary schools so each would serve particular grades and all Pinelands children in the same age cohort would study together and progress as a group through the system. The Green School's SGB rejected the proposal out of hand, citing practical problems such as the fact that it would involve more taxiing and meetings for parents with more than one child of primary age and that it would not be possible to pass uniforms down from one child to the next. Alf Turner of the Green School surmised that the real agenda of the proposal was to attract greater numbers from Pinelands. "Our governing board thought that we have a good thing going and that there is no reason to disturb it," he commented.

Racial Mix of Teachers in Formerly White Schools

Another important point to consider is how the opportunities to learn differ by race within and across schools. Black students in formerly white schools, for example, may face greater obstacles to learning than white students, owing to a lack of appreciation for their culture, outright racism, language challenges, and a dearth of black educators. The challenges related to cultural differences and racism in South African schools are amply documented elsewhere so are not further discussed here.[20] The large and complex issue of language is addressed in chapter 9. Here we briefly comment on the racial mix of teachers, using schools in Pinelands as an example.

In 1996 none of its three primary schools had any black teachers, and the high school had only three. By 2001 the Green School still had no black teachers, though 29 percent of students were now black. The Red School, with an evenly divided student body, had three black teachers out of a total of eleven, and the Blue School, which was 95 percent black, had only four black teachers out of eleven, although it had recently hired the school's first black principal. At Pinelands High, eight of the school's thirty-three teachers were coloured. With the exception of the Green school, the Pinelands schools had made some progress in changing the racial mix of their teachers but were still far from bringing that mix in line with their mix of learners.

These trends are much the same in the larger group of all formerly white schools in Western Cape. In 1996 they employed about 6,200 government-paid teachers, 99 percent of whom were white. As a result of national policy directives that required the downsizing of the teaching force in the Western Cape (see chapter 6), the total number of such teachers in these schools fell to 4,800 in 2001.[21] During that six-year period, the black share of teachers increased from 1 to 8.5 percent, with 384 of the black teachers being coloured. Thus, as was the case for the schools in Pinelands, the formerly white schools have been making some progress in diversifying their teaching force, but at a slower pace than

20. See, for example, Vally and Dalamba (1999).
21. Some of the reduction was offset by an increase in teachers paid by school governing bodies out of revenue collected from school fees. See chap. 6.

for racial diversification of the students. This outcome is not too surprising, particularly in light of the downsizing of the teaching force. Certainly it would have been easier for schools wishing to diversify their staff to do so had the number of teaching slots been expanding rather than contracting.

Conclusion

South African schools no longer prohibit students from enrolling simply because of their race. In that sense, the country's policies of equal treatment, or race-blindness, have had a major impact. Their strong message repudiating the race-based policies of the apartheid era has made it possible for substantial numbers of black students to enroll in previously all-white schools.

At the same time, the authority granted to local school governing bodies by the South Africa Schools Act has allowed many of the formerly white schools to maintain disproportionately white student bodies by pursuing admissions and related strategies that in effect limit black enrollments. Hence in some of those schools, including the Green School in Pinelands, class differences appear to be replacing racial differences as the criterion for entry. Since apartheid ensured that class and race would be highly correlated, any admissions policy that favors students with middle-class values indirectly discriminates against most black students from the townships and homelands.

It is important to remember that national policy regarding enrollment was essentially designed to promote race-blind behavior. The goal was deracialization, not necessarily equal access to schools by students of all races. Thus although formerly white schools are now racially integrated, most African and coloured students continue to attend schools that are essentially all black. That observation should surprise no one. Particularly in provinces such as Eastern Cape, where white learners constitute a tiny proportion of all students, racial integration will never play more than a minor role in determining the quality of the educational opportunities available to black students. Even in the Western Cape, where the proportion of white students is higher—about 10 percent in primary schools and 16 percent in secondary schools—the main determinant of educational opportunities and outcomes for black students will be the quality of the schools formerly designed to serve African and coloured students. In such situations the movement from race-based to race-blind policies with respect to admissions, while symbolically important, is essentially irrelevant.

To better understand racial equity, one needs to examine what happens within the schools, particularly those serving black students. The next four chapters turn to some important issues for those schools: funding policies (both public funding and private funding), curriculum policy, and educational outcomes.

six   **Financing Schools:**
Initial Steps
Toward Equity

The South African Constitution gives each person the right to a basic
education unqualified by any reference to the availability of resources. In
practice, of course, resource constraints are not irrelevant, and South
Africa has been forced to make difficult choices in its efforts to transform
its education system. In this chapter we deal with those related to the distribution of public resources both across and within provinces. Another
set of choices involves the use of school fees and is discussed in chapter 7.

Outside the scope of our analysis is an alternative form of resources—
those provided by nonprofit organizations (NPOs) supported by domestic or international donors. Among the domestic donors in the mid-
1990s was a group of large South African companies that, recognizing
the importance of a well-educated labor force, established the Joint Education Trust (JET) as a vehicle through which to provide funding for
more than 400 nonprofit education service providers. JET in turn was
able to leverage an even larger amount of funding from offshore donors
such as USAID, the European Union, and the Royal Netherlands
Embassy. Though the activities of such education organizations are
important, particularly in the areas of teacher training, adult basic education, and early childhood education, they are far less important in the
education sector in South Africa than in other social sectors, such as
health and housing and development.[1]

1. Robbins (2001). On the basis of their comprehensive survey of nonprofit
organizations (NPOs) in South Africa, Swilling and Russell (2002, table 9) find that

Equal Treatment

The new resource policies enacted by the government in 1994 were explicitly designed to eliminate the race-based disparities of the apartheid period and to treat all schools equally. Even after a significant increase in spending on black students in the waning days of apartheid, the amount per learner in white schools in 1994 was two and a half times that in schools serving African students in urban areas and more than five times that in schools serving African students in the most impoverished homeland.[2] With the formation of the nine new provinces—some consolidated primarily from former homelands with limited resources, others carved out of wealthier former provinces with more generous funding—the inherited race-based differences translated into large average differences in resources among the provinces.

The first task of the new government was thus to ensure that all provinces had access to similar amounts of funding for education. Others were to rationalize teacher salary schedules and to promote nationally uniform learner/educator ratios. Having almost no additional resources for education and working within the constraints of a federal system, the government could not accomplish all these tasks simultaneously. Nonetheless, it made significant and rapid progress toward equalizing education resources among provinces.

Funding

As noted in chapter 4, the 1996 constitution gave the nine new provinces and the national government joint responsibility for delivering major social services, including education, health, and welfare. Under this cooperative arrangement, each province was to receive an "equitable share" of the national revenue for such activities. In 1997 the national government began transferring an annual single unconditional grant to each province to be spent on these and other miscellaneous services.

---

the education NPOs account for less than 6 percent of the total NPOs, which is far less than the 23 percent for health, 21 percent for development and housing, and 21 percent for culture and recreation.

2. Hunter Report (1995, p. 15). Average spending per learner in 1994 was 2,222 rand. Per learner spending was 5,403 rand in white schools, 4,687 rand in Indian schools, 3,691 rand in coloured schools, and 2,184 rand in African urban (DET) schools. Across the homelands and self-governing territories, it ranged from 1,053 rand in Transkei to 2,241 rand in QwaQwa.

The size of the grant to each province is determined in a two-step process.[3] First, the national government decides how to divide its total revenue among the national, provincial, and municipal governments. Available revenue consists of nationally collected revenues minus payments for debt service and contingency reserves. Most of the remaining revenue is divided between the national and provincial governments.[4] Second, the available pool of funds is distributed to provincial governments on the basis of a weighted average of demographically driven formulas that apply to each major functional area, where the weights reflect the proportions of spending allocated to each expenditure category.[5] In the case of education, equitable shares are computed from actual school enrollments and school-age children, with the latter weighted double the former.[6] This formula ensures that each province, regardless of its wealth, will be able to spend the same amount on education per learner as any other province. To ease the transition to the new system, especially for provinces that would experience significant reductions, such as Western Cape, the formulas were phased in over five years.

Initially, the equitable share calculations were based on a 40 percent weight for education.[7] That does not translate into a 40 percent share of education spending in each province, however, in part because the education share of a province's total allocation depends on its demographic characteristics. All else constant, a province with a disproportionately large ratio of young people to its total population, for example, would receive a larger education share than other provinces. Furthermore, in

3. Ajam (2001).

4. Since the municipal governments are expected to raise most of their own revenue from local tax sources such as the property tax, they receive only a small share of the nationally collected revenue.

5. The Financial and Fiscal Commission (1995) first published a temporary formula as part of its recommendation for the 1996–97 financial year. The three main demographic factors determining the provincial shares were population (with rural people given an additional positive weight), school-age population, and use of private medical aid schemes.

6. In 1997 the single measure of the school-age population used in the initial temporary formula was replaced with this weighted average. It represented a middle-of-the-road solution to the problem raised by the fact that using school-age population alone offers provinces no incentive to decrease the proportion of that group not in school, while the use of actual student populations gives them no incentive to reduce the number of repeaters in the system. See Financial and Fiscal Commission (1998, p. 19).

7. That share was increased to 41 percent in 1999.

TABLE 6-1. Per Learner Budget Allocations, by Province,
1994–95 and 2000–01

| | Spending per learner (rand) | | Percent of national average | | |
Province[a]	1994–95	2000–01	1994–95	2000–01	Change in percent
Western Cape	4,074	4,230	183	130	−53
Gauteng	3,843	4,628	157	142	−15
Northern Cape	3,413	4,399	154	135	−19
Free State	2,317	3,604	104	111	+7
KwaZulu-Natal	2,969	2,643	93	81	−12
Mpumalanga	1,917	2,982	86	92	+6
North West	1,812	3,524	82	108	+26
Limpopo	1,669	2,780	75	85	+10
Eastern Cape	1,635	2,968	74	91	+17
All provinces	2,222	3,253	100	100	0
Coefficent of variation	0.39	0.22			

Source: Based on data from the Department of Education and the Department of Finance reported in Perry (2000), table 2.
a. Sorted by 1994–95 spending per learner.

the interests of strengthening democratic institutions, provincial legislatures are encouraged to make their own decisions about spending tradeoffs between education and other categories such as health and welfare. As a result, the provinces end up devoting somewhat different proportions of their budgets to education. In 1998–99, for example, poor provinces such as Eastern Cape, Mpumalanga, and Limpopo devoted more than 42 percent of their budgets to education, whereas the wealthier, more urban provinces such as Gauteng and Western Cape devoted only 36 to 37 percent.

Table 6-1 shows how the new funding policies affected the distribution of education spending across provinces between 1994–95—the last year before the new funding policies—and 2000–01. In the initial year, spending ranged from a high of 183 percent of the national average in Western Cape to a low of 74 percent in Eastern Cape. The three provinces that had the most resources in the early year—Western Cape, Gauteng, and Northern Cape—experienced the greatest declines in their relative positions, that of Western Cape being the most pronounced. Conversely, poor provinces such as Eastern Cape, Mpumalanga, Limpopo, and North West all experienced gains, indicating a significant convergence of spending across provinces.[8] By one measure of dispersion (the coefficient of variation, which is defined as the standard deviation across the nine provinces divided by the mean), the interprovincial variation in spending fell by more than 40 percent—from 0.39 in 1994–95 to 0.22 in 2000–01.[9] Thus although the process is not complete, it appears that South Africa has made remarkable progress toward equalizing spending across provinces.

Teacher Salaries

To rationalize teacher salaries, the government created a single schedule for all teachers regardless of the department for which they previously worked. This schedule was based on a new set of teacher qualification categories ranging from 10 to 17, where 10 represents the holding of a senior certificate and the higher numbers represent the number of years of additional training.[10] Salaries were adjusted as of July 1, 1996.

The conversion was progressive in the sense that teachers with lower qualifications in each new classification received the largest salary increases. As a result, teachers of black students with a given amount of educational training and experience no longer received lower salaries than comparable teachers of white students, although the latter still received higher salaries on average than the former owing to differences in qualifications between the two groups. Nevertheless, the new policy constituted an important symbol of the intent to treat all teachers the same.

Learner-Educator Ratios

In early 1996 the national Department of Education and the teachers' union agreed to a policy of "rightsizing" the public service with the intent of equalizing learner-educator ratios among and within provinces, aiming for 40:1 in primary schools and 35:1 in secondary schools.[11] These targets were based largely on international studies suggesting that

8. The only anomaly among the low-spending provinces is KwaZulu-Natal, where an increase in learner numbers and a relatively small education share of the budget led to a fall in its spending relative to the national average during the six-year period. (Perry 2000, p. 153).

9. More recent data provided by Wildeman (2003) indicate that by 2004–05 the coefficient of variation is expected to fall to 0.14. Also according to his figures, KwaZulu-Natal's spending rises to 97 percent of the national average.

10. Department of Education (1999).

11. This discussion relies heavily on Vally and Tleane (2001).

achievement is relatively constant in classes of twenty-five to forty students but that it falls off when the number is any higher.[12]

South Africa's policymakers may have arrived at these specific figures because they did not fully understand the distinction between learner-educator ratios and class sizes. The term "educator" includes school principals and heads of departments who are not in the classroom all of the time. Hence a learner-educator ratio of 40:1 translates into class sizes that are significantly larger than forty. Alternatively, policymakers may have been guided by what they perceived the country could afford. Once teacher salaries are set and the number of students known, simple arithmetic translates a learner-educator ratio into an aggregate expenditure for teachers that accounts for over 85 percent of the spending on schools.

After 1997 the national Department of Education had no direct control over decisions made in the provinces. Hence to implement the uniform learner-educator ratios it tried to require schools with a shortage of teachers to hire from a pool of teachers declared to be in "excess" at other schools. In addition, it called for voluntary severance packages (VSPs) designed to induce teachers to leave teaching and thereby to create room for others deemed to be in excess. By 1997 the total costs of the VSPs had risen to over a billion rand, and in a ruling that significantly curtailed the powers of the national government, the Cape High Court declared that the national Ministry of Education did not have the authority to force a Western Cape primary school to hire the excess teachers from other schools.[13] This court case effectively ended the mandatory redeployment policy.

The redeployment effort highlighted the tension between policymakers trying to set absolute standards at the national level and those making funding decisions at the provincial level. Since the national government was not explicitly paying for the required number of teachers in each province, there was no guarantee that a province could afford them. As a result of concern about what amounted to unfunded mandates, provinces were authorized to determine the total number of teacher positions, and hence class sizes, on the basis of what each province could afford.

In a 1998 agreement between the teachers' unions and the Depart-

12. The international studies were summarized in a 1995 World Bank study, cited by Vally and Tleane (2001, p. 183).
13. *Grove Primary School v. Minister of Education and Others,* 1997.

TABLE 6-2. Learners per Educator, by Province, 1996 and 2000
Number of learners

Province[a]	1996	2000	Change
Western Cape	26	31	+5
Northern Cape	27	26	−1
Gauteng	28	29	+1
North West	29	29	0
Free State	32	31	−1
Limpopo	33	31	−2
KwaZulu-Natal	34	34	0
Eastern Cape	35	32	−3
Mpumalanga	36	39	3
All provinces	32	32	0
Coefficient of variation	0.109	0.107	−0.002

Source: Monica Bot, "School Register of Needs 2000: An Update," *EduSource Data News*, no. 35, December 2001, table 3. Coefficient of variation calculated by the authors.
a. Sorted by 1996 number.

ment of Education, new national norms were established to guide the allocation of teachers within provinces. The new norms departed from the concept of uniform class sizes to allow for smaller classes and hence more teachers per student for certain subjects, most notably those on the national matriculation exam, technical subjects, and arts classes. They also called for more teachers in some grades than in others. Although the new norms for distributing slots were not based on race, they ended up favoring the previously advantaged schools, where demand for the subjects eligible for smaller class sizes was typically higher.

The effects of these policy initiatives on learner-educator ratios are shown in table 6-2, which summarizes results from two waves of a recent Department of Education survey. Its figures suggest much less convergence over time than was true for funding and relate much of what did take place to changes in Western Cape and Eastern Cape: between 1996 and 2000, the ratio rose from 26 learners per educator to 31 in Western Cape and fell from 35 to 32 in Eastern Cape. The province with the highest learner-educator ratio in 1996, Mpumalanga, is an outlier in that its ratio increased over the period. Overall, the coefficient of variation across provinces fell only slightly between 1996 and 2000 (from 0.109 to 0.107).

Our own calculations of the learner-educator ratio for Eastern and Western Cape show even greater changes, albeit for slightly different years.[14] Our numbers for the Eastern Cape decline from 47 in 1995 to 32 in 2000, and for the Western Cape they rise from 29 in 1996 to 37 in 2001 in primary schools and from 25 to 33 in secondary schools.

Thus it appears that much of the national convergence in funding across provinces may have been absorbed by the equalization of salaries rather than by the equalization of learner-educator ratios. It would be incorrect to conclude, however, that the effort to equalize learner-educator ratios had little or no overall effect on the distribution of resources among schools. Our analysis of the patterns across schools in 2001 in Eastern Cape and Western Cape, discussed at the end of this chapter, indicates that the national norms for allocating teacher slots within provinces appear to have significantly narrowed the differences across schools grouped by their former departments.

Large Loss of Teachers in Western Cape

As head of the Western Cape Department of Education, Brian O'Connell understood that cutting up to 8,500 teacher slots would inevitably require massive layoffs. In his view, the sooner the province began the adjustment, the better. His task was not made any easier by what he saw as the failure of the national government to take ownership of the policy. Instead of making a public plea for sacrifice in wealthy provinces such as Western Cape, it asserted that no teachers would lose their posts as their distribution across provinces and across schools became rationalized.[15] The unrealistic expectation was that excess teachers would simply be redeployed in other schools facing a shortage of teachers.[16]

As it turned out, the rationalization process in Western Cape led to large reductions in teacher slots not only in the formerly white schools

14. We calculated the Eastern Cape ratios as the total learners divided by the total educators for each year as reported in the Eastern Cape Department of Education, *Review of Education Indicators 1995–2000*. The total number of educators was not reported for 1996. Western Cape figures were calculated from data at the school level provided by the Western Cape Department of Education. For these calculations, intermediate schools are grouped with primary schools and combined schools with secondary schools.

15. Interview with Brian O'Connell, June 2002.

16. In response to the national government's effort to force schools to hire teachers from the pool of excess teachers, many of whom were coloured teachers from the coloured schools, the Grove Primary School, a preeminent former white school, went to court to assert its right to make its own hiring decisions. As mentioned earlier, the judgment in favor of Grove Primary essentially halted the teacher redeployment effort.

but also in coloured ones. The National Party had favored them with additional teachers during the buildup to the 1994 election in an effort to attract political support from the largely Afrikaans-speaking coloured population. As principals of coloured schools explained to us in 2002, this posed a clear difficulty. Riyaad Najaar, principal of Spine Road High School in the Mitchell's Plain section of Cape Town, said his staff plummeted from 53 teachers serving 1,100 learners in 1993 to 39 teachers for 1,300 learners in 2002. "They took away from us the only resources we had—human resources—and told us to compensate by cutting down on 'nonessential' services like health."[17]

Spine Road was not unusual. On average each formerly coloured high school lost more than 11 teacher positions between 1996 and 1999 while formerly white high schools lost about 6.7 teachers. In contrast, former African high schools gained a teacher.[18] Because the white schools were smaller than the coloured schools and were growing, however, the net adverse impact on schools as measured by the change in the ratio of learners to educators was largest in the former white schools. As figure 6-1 indicates, average learner-educator ratios rose in all types of schools in Western Cape, with the increases at both the primary and secondary level being the largest for the former white schools. The typical former white school experienced an increase of about 8 learners per educator at the primary level and about 10.5 at the secondary level.[19] As we show in chapter 7, however, former white schools had greater access to fee revenue and hence were in a better position than the coloured schools to offset the cuts in state-paid educators with privately funded educators. Thus the formerly coloured schools were indeed the group most adversely affected by the teacher rationalization process in the Western Cape.

To make things worse for the coloured schools, the teachers who left had higher average qualifications than those who remained. The typical teacher in coloured secondary schools in 1996 had nearly four and a half

17. Unless otherwise indicated, quotations in this chapter are from interviews with the authors between February and July 2002.

18. These figures are based on data provided by the Western Cape Department of Education. They understate the magnitude of the changes since they exclude any cuts in teachers between 1995 and 1996. The comparable changes for primary schools were −3.11 for former white schools, −3.01 for former coloured schools, and −0.22 for former African schools. We have not reported figures for former Indian schools since the number of such schools is so small.

19. The House of Delegates schools that serve Indian students are not included in the figure because of the small number of such schools and limited teacher departures.

FIGURE 6-1. Average Increases in Learners per Educator, by Former Department, Western Cape, 1996–99

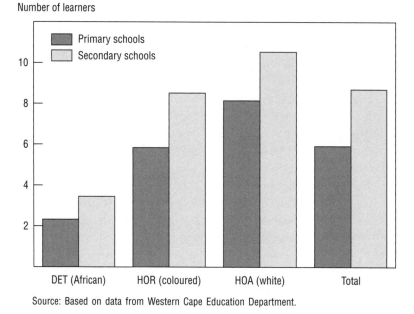

Number of learners

Source: Based on data from Western Cape Education Department.

years of education beyond the matriculation exam, but by the next year the typical teacher had one-third of a year less training. Our interviews with school principals suggest that the impact was particularly devastating for mathematics and science teachers, many of whom were quick to accept the VSP because they had ready access to attractive jobs in business and other sectors of the economy. Shadley Mohamed, principal of Crystal High School in Hanover Park, reported that "it was the good teachers who left, particularly in math and science, and this created huge gaps for disadvantaged schools." Rhoda Hendricks, the principal of another coloured school, Livingstone High School in Cape Town, called the voluntary plan "a total bungle. They should have tailored the cuts to our curricular needs," she said. "We lost thirteen of forty-nine staff members, especially math teachers, and now we can't find anyone to teach accounting. Some math teachers are beginning to go back, but they are very picky about the jobs they are willing to accept."

The national policy of moving teachers about caused a furor. In early 1996 teachers in Cape Town initiated a wildcat strike. Many there and

TABLE 6-3. Teacher Departures, 1997–2001, Western Cape

Departures	1997	1998	1999	2000	2001
Total departures	13,902	10,117	10,469	5,302	6,828
Schools with departures	1,359	1,211	960	953	1,069
Average per school	10.2	8.4	10.9	5.6	6.4
Departures by category					
Packages and contracts					
Package	379	1,946	18	2	483
Contract expiration	12,568	7,318	9,607	4,243	5,426
Subtotal	12,947	9,264	9,625	4,245	5,909
(percent of total)	(93.1)	(91.6)	(91.9)	(80.0)	(86.5)
Retirement, resignations, medical, and death					
Retirement	32	39	91	111	86
Resignation	389	392	429	577	560
Medical	305	306	254	275	197
Death	50	50	44	57	39
Subtotal	776	787	818	1,020	882
(percent of total)	(5.6)	(7.8)	(7.8)	(19.2)	(12.9)
Misconduct	168	53	16	34	30
Other	11	13	10	3	7

Source: Based on data from Western Cape Department of Education.

elsewhere, particularly married coloured teachers, were reluctant to move and left the profession.[20] Since the province was under pressure to reduce the total number of teachers by as many as 8,500, it could make no commitment to hiring new permanent teachers. As a result, many schools that needed to hire teachers were forced to engage temporary teachers on one-year contracts. By early 1998, however, budgetary constraints in Western Cape and other provinces kept them from renewing the appointments of many temporary teachers.

As table 6-3 indicates, the years 1997–99 witnessed a large number of teacher departures, the bulk of which represented the termination of short-term contracts.[21] Although some of these teachers were undoubtedly reappointed, the fact that contract expirations between 1997 and 1999 were nearly double the number in subsequent years indicates the heavy reliance on temporary teachers during that period. According to our figures, about 2,900 teachers opted for voluntary severance pack-

20. Fleisch (2002a, p. 44).
21. Note that the first big wave of departures that occurred before 1997 is not included in the table.

ages, and almost 2,000 left teaching in 1998 alone. Interestingly, the rates of teacher departure related to illness and death did not increase during the period, despite growing concern about HIV/AIDS (see chapter 9).

Equal Opportunity

A 1995 audit of teachers and the 1996 School Register of Needs dramatically highlighted the backlog of educational needs in the aftermath of apartheid. The national Reconstruction and Development Program (RDP) of the mid-1990s had promised an investment strategy to address those issues. Although the country has since made some progress in promoting equal educational opportunity through improvements to school facilities, teacher quality, and standards for nonpersonnel spending, much more remains to be done.

School Facilities

One of the most pressing problems in many of the poorer provinces has been the lack of schools and classrooms. As of 1991 there was a shortfall of 29,000 classrooms in primary schools and 14,000 in secondary schools for blacks throughout the country.[22]

Between 1996 and 2002 most provinces took steps to increase the number of classrooms. As a result, the ratio of learners to classrooms declined in all provinces except Mpumalanga, with the greatest declines in the two poorest provinces, Eastern Cape and Limpopo. With the building of new schools and classrooms in Eastern Cape, for example, the average number of learners per classroom dropped from 55 in 1996 to 43 in 2000.[23] Because the ratios fell somewhat more in the provinces that started with the highest ratios, some, albeit limited, convergence across provinces is apparent.

Many other facilities in the Eastern Cape remained poor, however. As of 2000, more than 40 percent of its 6,300 schools still did not have basic amenities such as telephones, water, or electricity, and 19 percent did not have toilets (table 6-4). In addition, 90 percent did not have library facilities ("media centers"), and 95 percent did not have computers. The situation in the Western Cape was much better: more than 95

22. These backlogs were based on a learner-educator ratio of 40:1 for primary schools and 35:1 for secondary schools. Reported in Nicolaou (2001, tables 4.1 and 4.2).
23. Monica Bot, "School Register of Needs 2000: An Update," *EduSource Data News*, no. 35, December 2001, table 2, p. 2.

TABLE 6-4. School Facilities, 1996 and 2000, Eastern Cape, Western Cape, and All Provinces

Percent of schools, unless otherwise noted

Physical facilities	Eastern Cape		Western Cape		All provinces	
	1996	2000	1996	2000	1996	2000
Number of schools	5,879	6,260	1,703	1,593	26,724	27,148
Telephones	19	59	94	98	41	65
Water	57	59	94	98	65	71
Electricity	22	40	88	96	43	55
Toilets	75	81	100	100	88	91
Computers	4	5	31	45	9	12
Media centres	7	10	52	58	17	20

Source: Monica Bot, "School Register of Needs 2000: An Update," *EduSource Data News*, no. 35, December 2001, pp. 2–4.

percent of the schools had the basic amenities and a relatively large proportion had media centers and computers.

The national picture more closely resembles that in the Eastern Cape. Figure 6-2 highlights the vast differences between the wealthy provinces such as Western Cape and Gauteng, on the one hand, and the poor provinces such as Limpopo and Eastern Cape, on the other. For example, more than half the schools in the wealthy provinces had media centers in 2000, whereas less than 10 percent had them in the two poorest provinces and less than 20 percent had them in four additional provinces.[24] We highlight media centers here because of their potential contribution to the successful implementation of the new outcomes-based curriculum discussed in chapter 8.

Despite the large backlog of unmet needs, capital spending decreased significantly during the late 1990s. Although it is impossible to obtain information on capital spending for the full post-apartheid period, the available data indicate that capital spending on school facilities declined by 41 percent between 1997–98 and 2000–01.[25] That fall occurred largely because most provincial departments of education had no money for capital projects after struggling to meet teacher payrolls.

The only other possible source of funding would have been conditional grants to the provinces, but few such grants were directed to edu-

24. Department of Education (2001, table 9).
25. According to one source, provincial allocations from the RDP for school building in 1996–97 were over R200 million for the Eastern Cape, KwaZulu-Natal, and Limpopo. *EduSource Data News*, no. 13, July 1996, p. 5.

FIGURE 6-2. Schools with Media Centers, by Province, 1996–2000

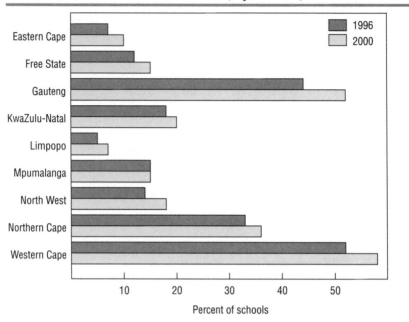

Percent of schools

Source: Department of Education, "Report on the School Register of Needs 2000 Survey," reported in *EduSource Data News*, no. 35, December 2001, table 9.

cation in the late 1990s and instead went to health, housing, and social development. Then in 2001 a conditional grant was approved for provincial spending on infrastructure of all types, including school facilities.[26] Though the effects on classroom construction remain to be seen, this new grant illustrates that the intergovernmental structure is in place to address pressing social needs when funds are available at the national level.

Qualifications of Teachers

The legacy of the past is also evident in the qualifications of teachers. The proportion of underqualified teachers (as determined by the standard of matriculation plus three years of training, denoted by 13 on the quality scale) dropped from about 45 percent of all teachers in 1990 to 36 percent in 1994 and 22 percent in 2000. Despite this progress, more

26. Republic of South Africa, National Treasury, *Intergovernmental Fiscal Review*, 2001, p. 36.

than one in five teachers was still underqualified at the end of that span.[27] The levels ranged from a low of 11 percent in Gauteng and Western Cape provinces to a high of 39 percent in North West, with the other six provinces falling in the range of 18 to 26 percent. These figures undoubtedly understate the extent of underqualification because many teachers received their education in the impoverished African or coloured schools of the apartheid system and their teacher training in one of the many low-quality teachers' colleges that have since been closed. Studies have shown that more than half of the math and science teachers were underprepared in those fields.[28]

Despite this legacy, spending on teacher education between 1997–98 and 2000–01 declined by 9 percent in nominal terms and by a far larger percentage if adjusted for inflation. This reduction corresponded to a drop in the number of universities and colleges that provide teacher training—from 122 in 1994 to 61 in 2000 and then to 31 in 2001—and to a corresponding decline in the number of students in preservice education training programs.[29] As with capital spending, the decline also reflects the pressures on provincial education budgets associated with increases in nationally negotiated teacher salaries. With respect to in-service training programs, a 2001 survey of all teacher training programs in the country indicated large variations in the number of teachers in in-service programs across the provinces. The number in such programs ranged from 30,000 or more in Gauteng to only about 2,100 in the Eastern Cape, where the needs were far greater.[30]

Even with the large number of unqualified teachers in the poor provinces, policymakers were hard pressed to spend more on the retraining of teachers since that would have required taking money from other ongoing programs that were also underfunded. In recognition of the national problem, a new Diploma in Education was introduced in 2001 supported by 50 million rand in bursaries. This program is designed to upgrade the qualifications of only 10,000 of the 77,000 teachers who were underqualified at that time.[31] Nevertheless, it highlights the crucial role that the national government must play in offsetting legacies of this type and puts a structure in place for addressing the problem.

27. Narsee (2002), based on information in CEPD (2001).
28. Narsee (2002, p. 8).
29. Vinjevold (2001).
30. Vinjevold (2001).
31. Narsee (2002, pp. 8, 12).

Norms and Standards for Nonpersonnel Spending

Though the equity concept of equal treatment provided the foundation for most of the new resource policies for education, a significant exception was the National Norms and Standards for School Funding, which took effect on January 1, 2000.[32] Since some schools and school communities were far more impoverished than others, this national program was designed to give the poorer schools more of the nonpersonnel funds in order to promote more equal educational opportunity. Nonpersonnel spending covers items such as utilities, maintenance, and teaching materials. To assure funds for such purposes, the national government had to work within the constraints of the new federal system. That meant that any redistribution of funds across schools had to be done within provinces, not across the country as a whole.

This program requires each provincial department to rank all its schools from poorest to wealthiest and then to allocate any funding for nonpersonnel purposes in a progressive way. At least 60 percent of the available funds must be allocated to the poorest 40 percent of the schools. In ranking its schools, each provincial department must apply a 50 percent weight to the poverty of the school community (as measured either by the characteristics of the parents of the children in the school or by the characteristics of the local community in which the school is located, or some combination thereof) and a 50 percent weight to the poverty of the school itself (as measured by characteristics such as whether the school has water and electricity).

While progressive in concept, this program had four drawbacks in practice. First, it put large technical demands on the provincial education departments. As a result, provinces varied in their ability to implement it. Not all provinces had the analytical capacity to rank schools according to the specified criteria. Lacking both capacity and funds, poor provinces such as Eastern Cape found the process particularly daunting and were slow to implement it. By 2002, however, all provinces appeared to have successfully implemented some version of the program.

Second, and most important, funds for this purpose are limited and consist of what remains after each province has met all its personnel commitments. In fact, the share of recurrent spending available for nonpersonnel spending varies both over time and across provinces. Of great concern to national policymakers in the late 1990s was the small (less

32. Department of Education (1998).

than 10 percent) share available nationally, a percentage deemed far too low to cover the costs of textbooks, municipal services such as water and electricity, equipment, and school maintenance. Funding for non-personnel purposes was especially low in impoverished provinces such as Eastern Cape, which devoted less than 5 percent of its recurrent budget to such spending in 1999–2000 and in 2000–01. Indeed, for the 2000 school year, Eastern Cape, lacking enough money to carry out the redistributive aims of the program, implemented it only in schools able to manage their own accounts.[33] Although most provinces expect to increase funding for nonpersonnel purposes somewhat over time, in 2002 the amounts were still well below the 15 percent of total spending deemed desirable by the national Department of Education.

Third, the degree of redistribution possible within each province depended on its mix of schools. A poor province with few wealthy schools could do much less in this regard than a rich province with a more even distribution of wealthy and poor schools. Not surprisingly, then, provinces vary greatly in the funds available for the learners in the poorest schools, and the current policy does not ensure that poor learners will be treated the same across provinces.[34]

Such an outcome is inevitable in a decentralized system in which the national government controls neither the total amount spent on educa-tion in each province nor how that money is allocated among uses. While poor learners throughout the country could in principle be given more equal treatment through some form of conditional grant to prov-inces based on their number of poor learners, the national government was apparently reluctant to interfere too much in the budgetary alloca-tion systems of the new provincial parliaments.[35]

Fourth, because the program is designed to distribute funds for recur-rent, not capital, spending to schools in a progressive manner, the case for having allocations depend in part on the infrastructure of the school is far from compelling. Indeed, schools with better infrastructure, including newly built schools serving previously disadvantaged students in township areas, are likely to have greater, not smaller, demands on

33. These are the section 21 schools. See Wildeman (2001a).
34. According to Wildeman (2001b, table 4), in 2001 the least poor group of learners in the Northern Cape received more than the poorest learners in Mpumalanga.
35. In recognition of some of these concerns, the Department of Education (2003) has proposed that the program be restructured to ensure more uniform treatment of poor learners across provinces.

their recurrent budget than schools without access to costly services such as electricity and water.[36] At the same time, one can sympathize with the spirit of the norms and standards initiative in that it provided a way for more funds to be distributed to schools in townships and home-lands that had been impoverished during the apartheid era without explicit reference to race or former education department. The norms and standards policy, however, clearly does not represent a substitute for direct capital grants to improve the infrastructure in those schools.

Educational Adequacy

Under an adequacy approach to funding, each school is supposed to receive sufficient resources to provide an adequate level of education to the students it serves. Thus unlike equal treatment and equal opportunity, this equity concept presumes an absolute standard, albeit one that is hard to define with any precision.

Because of its emphasis on the outcomes of education, an adequacy approach to equity typically calls for more money to be spent on some children than on others. More funding is needed in part to offset the past differences in the quality of educational facilities and teachers that prevent some schools from giving their students an adequate education. In this sense, the adequacy and equal opportunity approaches both attempt to address racial differences in school resources.

From an adequacy perspective, however, the fact that black students in South Africa typically come from more impoverished and less well-educated families than do white students provides added justification for differential funding for such students. More spending would be needed in schools or school systems serving a disproportionate number of disadvantaged students to cover the differentially high costs of edu-cating students who come to school less ready to learn. For example, children whose parents have little income or limited education may require smaller class sizes and more individual attention at school than children from more affluent backgrounds. Similarly, it may take more or better-trained teachers to educate students whose language at home dif-fers from the medium of instruction in school. Here the goal need not be

36. Apparently many poor schools around the country are not able to spend all the money they receive through the norms and standards allocation because they do not have the basic infrastructure that would give them access to municipal services such as electricity and water. See Wildeman (2001a).

to ensure equal outcomes for all students regardless of their socioeconomic background—a goal that would be asking too much of the education system. Rather, it should be to ensure that, at a minimum, all students receive the basic education they need to participate in the political and economic life of the country. Even this goal may require policies such as school feeding programs that may or may not be within the purview of the Department of Education.

Thus an adequacy approach to funding equity would have required the national government to provide each province with sufficient revenue to meet the basic educational needs of all of its students, including those who cost more to educate because of their educational disadvantage. Such an approach would be implemented from the bottom up, the first step being to determine those costs. That total cost would in turn be used to determine how much money the national government should distribute to the provinces, with more money per learner going to the provinces whose students cost more to educate.

In its recommendations for the period 2001–04, the country's Financial and Fiscal Commission (FFC) proposed an adequacy approach. The idea was to have the national government specify norms for each functional area (education, health, and social welfare), determine the costs of achieving those norms, and then provide each province with an equitable share grant sufficient to meet the norms. The educational norms were to be specified not in terms of inputs such as pupil/teacher ratios but in terms of outcome measures such as reading proficiency or examination performance. In theory, cost estimates would then take into account not only the average costs of achieving those norms but also the differential costs of achieving those norms across provinces owing to factors outside the control of provincial school officials, such as family poverty and rural residence. Determining those costs is not a simple task and would require significant research into the determinants of the desired outcomes and how much they would cost.

This "costed-norms" approach, the FFC argued, would promote the development of the type of "outcomes-based and costs sensitive budgeting regime" envisioned by the Public Finance Management Act of 2000.[37] The use of national outcome norms as the starting point would encourage clearer thinking about the definition of minimum standards, and the required cost estimates would focus greater attention on costs and on more efficient use of resources than would otherwise be the case.

37. Financial and Fiscal Commission (2000, pp. 1, 19–22).

In addition, once funding was brought into line with these norms, it would be easier to hold provinces and schools accountable for their performance. The approach might also have beneficial effects on nationally negotiated teacher salaries because any increase in those salaries would translate directly into higher required grants to the provinces for education.[38]

In the end, however, the government rejected the FFC's proposal and essentially maintained the previous system, thereby restricting itself to a relatively even distribution of inputs across provinces. It argued that a bottom-up approach was not an appropriate way to set budget priorities in view of the necessary political trade-offs among competing demands.[39]

The overall resource constraint is also relevant here. In order to take seriously one of the key insights of the adequacy approach—namely that it is more costly to educate disadvantaged students than other students—there would have to be a significant shift in resources away from the wealthier provinces with lower proportions of needy students and toward the poorer provinces. One study has shown that the allocation to Eastern Cape would have risen by 19 percent, while that to Western Cape would have declined by 38 percent, adjustments that would have had profound political consequences.[40]

Another important consideration is that the level of resources needed to achieve adequacy is difficult to determine even in the best of circumstance and nearly impossible to calculate in the South African context [41] To do it correctly, one would need educational outcome measures that do not yet exist in South Africa, as well as a solid understanding of the relationship between resources and educational outcomes. The only outcome measure currently available is the pass rate on the senior certificate exam, which, for reasons discussed in chapter 9, is not well suited to measuring adequacy. In addition, the combination of huge inefficiencies in the delivery of education and high aspirations for adequacy could well lead to required spending that the country could not afford. A natural prior step consistent with an eventual move in the direction of ade-

38. Reschovsky and Chernick (2001).
39. Republic of South Africa National Treasury (2001).
40. Firoz Patel, "A Review of School Funding," *EduSource Data News*, no. 36, March 2002, pp. 10–23.
41. For a full discussion of the concept of adequacy and the challenges of implementing it in the U.S. context, see Ladd and Hansen (1999), and Ladd, Chalk, and Hansen (1999).

quacy of funding would be the development of new systems of quality assurance. As we discuss in chapter 9, those systems are only now being developed.

Thus it is far too early to see much serious progress toward funding equity in the sense of educational adequacy At the same time, one can hope that the concept of educational adequacy will play an increasingly important role in the further development of South Africa's education system. Focusing on the ends of education and not just the inputs forces policymakers to measure outcomes and to promote more effective use of educational resources.

Resource Patterns across Schools within Provinces

Though some of the policies described in this chapter were designed to equalize resources or opportunities across provinces, others focused explicitly on the distribution of resources within provinces. Of particular interest is the extent to which resources have been equalized across schools grouped by their former departments. Once again, we use Western Cape and Eastern Cape to illustrate the patterns.[42]

Western Cape

As in chapter 5, we group Western Cape schools by their four former departments—DET (African), HOR (coloured), HOD (Indian), and HOA (white)—since those categories capture the relative degrees of privilege during the apartheid period (see tables 5-1 and 5-2 for the racial mix of learners). Students in white schools typically had access to the most resources, followed by the students in the Indian and the coloured schools, with the students in the African schools having the fewest resources. According to additional analysis (not reported here), the former DET schools serve predominantly poor communities, the HOR schools serve somewhat richer communities, the HOD schools serve those that are richer still, and the HOA schools serve the most affluent communities.[43]

42. See van der Berg (2001) for similar analyses for the whole county based on 1997 data.
43. These conclusions are based on measures of community poverty developed by the Western Cape Education Department (WCED) in connection with its ranking of schools as required for the norms and standards funding program. The WCED calculated measures of community poverty by combining information from the 1996 census on the characteristics of residents in local school communities and on survey

Information on average learner ratios, teacher qualifications, and financial resources for primary (table 6-5) and secondary schools (table 6-6) indicates that the former DET or HOR schools have the least resources. The one exception is the per learner allocations under the norms and standards program, which by design favor poor schools. However, the amount of money distributed to schools under that program pales in comparison with the amount spent on the teachers in each school and is far from sufficient to compensate the DET and HOR schools for differences in spending on teachers that favors the former HOA schools.

In the case of the primary schools, learner-educator ratios range from a high of 38.4 in the DET schools to a low of 35.9 in the HOA schools. These differences reflect the fact that the former white schools offer more of the subjects that qualify for additional personnel. A shortage of classrooms in the African schools widens the difference between categories in terms of learners per classroom. A major problem is the small number of administrative staff in the African schools. Given the reporting demands on schools, not to mention the demands on schools related to the serving of parents and students, the number of administrators in African schools is clearly inadequate.

Our analysis of teacher qualifications in each school uses the standard 10–17 qualification scale. The minimum qualification to be a teacher is 13, which represents senior certificate plus a three-year program. Average qualifications range from a low of 13.10 in the coloured schools to 14.05 in the white schools. Consistent with that pattern is the fact that in the typical coloured primary school almost 21 percent of the teachers are underqualified. The average salaries and benefits paid to educators per learner within each school are determined by the uniform salary schedule negotiated at the national level. This amount captures differences both in the numbers of educators and in their qualifications level. The per-learner payments to educators in the African schools are 20 percent lower than those to educators in the HOA schools.

Consistent with the goals of the norms and standards program, sig-

information on the characteristics of the families of students in each school. Using these measures, we divided schools into quintiles (separately for primary and secondary schools) and examined how students in the schools in each department were distributed among the quintiles. At the secondary level, for example, we found that three out of four students served by the former DET were in schools in the poorest quintile and that seven out of ten students served by the former HOA were in schools in the top quintile.

TABLE 6-5. Resources in Primary Schools, by Former Department, Western Cape, 2001[a]

Resources	DET (African)	HOR (coloured)	HOD (Indian)	HOA (white)	Total
Learner ratios					
Per state-paid teacher	*38.4*	36.3	37.1	35.9	36.6
Per classroom	*41*	26	26	24	27
Per administrator	*916*	431	419	311	459
Teacher qualifications[b]					
Average	13.4	*13.1*	13.5	14.1	13.3
Percent of unqualified teachers	6.5	*20.9*	9.4	0.8	15.0
Salary (plus benefits) per learner	*2,000*	2,246	2,273	2,573	2,254
Publicly provided resources per learner (rand)					
Personnel spending	*2,815*	3,444	4,020	3,785	3440
Allocation (norms and standards)	187	169	122	*72*	154
Total public funds	*3,002*	3,613	4,142	3,857	3,594
Index[c]	*1.00*	1.20	1.38	1.28	1.20

Source. Based on data from Western Cape Education Department.
a. Figures in bold italic represent the least resources within each row.
b. Teacher qualifications are on a scale of 10 to 17, with 10 representing matriculation from secondary school and the numbers above the years of additional training. A qualified teacher is one who has passed the matriculation exam and has three additional years of training (13 = 10 + 3).
c. Publicly provided resources in each department relative to the resources provided to schools in the DET department.

nificantly more money goes to the relatively impoverished DET and HOR schools than to the relatively wealthy HOA schools. However, the total public resources available to the DET schools still fall far short of the public resources available to the HOA schools because the targeted funding for nonpersonnel purposes is insufficient to offset differences in personnel funding. As a result, spending on behalf of learners in the HOA schools exceeds that in the DET schools by 28 percent and exceeds that in the HOR schools by 7 percent, but it falls short of that in the HOD schools by 7 percent.

Secondary schools follow a similar pattern, with the DET secondary schools even more consistently at the bottom of the scale than was the case for the primary schools, while the HOA schools are even more consistently at the top. As a result, total public spending on behalf of learners in the HOA schools exceeds that on behalf of those in the DET

TABLE 6-6. Resources in Secondary Schools, by Former Department, Western Cape, 2001[a]

Resources	DET (African)	HOR (coloured)	HOD (Indian)	HOA (white)	Total
Learner ratios					
Per state-paid educator	**33.6**	33.2	35.3	32.4	33.1
Per classroom	**44**	27	38	23	29
Per administrator	**1,117**	958	579	390	776
Teacher qualifications[b]					
Average	**13.8**	14.1	14.2	14.5	13.3
Percent of unqualified teachers	**2.6**	0.8	1.2	0[b]	0.9
Salary (plus benefits)					
per learner	**2,367**	2,712	2,440	2,961	2,704
Publicly provided resources per learner (rand)					
Personnel spending	**3,193**	3,807	3,644	4,337	3,892
Allocation (norms and standards)	209	165	159	**82**	141
Total public funds	**3,402**	3,972	3,803	4,419	4,034
Index[c]	**1.00**	1.17	1.12	1.30	1.19

Source: Based on data from Western Cape Education Department.
a. Figures in bold italic indicate the least resources within each row.
b. Teacher qualifications are on a scale of 10 to 17, with 10 representing matriculation from secondary school and the numbers above the years of additional training. A qualified teacher is one who has passed the matriculation exam and has three additional years of training (13 = 10 + 3).
c. Publicly provided resources in each department relative to the resources provided to schools in the DET department.

schools by 30 percent, that in the HOR schools by 11 percent, and that in the HOD schools by 16 percent.

These patterns can be interpreted positively or negatively, with both views correct. In the positive interpretation, the levels are far more uniform across departments than was the case during the apartheid period. A more negative view is that significant disparities remain in public funding levels. As chapter 7 makes clear, the disparities in public funding are exacerbated by disparities in private funding.

Patterns and Changes over Time in Eastern Cape

Comparable information on educator qualifications and learner-educator ratios over time in Eastern Cape (table 6-7) indicates that qualifications at all levels increased between 1997 and 2001 but were still far below those in Western Cape in 2001. The typical teacher in both

TABLE 6-7. Teacher Characteristics and Ratios, Eastern Cape, 1997–2001[a]

Teacher and school characteristics	1997	1999	2001
All schools			
Average qualifications	12.8	12.8	13.0
Percent underqualified teachers	32.0	30.6	23.6
Learners per educator	40.5	38.3	33.6
Number of schools	5,781	6,227	6,029
Primary schools			
Average qualifications	12.6	12.7	12.9
Percent underqualified teachers	37.3	35.4	26.9
Learners per educator	40.0	38.5	32.1
Number of schools	2,567	2,696	2,707
Combined schools			
Average qualifications	12.6	12.7	12.9
Percent underqualified teachers	34.2	32.6	26.3
Learners per educator	43.7	40.1	36.7
Number of schools	2,313	2,488	2,479
Secondary schools			
Average qualifications	13.6	13.7	13.8
Percent underqualified teachers	7.1	6.1	5.8
Learners per educator	33.6	34.3	29.0
Number of schools	791	851	842

Source: Based on data from Eastern Cape Department of Education.
a. Teacher qualifications are on a scale of 10 to 17, with 10 representing matriculation from secondary school and the numbers above the years of additional training. A qualified teacher is one who has passed the matriculation exam and has three additional years of training (13 = 10 + 3).

primary and secondary schools in Eastern Cape in 2001 was underqualified according to the qualification standard of senior certificate plus three years. Perhaps more important, most teachers in Eastern Cape received their training in teacher colleges under the apartheid system. Because of their low quality, these colleges have since been either shut down or incorporated into universities or technikons.

As seen in tables 6-7 and 6-5, respectively, the number of learners per educator in primary schools as of 2001 was lower in Eastern Cape (32.1) than in Western Cape (36.6). We find little or no evidence to support one potential explanation for this difference, namely the presence of a large number of very small schools in rural areas. In fact Transkei, the most rural part of the province, has more than forty-four learners per educator in the typical primary school. An alternative, and more plausible, explanation is that the disarray in the Eastern Cape Depart-

TABLE 6-8. Variation in Teacher Qualifications and Learners Per Educator, by Former Department, Eastern Cape, 2001[a]

All schools	Transkei	Ciskei	DET	HOR	HOA
Average qualifications	12.9	13.2	13.0	13.1	14.0
Percent of underqualified teachers	26.0	19.4	25.97	20.5	4.8
Learners per educator	36.9	27.4	27.0	27.8	33.4
Learners per classroom	48.1	27.7	28.2	27.4	26.7
Number of schools	3,548	771	965	293	172

Source: Based on data from Eastern Cape Department of Education.

a. Teacher qualifications are on a scale of 10 to 17, with 10 representing matriculation from secondary school and the numbers above 10 the years of additional training. A qualified teacher is one who has passed the matriculation exam and has three additional years of training (13 = 10 + 3).

ment of Education has led to some "double-parking" of teacher slots; that is, some schools are hiring new teachers before "excess" teachers in other schools are actually laid off.[44]

However, fewer numbers of learners per educator need not imply smaller classes. The shortage of physical classrooms in Eastern Cape pushed its average number of learners per primary school classroom in 2001 to forty or more, which far exceeded the number of learners per educator. Another problem we observed in rural schools in Transkei was that a number of school principals were essentially nonfunctional and their duties were being performed by a teacher. During apartheid the only qualification necessary for a school principal was seven years of teaching experience. As a result, many existing principals do not have the skills needed to do the job yet remain on the payroll doing little work.

As table 6-8 illustrates, teacher qualifications and learner ratios vary across the major former departments in Eastern Cape: the homelands of Transkei and Ciskei, DET schools for Africans in urban areas, HOR schools for coloured students, and HOA schools for white students (see table 5-3 for the racial breakdown of students by department). By the four measures given in the table's rows, the 3,500 schools in Transkei are the worst off. Their educators have the lowest average qualifications, and their schools have the highest average proportion of underqualified educators, the highest average ratio of learners to educators, and the highest average number of learners per classroom. Low teacher

44. "Double-parking" was a widespread phenomenon throughout the teacher rationalization process. See Fleisch (2002a, chap. 3).

qualifications also appear to be a significant problem in the DET schools.

Once again, the figures do not adequately capture the challenges facing many schools in Eastern Cape, as quickly became evident during our tour of schools in the town of Umtata and in rural areas surrounding it in Transkei. Mkatini Primary School, for example, does not have enough classrooms for the 610 learners in grades 1 to 7, so teachers take turns using those that are available. The school has no toilets or electricity, and learners are usually hungry when they arrive at school. The senior teacher, Mandisa Memela, explained: "We had a feeding scheme that provided a piece of biscuit for learners up to grade 3, but that was taken away." She was referring to the fact the Eastern Cape's school feeding program had to be suspended because of corruption. Asked what the first priority would be if the school were to be given some additional funds, she replied, "Fencing to protect the school, then more classrooms."

The Mandela Park Junior Primary School was established in 1996 by residents of an informal settlement in the area where Nelson Mandela held his first public meeting after his return to his native Transkei. The school, which receives nine teachers but no other support from the local department of education, occupies two large halls that the community uses on weekends for agricultural shows. Teachers and students pile up the furniture and the twelve small chalkboards in a corner every Friday and then put things back on Monday. "Theft is a problem," said Xolisani Neti, the principal. "We lost some furniture and had to ask the police to help get it back."

Lack of textbooks and other teaching supplies is a general problem. "The government is supposed to provide textbooks, but sometimes it fails to do so," reported Victoria Mabengu, senior teacher at the Umtata Community School, which has 21 educators for nearly 1,100 learners. "We have one class that has 20 books for 140 learners. Sometimes we order one book but get another." The school has no library but has managed to obtain six computers. The latter had yet to be made available to students pending security arrangements for the computer room.

Conclusion

In this chapter, we used the three concepts of equity introduced in chapter 1—equal treatment, equal educational opportunity, and educational adequacy—to evaluate South Africa's progress toward a more equitable funding system for education. Our analysis of funding policies shows significant movement toward equity in the sense of equal treatment. Much less progress has been made toward the other two concepts of equity.

New policies driven by the equity standard of equal treatment in South Africa have significantly reduced disparities in public funding across provinces. The convergence of funding is particularly impressive because it was accomplished with essentially no increase in public revenue for education and primarily through reductions in the wealthier provinces.[45] That outcome is attributable in large part to the country's decision to maintain as a central function the task of raising revenue for education and other social services and then distributing those funds by formula to the provinces. Given the large disparities in income and wealth across the provinces, had they been forced to rely on revenue from their own taxes for education, interprovincial disparities in public spending on education would undoubtedly be far greater than they now are.

It is easy to understand why policymakers focused on equal treatment during the initial post-apartheid period. First, the previous racially defined system had created enormous disparities, and addressing them decisively sent out an important political signal regarding the values of the new government. Thus symbolically these changes were crucial. Second, given the absence of new funding for education, the only option open to education policymakers during the late 1990s was to redistribute resources among provinces and schools. Owing to the combined effects of GEAR (the country's austere budget policy described in chapter 4) and the economic slowdown, they simply did not have the luxury of investing large amounts of new funds in the poor provinces or the poor schools.

The progress toward equal treatment to date is but an initial step, albeit an essential one, toward the development of an equitable funding system for education. There are still glaring racial gaps in the support for school facilities and in the qualifications of teachers. Moreover, as we document in chapter 9, the country has a long way to go to achieve outcomes that are consistent with the concept of educational adequacy.

45. Interestingly, many U.S. states have been ordered by the courts to equalize resources across schools districts within states. To the extent they have succeeded in doing so, it is primarily by increasing resources in the low-spending districts, not by reducing it in the wealthier districts. Evans, Murray, and Schwab (1999).

The good news is that South Africa's intergovernmental system is basically sound and generally well designed for the purposes of fiscal equity. Thus structures are in place to direct more funds to the poor provinces and poor schools over time as more resources become available. While additional funding for poor provinces and poor schools is part of the solution to the equity challenge, it is certainly not the whole answer. Managerial capacity also plays an important role, and changes must also be initiated there, as in many other areas, in the quest for racial equity in education.

seven Balancing Public and
Private Resources

A weighty question for policymakers everywhere is how to achieve the right balance between public and private resources in the provision of primary and secondary education.[1] The question is particularly troubling for developing countries, which typically lack the tax-generated resources to fund education at an adequate level. The 1990 World Conference on Education for All, which formalized the global commitment to universal basic education, established a context for the discussion of school fees and other user charges in developing countries. Such fees are controversial, though, and there is growing international pressure to abolish them, especially at the level of primary education.

South Africa came face to face with the issue when abandoning its apartheid past and embarking on the difficult process of restructuring its education system to serve the needs of the new democracy. The post-apartheid government decided to encourage public schools to supplement public funds with revenue from school fees. It did so despite the declared aspirations and promises of the African National Congress (ANC) during the final years of apartheid that all children should have access to a free basic education. South Africa has continued that policy, although fee policy remains a topic of current debate. It received significant attention in a March 2003 Department of Education Report to the Minister of Education, which recommended that the department monitor fee-setting processes more strictly and provide fairer and more effec-

1. This chapter draws heavily on Fiske and Ladd (2004).

tive means of permitting exemptions to alleviate poverty.[2] A June 2003 plan called for discouraging the use of fees in poor schools.

South Africa adopted its fee-based policy for a variety of reasons, including limited public resources and pressure for local control over education. Most decisive, though, was the argument that fees would forestall a flight of the middle class to private schools, thus providing continuing political support for the state education system and avoiding the creation of yet another bifurcated educational system in South Africa. As our analysis shows, the fee policy did indeed succeed in keeping most middle-class students in the public school system and, contrary to the effects of fees in many other developing countries, apparently did not keep poor children out of primary school to any significant extent. At the same time, the fees have affected the way in which students sort themselves among schools, with class beginning to replace race as the primary determinant of who is able to gain access to the formerly white schools. Furthermore, fees have failed to increase resources at schools serving historically disadvantaged students; instead, they have reinforced the advantages enjoyed by the formerly white schools. Therefore it would now be appropriate to consider changes to the fee policy that would work to the advantage of the historically disadvantaged schools.

Fees as a Revenue Source for Schools

For reasons explained in chapter 4, responsibility for managing South Africa's schools was vested in each school's elected governing body, which by design is dominated by parents.[3] Two of the body's tasks are to set admissions policy, subject to nondiscrimination requirements, and to make recommendations to the provincial department of education regarding the appointment of teachers and staff.[4] The mandate of concern in this chapter stipulates that "a governing body of a public school *must take all reasonable measures within its means to supplement the resources supplied by the State* in order to improve the quality of education provided by the schools to all learners at the school" (emphasis added).[5]

This provision refers not only to school fees but also to voluntary contributions from the community. The setting of school fees is optional

2. Department of Education (2003).
3. South African Schools Act (SASA) (1996, p. 16).
4. SASA (1996, p. 14).
5. SASA (1996, p. 21).

FIGURE 7-1. Annual Fees Charged by Primary Schools, Eastern Cape and Western Cape, 2001

Percent of students

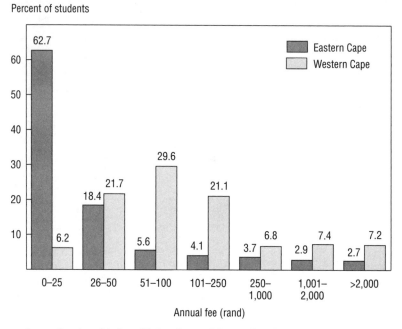

Annual fee (rand)

Source: Based on data from Western Cape and Eastern Cape Departments of Education.

in the sense that a school can impose such fees only when authorized to do so by a majority of parents attending a budget meeting at the school.[6] Once a fee is approved, however, all parents are required to pay it except those who, under a provision added in 1998, are exempted from doing so by action of the governing body because of their low income. Although a child cannot be denied admission for failure to pay the fee, schools can sue parents for nonpayment.[7] Money collected from school fees is put into a school fund that can be used for any school purpose, including the hiring of additional teachers. Teachers hired out of locally raised funds are referred to as school governing body (SGB) teachers.

Figure 7-1 shows the amounts and variation in the fees charged by schools in Eastern Cape and Western Cape in 2001. In the very poor province of Eastern Cape, fees were low, and nearly two-thirds (63 per-

6. SASA (1996, p. 21).
7. SASA (1996, pp. 5, 23).

FIGURE 7-2. Annual Fees Charged by Secondary Schools, Eastern Cape and Western Cape, 2001

Percent of students

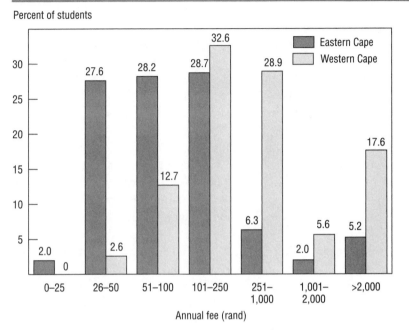

Annual fee (rand)

Source: Based on data from Western Cape and Eastern Cape Departments of Education.

cent) of students at the primary level attended schools with fees of less than 25 rand per year. Fees were generally higher in Western Cape, where the median primary school student was subject to a fee in the range of 51 to 100 rand. Some public primary schools in both provinces have quite high fees, as much as 1,000 rand for 5 percent of the students in Eastern Cape and 14 percent of those in Western Cape.

The fees are uniformly higher for secondary schools (figure 7-2). The typical, or median, secondary school student in Eastern Cape faced a fee of 51 to 100 rand, while in Western Cape the fee was more than 250 rand. Close to 18 percent of the secondary school students in Western Cape encountered fees in excess of 2,000 rand.

In 2001 average public spending per pupil in Western Cape was about 3,600 rand for primary school students and about 4,000 rand for secondary school students. Thus a fee of 100 rand would augment spending at the primary level by about 3 percent. The median fee at the secondary level, about 250 rand, would increase spending by about 7 percent, while a fee of 2,000 rand would do so by about 50 percent. We say more about the relative magnitude of fees for various types of schools later in the chapter.

Public funding, it should be made clear, refers to revenue from general taxes, with the amounts determined by collective choice and allocated to public purposes. With public funding of schools, the burden of financing is spread among all taxpayers, not just those who benefit directly from the schools, and the taxes are compulsory. By contrast, private funding, which takes the form of parental fees, typically places the financing burden on a smaller group of people, albeit a group that directly benefits from the schools.[8]

Many developing countries allow the state education system to levy school fees, which might include payment for tuition, textbooks, uniforms, financial contributions, and other school needs. A recent survey of seventy-nine of the World Bank's client countries indicated that seventy-seven of these countries required such payments and that sixty-nine had more than one type of fee.[9] In most cases, such fees simply supplement public funding for education that is deemed inadequate. In that sense, fees are simply another source of revenue and are similar to taxes, except that the group who pays them is limited to parents. School fees are most like taxes when they are obligatory, do not vary with the quality of service provided, and for all practical purposes substitute for public funding.

There is, however, another way to look at fees. To the extent that they operate like user charges, they could lead to more efficient delivery of educational services in the same way that market prices promote efficiency in the private sector.[10] School fees resemble user charges when they vary with service quality, when the fee revenue remains at the school, and when parents have some control over whether they pay fees, either through collective choice in a particular school or through an individual decision of the school to which they send their children. Though appealing in some situations, the efficiency argument holds little water for schools serving students from low-income families.

8. Although private funding can include funding from donors, such as private corporations or nongovernmental organizations, we use the term to refer to fees paid by parents.

9. Burnett and Bentaouet-Kattan (2002).

10. Local financial contributions from municipal governments and parent-teacher associations, along with fees paid by parents, were found to have some salutary effects, especially in terms of cost-effectiveness, in a study of 586 primary schools in the Philippines. See Jimenez and Paqueo (1996).

Why Were School Fees Permitted and Encouraged?

International experience suggests that school fees have become widespread in developing countries primarily because their governments are unable to provide free basic education at public expense. Although insufficient public funding was certainly a relevant factor in South Africa, it was only one of several favoring the use of fees, including political economy considerations that reflected the legacy of apartheid.

Limited Public Resources

Once in power, the African National Congress and its allies recognized that there would be insufficient public funds to equalize public funding at anywhere near the level needed to provide all learners with the quality of education previously available to whites. Given that white people accounted for less than 12 percent of the total population of South Africa, any redistribution of funds from the formerly white schools to all the others in the country would be spread so thinly that historically disadvantaged schools would experience little benefit.

At the time, many believed that the new government should view education as an investment in South Africa's future and hence direct substantial new sums to schooling for the long-deprived black majority. Such arguments were thwarted by the constraints on spending described in chapter 4. When it became clear that additional public funds would not be forthcoming, the only alternative seemed to be to turn to the private sector and allow schools to charge user fees. In recognition of this reality, the report of the 1995 Committee to Review the Organization, Governance, and Funding of Schools (henceforth referred to as the Hunter Report) laid out three policy options, all of which called for school fees in some form to supplement public funding.

Promotion of Local Control and Efficiency

The South African Schools Act of 1996 gave significant control over schools to elected SGBs with the hope that local control would overcome some of the deep distrust of schools rooted in the apartheid era. Although school fees need not have been part of the self-governing package, they were seen as a way of giving school governing bodies both discretionary funds and a significant incentive to use funds wisely. For this reason, some advocates of school fees in South Africa argued that they would promote efficiency in the provision of schooling.[11]

Mobilization of Private Resources to Egalitarian Ends

The ANC and its allies initially opposed school fees but eventually came to accept the Department of Finance argument that, by providing local schools with an independent source of revenue, fees paid by wealthier communities would release scarce state funds for poor schools, which in turn would increase equal educational opportunity.[12] This argument lay behind the Hunter Report's preferred "partnership funding" option, which called for a combination of obligatory fees and voluntary contributions to supplement public funding of schools for nonpersonnel purposes. Very poor families would pay no fees, and others would pay fees on the basis of a sliding scale related to their family income. The obligatory fees were intended to help poor students not only by freeing up public funds to be distributed to schools serving poor students but also by making it possible for children from poor families to have access to a range of public schools rather than being restricted to low-quality schools with no school fees.

Perhaps the most persuasive case for school fees came from Luis Crouch and Christopher Colclough, a pair of international consultants. If schools were not allowed to charge fees and use them for purposes such as the hiring of additional teachers, they argued, the quality of the formerly white schools would deteriorate. That in turn would induce many key "opinion- and decisionmakers" to pull their children out of the public school system and enroll them in private schools (called independent schools in South Africa), which were specifically permitted under the 1996 South African Schools Act (SASA).[13] Independent schools are financed primarily by private tuition but also receive some public subsidies on a sliding scale, the most going to the poorest and the least to the well endowed. Since 2000, independent schools with fees more than 2.5 times the average provincial per capita norms and standard expenditure on public schools have received no subsidy. Schools with fees below that level continue to receive a subsidy, with the poorest schools getting the maximum amount of 60 percent of average provincial per capita nonpersonnel spending on public schools.

11. See, for example, Crouch (1995).
12. Pampallis (1998, pp. 168–69). See also Donaldson (1992).
13. SASA (1996, p. 24).

Once outside the state education system, both Crouch and Colclough argued, families would have little reason to exert political pressure for more spending on public schools. Like the Hunter Report itself, the consultants were careful to emphasize that the argument was not an elitist one designed to privilege the middle class but rather a means of improving schools for the poor.[14]

Crouch and Colclough proposed a fee policy similar to the one subsequently embodied in SASA, and their work proved to be compelling to policymakers.[15] This policy called for the governing body of each school to be empowered, indeed encouraged, to charge fees after discussion with the parents. The consultants recommended that children from families with incomes below some national threshold be exempt from school fees. Such a policy was not immediately adopted, but in 1998 a provision was added that required school governing bodies to issue full or partial exemptions from fees for families whose annual income fell below thresholds defined by the size of the school fee. To offset any incentive for schools to exclude exempted children, both consultants recommended that richer schools be required to reserve a certain number or proportion of spaces for students not paying fees.[16] That provision, however, has not been enacted.

Allowing schools to charge fees thus provided a mechanism to enhance limited public resources in a way that respected the agreements already reached between white persons and the ANC regarding local governance. It also served to maintain support for the state education system among privileged classes that were no longer defined primarily by race. By joining with whites to preserve the independence and quality of the former Model C schools, black political leaders were able "to silently permit their own class interests to be taken care of without confronting (or clashing with) their own, largely poor, constituencies."[17]

South Africa's Approach to Fees in an International Context

South Africa's decision to permit local governing bodies to impose compulsory school fees came just as global sentiment began mounting in opposition to such a policy. Since then the United Nations Children's

14. Crouch (1995, p. 12).
15. Pampallis (1998, p. 158).
16. Colclough (n.d., p. 2); Crouch (1995, p. 12).
17. Karlsson, McPherson, and Pampallis (2001, p. 151).

Fund (UNICEF) has organized a campaign to eliminate primary-level fees and other costs in Africa, and in 2000 a group of nongovernmental organizations and teachers' unions formed the Global Campaign for Education around the belief that "free, quality basic education for every girl, boy, man and woman is not only an essential right but an achievable goal." In April 2000 at a meeting in Senegal, representatives from 185 countries, including South Africa, approved the Dakar Framework for Action as a means of ensuring that all children would "have access to, and complete, free and compulsory primary education of good quality" by 2015.[18]

The principal argument in the international literature for opposing fees is that they are a major cause of nonenrollment among the poor. Indeed, a number of countries that have eliminated fees have seen a significant increase in access to schooling. When the rulers of Malawi fulfilled an election campaign pledge in 1994 by abolishing school fees and enacting a policy of free primary education, primary school enrollment soared by more than 50 percent, from approximately 1.9 million in 1993–94 to nearly 3 million the following year.[19] Similarly, when Uganda eliminated tuition fees for primary schools in 1997 under its Universal Primary Education initiative, school enrollment increased by 70 percent.[20] The most recent country to curtail school fees is Kenya, where the newly elected president, Mwai Kibaki, fulfilled his campaign promise to eliminate fees in the country's 17,500 primary schools. The response was an immediate surge in enrollment that forced some schools to put new students on a waiting list for the next term.

Although fees are clearly a deterrent to enrollment among the poor in certain situations, some cross-country studies suggest that the elimination of such user charges will help improve enrollment only to a point. For one thing, fees are not the only factor to deflate demand for education among the poor. Other obstacles include books and other direct costs of schooling, the opportunity costs of having children in school rather than working in the home or fields, expectations of low economic returns from a primary education, social norms that discriminate against girls, and the burdens families face in dealing with AIDS. If demand for

18. Dakar Framework for Action, Section 7 (ii) in UNESCO (2000a).
19. Kadzamira and Rose (2001). Of course, rising enrollment brings its own challenges in the form of the need for additional teachers and classrooms. Without more resources, the quality of education is likely to fall.
20. Hillman and Jenkner (2002).

education is low for such reasons, eliminating fees may have little effect on parents' decision to send their children to school.[21] Furthermore, it is not clear that fees in South Africa in the 1990s prevented large numbers of families from enrolling their children in primary school.

Impact of Fees on Access to Schooling

As far as we can tell, underenrollment of children at the primary level was not a serious problem in South Africa in the mid-1990s, when the current funding policies were introduced. Nor does it appear to be a big problem today. By contrast, many potential secondary-level students are not in school, and the dropout rate appears to have risen over time. Hence it is hard to rule out fees as one of the factors negatively affecting secondary school enrollments, though is is probably not the most important.

Because of the difficulty in determining the overall enrollment rate in South African schools, we have estimated it in a variety of ways, as described in appendix table A. Our figures are based on different types of data, such as information from household surveys or census reports, and highlight different definitions of the concept. The most straightforward approach is to estimate the proportion of students enrolled in school by age. According to 1995 enrollment data from the national Education Management Information System (EMIS) and national demographic data from a different source, the proportion of children aged seven to thirteen enrolled in school throughout the country was close to 100 percent. This figure could well overstate the enrollment rate because schools may inflate their enrollments to obtain more funding. A second estimate of 96.2 percent enrollment, not subject to this upward bias, emerges from the 1995 October Household Survey (OHS). Providing additional credibility to that estimate is a third estimate of 95.3 percent based on a separate survey by the Southern Africa Labour Development Research Unit (SALDRU).[22] That slightly lower estimate could reflect

21. Oxfam (2001); and Hillman and Jenkner (2002)

22. The 1996 census raised some questions about the validity of all of these figures, in that its estimate of the proportion of seven- to twenty-four-year olds in school suggested a much lower enrollment rate for the younger ages than is consistent with the figures just reported. Careful analysis by Crouch (1998) suggests that the higher rates in appendix table A are the more believable figures, largely because they emerge from three different sources—one based on a full census of schools and two from separate household surveys.

the fact that the respondents include fourteen- and fifteen-year-olds, who have somewhat lower enrollment rates than the seven- to thirteen-year-olds in the previous two estimates.[23]

We also estimated both gross and net enrollment rates by grade grouping. The gross enrollment rate is the ratio of the total number of students enrolled in the relevant grades to the total number of children in the appropriate age range for those grades. Because the numerator includes both underage and overage children, the gross enrollment rate can exceed one. The net rate, in contrast, counts in the numerator only those enrollees who are in the appropriate age range for those grades and hence—in the absence of data errors—should not exceed one. Differences between gross and net enrollment rates are sometimes used as one indicator of the efficiency of an education system. The higher the gross enrollment rate in relation to the net rate, the more pupil-years of resources are required to educate a student. However, a distinction should be made between overage students who were retained and those who dropped out of school for nonschool reasons, such as to take care of an ailing parent or to earn income, and then returned to school. Also the presence of underage children in primary school could well indicate that parents have no other child care options. (For additional discussion of internal efficiency indicators, see chapter 9.)

As of 1999, the estimated net enrollment rate in South African primary schools was about 93 percent. Whether this estimate is biased upward or downward is unclear. On the one hand, it may be too high because it is based on school enrollment data that could be inflated. On the other hand, it could be misleadingly low because it excludes any twelve- and thirteen-year-olds who have already progressed to eighth grade.[24]

In any case, this 93 percent rate is high in comparison with net enrollment rates for primary schools in other countries. The EFA 2000 Assessment, which examined the status of basic education in 180 countries, reported that the net enrollment rate for all countries in 1998 was 84 percent, with rates ranging from 82 percent in less developed regions to

23. Enrollment ratios for fourteen- and fifteen-year-olds calculated from the EMIS and Demographic Information Bureau Data Set were 0.91 and 0.88, respectively, and were 0.97 and 0.94 when calculated from 1995 OHS data. See Luis Crouch and Thaba Mabogoane, "Aspects of Internal Efficiency Indicators in South African Schools: An Analysis of Historical and Current Data," *EduSource Data News*, no. 19, December 1997, table 1.

24. Our own estimates of net enrollment rates based on EMIS data for primary schools in Eastern Cape and Western Cape are slightly higher.

98 percent in more developed ones. The average rate for countries in sub-Saharan Africa was only 60 percent.[25]

Our various estimates of South African enrollment rates at the primary level provide no evidence of a decline in enrollment over time. They do indicate, however, a significant drop in the net enrollment rate between the two levels of schooling—from more than 90 percent at the primary level to about 62 percent at the secondary level.[26]

Though admittedly imperfect, these estimates of enrollment rates provide no evidence that school fees have kept significant numbers of South African children from enrolling in primary schools. This outcome may be attributed in part to the existence of national policies designed to minimize the effects of fees on poor families. These include the prohibition against denying admission to children who cannot pay fees and the introduction in 1998 of the fee exemption policy for low-income families. According to that policy, a child is eligible for a full exemption if the combined gross income of the parents is less than ten times the annual school fee per learner, and the child is eligible for a partial exemption if the income is between ten and 30 times the amount of the school fee. As we show shortly, however, the fee exemptions have not been widely used even in situations of widespread poverty.

Another factor limiting the deterrent potential of fees, as indicated in our interviews with the principals of schools serving poor students, is that they may not be easy to collect, even when they are as low as, say, 20 rand per year. The fee at Mkatini Primary School in Umtata is 80 rand a year, yet "most parents are unable to pay even this amount," reports principal Xolisani Neti.[27] At the Mandela Park Junior Primary School, also in Umtata, less than 10 percent of families pay the nominal fee of 50 rand. Shadley Mohamed of Crystal High School in Hanover Park in Cape Town said that his governing board established a fee of 250 rand, but he estimated that only about 40 percent of families pay it. "As an incentive, we give workbooks to learners who pay 150 rand up front, and then we give them to the rest two weeks later," he said.

Such principals typically report that, despite time-consuming efforts by themselves and their teachers to pressure parents into paying, they

25. UNESCO (2000a, fig. 1, p. 11).

26. Consistent with these national rates, we estimate net enrollment rates for grades 8 to 12 in 2001 of 0.59 in Eastern Cape and 0.66 in Western Cape.

27. Unless otherwise indicated, quotations in this chapter are from interviews with the authors between February and July 2002.

rarely collect the designated fee from a majority of families. Although schools have the option of taking nonpaying parents to court, it is typically not worth the time and effort involved, given the small amounts that would be realized if successful and the ill will that would ensue. Thus the reality is that many low-income families in poor communities pay little or no school fee.

There is a greater chance that fees have kept some students out of secondary school. However, secondary school enrollments at one point in time are hard to evaluate because there is no clear goal, such as 100 percent enrollment, in developing countries to serve as a basis of comparison. Rising dropout rates during the late 1990s in Western Cape could be consistent with a negative effect of fees except that other factors were at work as well (see chapter 9). When the national Department of Education called on secondary schools to increase their pass rates on the matriculation exam, some schools apparently responded by encouraging students who were not likely to pass to drop out of school.

Impact of Fees on Enrollment Patterns

Although it is not at all clear that fees at the primary level have deflated the overall enrollment rate in South Africa, they appear to have significantly affected enrollment patterns among schools. That is because parents who accept the need to pay fees tend to sort themselves into schools partly in line with the fees that they are willing and able to pay. In schools serving richer communities, both the level of fees and the collection rate are generally much higher than in schools serving the poor. Hence children who attend those schools are either middle-income students whose parents can afford the fees or lower-income students who are accepted by those schools and who are eligible for a full or partial fee exemption. Fees thus constitute an incentive for parents to sort themselves by income in their selection of schools.

Two sets of factors are at work here. The first is the preferences of families for certain types of schools, such as those within walking distance or those with particular types of educational programs, combined with their ability and willingness to pay the fees charged by a particular school. The second factor is the type of decisions that school governing bodies make regarding their general admissions policies. Some SGBs may want to minimize the admission of low-income students eligible for fee exemptions in order to prevent more affluent parents from paying substantial cross-subsidies for such students.[28] Though schools have to be careful not to discriminate against poor students in an unlawful way, such as by race, there is little doubt that many schools consider a family's likely ability to pay their fee when making admissions policy.

In 2001 average annual fees at the primary level in Western Cape ranged from 45 rand in the former DET schools to over 2,000 rand in the formerly white (HOA) schools (table 7-1). At the secondary level they ranged from 105 to 2,700 rand. In the absence of fee exemptions, the high fees in the formerly white schools would put them out of the range of all but middle- and upper-middle-class families. Note, too, that more than 99 percent of the students in DET schools were African at that time, 91 percent in the HOR schools were coloured, and 65 percent in the HOA schools were white (see tables 5-1 and 5-2).

We categorize each school into one of five fee quintiles ranging from low fees to high fees. We divided schools in this manner because of our prediction that the incentive for families to apply for fee exemptions would be greater when the fee is higher and the school more likely to try to collect it. Not surprisingly, the DET schools are disproportionately found in the low-fee quintiles, while the formerly white schools are disproportionately in the high-fee quintiles. In primary schools, only 2.5 percent of the students overall and 4.1 percent in the formerly white schools receive fee exemptions. We interpret the 4.1 percent figure to mean that the other 95.9 percent of the students in the formerly white schools can afford the high fees charged by those schools. A similar pattern emerges at the secondary level, where we find that only 5.7 percent of the students in the formerly white secondary schools receive full or partial fee exemptions.

Thus either as a result of the fee policy or other factors, the formerly white primary and secondary schools serve primarily families with a relatively high income, whether they be black or white. This pattern suggests that to some extent race is being replaced by economic class as the determinant of who is able to go to the formerly white schools.

Impact of Fees on School Quality

Fees may affect school quality directly by enabling schools to purchase additional resources, including teachers, that may enhance student performance. As argued by the international consultants, school fees may

28. See Crouch (1995); and Colclough (1995).

TABLE 7-1. Percent of Students with Fee Exemptions, Primary and Secondary Schools, by Former Department, Western Cape, 2001[a]

School category	DET (African)	HOR (coloured)	HOA (white)	Total
Average annual fee charged (rand)				
Primary	45	99	2,077	443
Secondary	105	333	2,701	1,126
Percentage of students with fee exemption				
Primary schools[b]				
1 (low)	1.9 (67)	3.6 (159)	*	2.5 (226)
2	1.7 (37)	1.7 (188)	*	1.7 (225)
3	4.3 (6)	1.9 (219)	*	2.1 (225)
4	13.3 (4)	2.3 (218)	10.6 (2)	2.7 (225)
5 (high)	0 (1)	1.3 (26)	4.1 (197)	3.7 (226)
Total	2.5 (115)	2.2 (810)	4.1 (199)	2.5 (1,127)
Secondary schools[b]				
1 (low)	0.9 (46)	1.7 (20)	0 (2)	1.1 (68)
2	2.5 (9)	3.6 (56)	0 (1)	3.4 (66)
3	*	4.0 (63)	*	4.2 (66)
4	*	3.8 (15)	6.9 (51)	5.9 (66)
5 (high)	*	*	5.1 (65)	5.1 (65)
Total	1.2 (55)	3.6 (154)	5.7 (119)	3.7 (331)

Source: Based on data from Western Cape Education Department.
*No schools in this category.
a. Included in the totals are three HOD (Indian) primary schools and three HOD secondary schools that are not shown separately. Excluded completely from the table are three primary schools without fee data and three HOR secondary schools without fee data.
b. By fee quintile. Numbers of schools in parentheses.

also exert an indirect effect by keeping key decisionmakers engaged in the public schools.

Direct Effects on School Quality

School fees can directly affect school quality only to the extent that they permit schools to significantly augment the resources provided by the state. As shown in table 7-2 for primary schools and table 7-3 for secondary schools in Western Cape, this criterion is met only for the former HOA (white) schools. Assuming that all fees were collected and that there were no fee waivers, fee revenue for the DET (African) schools would account for only 1 percent of their total revenues. In contrast, the average fee of 2,077 rand per learner in the formerly white

TABLE 7-2. Public and Private Resources in Primary Schools, by Former Department, Western Cape, 2001

Unweighted averages across schools, except where noted

Resource	DET (African)	HOR (coloured)	HOD (Indian)	HOA (white)	Total
Per student (rand)					
Annual fees charged	45	99	327	2,077	443
Total public funds per learner	3,002	3,613	4,142	3,857	3,594
Teachers and qualifications[a]					
Number of SGB teachers per school[b]	0.16	0.29	1.33	3.82	0.90
SGB teachers as percent of state-paid teachers	0.6	2.2	12.5	28.5	6.3
Learners per state-paid teacher	38.4	36.3	37.1	35.9	36.6
Average qualifications	13.41	13.10	13.51	14.05	13.30
Percent of unqualified teachers	6.5	20.9	9.4	0.8	15.0

Source: Based on data from Western Cape Education Department.

a. Teacher qualifications are on a scale of 10 to 17, with 10 representing matriculation from secondary school and the numbers above the years of additional training. A qualified teacher is one who has passed the matriculation exam and has three additional years of training (13 = 10 + 3).

b. Weighted average, calculated as the total number of teachers hired by school governing bodies (SGB) divided by the number of schools.

schools would augment total public funding in those schools by 54 percent (see table 7-2).[29]

Income from fee revenue permitted the typical African primary school to hire less than one-fifth of an additional teacher (table 7-2). This contrasts sharply with the situation of the typical formerly white school, which was able to hire close to four additional teachers and to supplement its government-funded teaching force by close to 30 percent. Furthermore, such schools also benefited somewhat in terms of the quantity and quality of state-funded teachers: they have slightly lower learner-to-teacher ratios, their teachers have high average qualifications

29. Because the entries in the first row represent the fees charged per student rather than the fees actually collected by the schools, they most likely understate the true disparities in fee revenue across types of schools. That is because the formerly white schools collect fees more readily. At the same time, fee exemptions are more common in the formerly white schools than in the schools of the other departments.

TABLE 7-3. Resources in Secondary Schools, by Former Department, Western Cape, 2001

Unweighted averages across schools, except where noted

Resource	DET (African)	HOR (coloured)	HOD (Indian)	HOA (white)	Total
Per student (rand)					
Annual fees	105	333	283	2,701	1,126
Total public funds per learner	3,402	3,972	3,803	4,419	4,034
Teachers and qualifications[a]					
Number of SGB teachers per school[b]	0.13	0.94	0.67	5.96	2.60
SGB teachers as percent of state-paid teachers	0.4	3.0	2.5	29.5	9.4
Learners per state-paid teacher	33.6	33.2	35.3	32.4	33.1
Average qualifications	13.83	14.10	14.17	14.48	13.30
Percent of unqualified teachers	2.6	0.8	1.2	0*	0.9

Source: Based on data from Western Cape Education Department.
0* = less than 0.1 percent.
a. Teacher qualifications are on a scale of 10 to 17, with 10 representing matriculation from secondary school and the numbers above the years of additional training. A qualified teacher is one who has passed the matriculation exam and has three additional years of training (13 = 10 + 3).
b. Weighted average, calculated as the total number of teachers hired by school governing bodies (SGB) divided by the number of schools.

(as measured on the 10 to 17 scale), and a smaller share of them are underqualified.

Similar patterns emerge for secondary schools. As table 7-3 shows, the formerly white schools had sufficient fee revenue to expand their teaching staffs by over 29 percent on average, which sometimes produced marked disparities. For example, Phoenix Secondary School in the Manenberg township of Cape Town, which has nearly 900 students, and Westerford High School, a former Model C school in Cape Town that has invested heavily in governing body teacher positions, each were allocated twenty-six publicly supported teachers. However, as the Phoenix principal pointed out, Westerford "actually has fifty-one for the same number of students. That's where the field has to be leveled."

Although one might assume that these resource differences would translate into differences in educational outcomes, that assumption has been challenged in other contexts.[30] To examine its validity in South Africa, we conducted a relatively crude statistical analysis using school-level data in Western Cape and compared the results with findings from a more sophisticated study based on South African household survey data. Taken together, the results support the view that school resources, particularly the quantity and quality of teachers, do affect educational outcomes in South African schools. Thus the use of revenue from school fees to purchase more teachers appears to have helped many schools maintain school quality.

Our statistical strategy was to examine the relationship between pass rates on the senior certificate exam and school resources across schools in Western Cape with close attention to other relevant factors, such as household income, that may also affect student outcomes.[31] Specifically, we used multiple regression to explain variation across the 277 secondary schools in Western Cape in the matriculation pass rate for twelfth graders, with the passes of students who did sufficiently well on the exam to qualify for university weighted at 1.33 an ordinary pass.[32] (See appendix table B for the estimated equations.) Our equation includes four measures of teacher resources: the ratio of state-paid educators to learners, the number of school governing body teachers expressed as a ratio of state-paid educators, and two measures of the quality of state-paid educators (the average quality and the fraction of unqualified educators). In addition, our basic model contains three control variables: a

30. Eric Hanushek has contested the proposition in the U.S. context in meta-analyses of the effects of resources. See, for example, Hanushek (1986, 1997). His conclusions have been challenged by more sophisticated meta-analyses (Hedges, Laine, and Greenwald 1994). For a survey of comparable studies in developing countries, see Fuller (1987). For a summary of research in South Africa, see Taylor, Muller, and Vinjevold (2003).

31. Note that our data are at the school level, our only outcome measure is the (weighted) pass rate on the senior certificate exam, and we do not have as complete a set of family and student background measures as desirable for a study of this type. At the same time, we are able to separate the effect of the fee charged by the school—which we interpret as a family background variable—from that of the teachers hired with the revenue from the fees.

32. The results are similar, but slightly less strong, when the dependent variable is not weighted. When ordinary pass rates are used, much of the variation at the high end of the distribution is lost because many schools have pass rates of 100 percent. In a comparable study of matriculation outcomes in Western Cape, van der Berg and Burger (2002) addressed this issue by using as their outcome variable an overall performance index and a mathematics performance index calculated from the grades on the subject exams.

measure of the poverty of the school community, the annual school fees charged as a measure of the willingness and ability of parents to pay for good schooling for their child, and an index of the poverty of the school's nonteaching resources. A second equation also includes indicator variables for the former department of each school.

Both equations indicate strong and statistically significant relationships between weighted test scores and three of the teacher variables (and all four of them in the basic model). With respect to the quantity and quality of teachers in an average school, a higher learner-to-educator ratio is associated with a lower (weighted) pass rate, a more highly qualified group of teachers with a higher pass rate, and a larger proportion of school governing body teachers with a higher pass rate. In particular, the ability to augment the number of state-paid teachers by 30 percent with school governing body teachers (as in the case of the typical formerly white school) is associated with a 5 to 7 percentage point difference in the (weighted) pass rate of the school.

Though the relationships just described are valid in a descriptive sense, one needs to be cautious in attributing causation because students who are likely to do well on the senior certificate may be more likely than others to choose schools offering small classes taught by high-quality teachers. As a result, we cannot rule out the possibility that the observed relationships reflect, at least in part, this reverse causation rather than the effects of the teachers on outcomes. Treating the annual school fee as a separate variable helps to mitigate this problem to the extent it measures family and student commitment to education, but it does not do so completely.

Our findings are fully consistent with a more extensive study of the effect of school resources in South African schools based on a nationally representative survey of households at the end of apartheid.[33] The American researchers who carried it out argued convincingly that the large variation in the average ratio of learners to educators across magisterial districts, particularly the variation in black areas, was the result of a process that had little to do with student or teacher mobility among schools or with parental pressure. Hence reverse causation is not a concern there, and it seems clear that the variation in average learner-to-educator ratios across magisterial districts contributed to differences in three educational outcomes for students: educational attainment, the probability that an adolescent would be in school, and scores on a

33. Case and Deaton (1999).

TABLE 7-4. Students in Independent Schools, 1995 and 2000

Province	Students in independent schools[a]		All students		Independent students/all students (percent)	
	1995	2000	1996	2000	1995	2000
Eastern Cape	n.a.	8,049	2,233,997	2,105,579	n.a.	0.4
Free State	6,691	10,539	789,933	743,030	0.8	1.4
Gauteng	85,727	117,531	1,427,872	1,554,495	6.0	7.6
KwaZulu-Natal	20,333	43,729	2,598,573	2,668,676	0.8	1.6
Limpopo	8,782	15,247	1,903,020	1,845,265	0.5	0.8
Mpumalanga	3,487	10,209	904,593	893,596	0.4	1.1
North West	4,840	7,650	958,120	908,990	0.5	0.8
Northern Cape	1,385	2,625	196,441	200,871	0.7	1.3
Western Cape	16,366	28,133	885,416	916,384	1.8	3.1
South Africa	n.a.	243,732	11,897,965	11,836,906	n.a.	2.1

Sources: South African Institute of Race Relations (2001, pp. 252, 254) for all figures except 1996 entries, which are from South African Institute of Race Relations (1997, p. 143). Note that the 1995 ratios were calculated using the 1996 estimates for "all students."

n.a. Not available.

a. Enrollment figures are not strictly comparable over time. The 1995 figures are from the Education Foundation and the 2000 figures are from the Department of Education. The independent school figures include students in registered independent primary, secondary, combined, intermediate, and middle schools. All students include learners from grade 1 to 12, preprimary enrollments, public with special needs at public schools, and pupils at combined, intermediate, and middle schools.

numeracy test administered as part of the survey. Their study thus provides compelling evidence that greater school resources, as measured by the inverse of the ratio of learners to educators as a proxy for a more general set of resources, do generate better educational outcomes for students in South African schools.

Indirect Effects on School Quality

Consistent with the predictions of the international consultants, the ability of the formerly white schools to maintain quality is undoubtedly a major explanation for the relatively low rates of flight to the independent schools. Only 2.1 percent of the students in the country were apparently enrolled in such schools in 2000 (see table 7-4). However, the percentages were higher in the wealthier provinces of Gauteng, where the rate was 7.6 percent, and Western Cape, where the rate was 3.1 percent. These provinces are the home of many of the political decisionmakers about whom the consultants were concerned. Thus the higher rates there, along with the fact that the rates everywhere have been rising over time, could gradually undermine the goal of keeping most children in the public school system. In addition, the table entries may slightly understate the number of students in independent schools since they exclude students in independent schools that are not registered. Nonetheless, most South Africans, including many middle-class South African families, have apparently kept their children in the public school system.

The evidence that resources affect educational outcomes strengthens the case for maintaining strong public support for education funding. One key prediction of the international consultants in this regard was that if key decision- and opinionmakers were induced to keep their children in the public schools, public funding for education would be higher than it would have been without their engagement. In fact, however, it was virtually impossible for such opinionmakers to have much impact on the amount of public resources available for education. South Africa's restrictive macroeconomic strategy and its high spending on education in comparison with that in other countries forced the government to limit the resources available for public spending on education during the late 1990s and the early 2000s.

Overall Evaluation

On the positive side, South Africa's decision to encourage schools to levy fees appears to have induced most middle-class families to keep their children in the public school system. That is an important achievement in light of South Africa's apartheid history and the inclusive values on which the new democracy has been built. In replacing the fragmented education system under apartheid, it was essential for the new government to avoid setting up yet another bifurcated system of education.

Moreover, permitting the formerly white schools to charge school fees headed off the temptation to seek equity by destroying the islands of educational excellence that existed under apartheid. South Africa needed all the trained workers and citizens it could muster, and it made little sense to undermine the quality of schools with strong academic programs, especially at a time when the constituency of those schools was being widened to include all races. In addition, for schools serving affluent families the option of using revenue from school fees to purchase additional teachers undoubtedly facilitated their general willingness to go along with the policies to redistribute public resources across provinces and across schools within provinces. Thus it made sense for

South Africa to rely on the private sector as well as the public sector to marshal the resources needed for the new education system during the initial stage of the reform effort.

Contrary to some expectations, however, the fee policy is doing little, if anything, to help the historically disadvantaged schools. The policy as implemented includes no explicit provision to free up more funds to be distributed to those schools, as would have been the case under the preferred option of the Hunter Report. Also the GEAR economic policy provided little leeway for public funding on education to respond to political pressure for greater spending. The expectation that school fees might improve schools serving low-income students by making them more efficient did not materialize because such schools found it difficult to collect fees, were forced to use scarce resources to do so, and generally ended up with fee revenue that was too small a portion of the overall budget to have much effect on school operations.

Has the time come, then, to change the policy toward school fees? The national Department of Education appears to believe that it has, and we agree.[34] One issue that needs to be addressed is whether poor schools should continue to be encouraged to charge fees. Our answer would clearly be "no," on the ground that basic education, as a fundamental human right, is more appropriately financed by broadly based taxes on the entire community than by some mix that includes user charges paid by parents. A necessary corollary to eliminating fees for poor schools, however, would be to provide additional public funding for such schools.

A second question is whether the power of schools serving more affluent students to levy fees should be capped in some way. On the one hand, such capping might encourage more families to move their children to private schools. On the other, if school fees are not capped, many public schools will function increasingly like private schools, albeit with some public funding. That in turn could generate the same undesirable effects that troubled observers to begin with, namely, that

34. On June 11, 2003, the cabinet approved an "Action Plan" based on a review carried out by the Department of Education and released for public comment in March 2003. The action plan provides, among other things, for "the abolition of compulsory school fees, where adequate levels of resourcing is reached, for the 40% of learners in the poorest schools." See Kader Asmal, press statement issued June 17, 2003, on the release of "Action Plan Arising from the Review of the Financing, Resourcing, and Costs of Education in Public Schools."

support for public school funding would decline. Why should affluent families support higher public funding for all schools when they can improve their own schools simply by paying higher fees? If, instead, revenue from school fees were capped at something like 20 percent of the resources provided by the government, families in schools that had reached the cap would in principle have a powerful incentive to support higher public spending on education.[35] Whether any such cap could be achieved politically in the current environment in which many schools already charge fees far higher than any reasonable cap is not a question we can answer here. However, it is, in our own view, decidedly an option worth considering.

An alternative strategy for directing more public funding to poor schools while still maintaining some use of private resources is to give schools public money if they choose not to use fees. Under this approach all schools would receive a basic allotment of teacher slots and funding for nonpersonnel purposes. Additional funding would then be made available for more teaching slots or other uses—but only for those schools that gave up the right to charge fees. Most likely, schools serving the wealthier families would choose to continue to charge fees on the ground that the quality of their schools was worth the cost of the additional fees even at the loss of some public funding. Poorer schools, in contrast, would be more likely to give up fees in return for more public funding. The overall result would be that additional public funds would be channeled to the needier schools without interfering with the power of the wealthier schools to use private funding to maintain their school quality. From a political point of view, the viability of this approach would depend on whether the more affluent families would be willing to see more public funds go to poor schools in exchange for the unlimited right to make heavy use of fee revenue in their own schools.

This proposal reflects in part the spirit of the partnership funding initially proposed in the Hunter Report, but, unlike that report, it extends the principle beyond nonpersonnel spending to the hiring of teachers. Such a policy would not keep the former Model C schools that once served the white elite from having far greater access to resources than other schools. It would, however, most likely reduce some of the current

35. Loeb (2001) develops a similar argument more fully in the context of whether school districts in the United States should have an unlimited right to supplement the amount they receive from the state government in the form of a basic grant for education.

fee-related disparities in quality among wealthy and poor schools by enhancing the teaching staffs of the poor schools. In doing so, it would address what we consider the most urgent priority: finding ways to direct more resources to the schools serving low-income and historically disadvantaged families. Ultimately, there is no substitute for additional public funding for those schools.

eight   Outcomes-Based
Education and Equity

On March 24, 1997, Education Minister Sibusiso Bengu presided over a festive ceremony at Parliament in Cape Town marking the release of a new curriculum for the state education system known as Curriculum 2005. With drummers, singers, and dancers providing a musical backdrop, 2,005 balloons in the colors of South Africa's new flag were released, and the minister proclaimed, "Today heralds the dawning of new hope for the learners of our country."

Curriculum content and structure carry high symbolic value for all countries engaged in the transition from one social system to another. Just as the National Party had used state schools to reinforce the ideology of apartheid and to sustain white privilege, education policymakers in the new democratic government understood the importance of sending powerful signals that the state education system had broken with this discredited past and entered a new era. Specifically, they needed a new curriculum that would meet three requirements relating to both content and pedagogy.

First, instruction had to reflect the *social values that define the new South Africa*—values that Nelson Mandela summarized in his inaugural address as "peace, prosperity, nonsexism, nonracialism, and democracy." The new curriculum needed to reflect the emphasis in the new constitution on equity and human rights and, in sharp contrast to its predecessor, had to foster universal access and common expectations for all learners. It needed to stand as a statement of what all citizens of the new South Africa should know and be able to do as workers, citizens, and fulfilled individuals.

Second, the content of the new curriculum had to be *nonauthoritarian*. Whether delivered in white schools or black, apartheid-era instruction had been doctrinaire and its content defined at the center. The post-1994 climate would not tolerate the mere substitution of one orthodoxy for another. Local schools and communities had to be able to participate in shaping curriculum content.

Third, the new curriculum needed to be *delivered in a democratic fashion*. Instruction in the apartheid era had been universally teacher-centered and emphasized rote learning rather than critical thinking and open-ended problem solving. Instead, the new curriculum would focus on the child, promote active learning, and give each learner some responsibility for the shaping of his or her own education. Consistent with the themes of the "people's education" movement of the 1980s described in chapter 3, the new instructional framework had to be seen as a curriculum of liberation. It also had to be readily implemented in thousands of schools with vastly different resources and serving learners with a wide variety of backgrounds.

Outcomes-Based Education

Debate over the shape and content of a new curriculum for South Africa took place in a variety of forums from the late 1980s through the formal promulgation of a new national curriculum in 1997. The first changes were initiated by the National Party itself in 1990, the year in which it was forced into releasing key political prisoners and legalizing the African National Congress (ANC) and other banned political organizations. In anticipation of further changes down the road, the Nationalists published *A New Curriculum Model for South Africa* that instituted necessary reforms while preserving as much of the old curricular approach as possible. Among other things, these reforms rationalized the multiple apartheid-era syllabi and subject requirements for different grades and phases of schooling. They also defined core learning areas that linked education strongly to economic development and emphasized vocational education.

At the same time, a vigorous debate was under way among educational and other groups over how to structure an appropriate new curriculum once the expected new political order was established. This debate took on new urgency after the Government of National Unity came into being in 1994, and the new Department of Education actually set about designing a curriculum for the post-apartheid era. The curricular debate was carried out in what Kader Asmal, who became minister of education in 1999, described as "an extraordinarily complex environment." Policymakers were being called on not only to establish national and provincial departments of education, but also to set up frameworks for governance and financing; address issues of equity and capacity in the distribution of teachers, facilities, and other resources; enhance professionalism; and, while they were at it, design a whole new approach to instruction. In addition, he recalled, "We went about the tasks knowing we had to operate an existing educational system."[1]

Discussions leading up to the publication of a new curriculum in 1997 were marked by disagreements over the importance of liberal education versus vocational training, the demands of economic development and social transformation, competing views of how learning occurs and, in Asmal's words, how to "strike a sensible balance between centralized design and control of curriculum (with inevitable reductions in diversity) and devolution of curriculum responsibilities to schools, districts and provinces?"[2] In particular, many anti-apartheid activists wanted to eliminate prior distinctions between education and training, which were seen as a means of limiting the vocational prospects of poorly trained workers. By linking education and training, the argument went, workers who had historically been denied access to social or job mobility would be in a position to gain new skills and knowledge that would be formally recognized.[3]

Such discussions had been of particular interest within the Congress of South African Trade Unions (COSATU), where consensus emerged around defining educational objectives in terms of "competencies." The business community called for more emphasis on vocational and entrepreneurial education, and it found allies in both COSATU and the ANC in forging a new National Qualifications Framework, which integrated academic and vocational skills and was eventually established in 1996. Foreign donors such as the U.S. Agency for International Development were urging more attention to early childhood and adult education.[4]

1. Department of Education (2001, sec. 3.2).
2. Department of Education (2001, sec. 3.2).
3. Fleisch (2002a, p. 108).
4. Jansen and Christie (1999, pp. 4–5).

On February 26, 1997, the Council of Education Ministers decided to embrace "outcomes-based education"(OBE) as the guiding principle for a post-apartheid curriculum in South Africa at both the compulsory (general education and training) level, which runs through grade 9, and at the secondary (further education and training) level.[5] OBE is, in essence, an instructional method in which curriculum planners define the general knowledge, skills, and values that learners should acquire. Teachers then work backward to design teaching strategies for reaching these outcomes tailored to the situation and needs of their particular learners. It thus differs in a fundamental way from traditional instruction, in which curriculum planners define quite specific sorts of knowledge and skills that are to be transferred from teacher to pupil and teachers enjoy somewhat less freedom of operation.

OBE has its roots in the behaviorist psychology of B. F. Skinner, the pedagogical principles of Paolo Freire, the mastery learning techniques of Benjamin Bloom, and the curriculum objectives of Ralph Tyler. It is also consistent with progressive learner-centered educational principles nurtured by English private schools. Its adoption in South Africa in the mid-1990s can be explained in part by the fact that at the time OBE was enjoying considerable popularity in other English-speaking countries, most notably Australia and New Zealand. The Department of Education was particularly influenced by William Spady, an American proponent of the method who visited South Africa as a consultant.[6]

Despite OBE's outside origins, South African policymakers gave it a distinctively local flavor. Whereas Spady and other proponents started with a clear picture of what students should be learning and then organized instruction and assessment to make sure that this took place, South African policymakers introduced broader values, such as access, equity, and development, that were driving social change in the post-apartheid period. Designers put heavy emphasis on "progressive pedagogy such as learner centeredness, teachers as facilitators, relevance, contextualized knowledge and cooperative learning."[7] It was an eclectic approach to curriculum reflecting various constituencies and consistent with the spirit of reconciliation that characterized the new democratic South Africa. Spady eventually distanced himself from the South African

5. Kader Asmal, Briefing Notes for the Minister's Meeting with Edward B. Fiske and Helen F. Ladd, July 1, 2002.
6. Jansen (1999, p. 146).
7. Department of Education (2000, pp. 1–6/15).

version of OBE, describing it as "a professional embarrassment."[8] As a guiding principle for a post-apartheid national curriculum, OBE met the initial requirement of signaling a dramatic repudiation of the past in three important respects.

DEMOCRACY WITH RESPECT TO TEACHERS. OBE offers teachers considerable latitude in determining both the content and the pedagogical methods they will employ in order to achieve the desired educational outputs. As a Department of Education booklet put it:

> The new curriculum does not provide detail about content. . . . Educators are recognized as professionals who can make curriculum decisions in the best interests of learners and who do not have to rely on the dictates of a centrally devised syllabus. This means the same outcomes can be achieved through a wide range of learning activities and contexts, and educators must choose the content and locate the activity in contexts of relevance for their particular learners.[9]

DEMOCRACY WITH RESPECT TO LEARNERS. OBE opposes the prescriptive and teacher-centered instruction of the apartheid era and favors a child-centered approach. Whereas accountability in the past focused on normative benchmarks such as grades, OBE in South Africa looks at measures of individual student progress and, consistent with the tradition of "people's education," tends to favor social promotion rather than holding back students who have difficulty mastering the material. It places considerable emphasis on learning through group work and downplays rote learning. It is also constructivist in nature in that it respects not only formal school knowledge but the everyday knowledge with which all children come to school.

EQUAL EXPECTATIONS FOR ALL LEARNERS. OBE asserts that every student, regardless of race, can and must acquire the critical skills that he or she will need to function as citizen and worker. It also puts skills on the same level as content knowledge and blurs the distinction between education and training.

OBE has turned out to be an enormously popular approach to curricular reform in South Africa among both educators and the public at large. OBE made intuitive sense to most South Africans, who came to see it, in Linda Chisholm's words, as "the pedagogical route out of

8. Department of Education (2000, pp. 1–7/15).
9. Cited in Chisholm (2001, p. 6).

apartheid education."[10] Support for OBE as a guiding principle has remained strong even among educators who struggled under the burden of implementing it.

Curriculum 2005

The principles of outcomes-based education were encoded in Curriculum 2005 (C2005), a set of national curriculum guidelines to be fully implemented at both the compulsory and secondary levels of schooling by that year. In practice, official documents do not clearly distinguish between OBE and C2005, and South African educators often use the terms interchangeably.

Everyone understood that Curriculum 2005 was significant not only as a guide to future pedagogy but, like OBE itself, as a symbol of the new educational order. In a May 2000 analysis of its implementation, the Review Committee on C2005 described it as "probably the most significant curriculum reform in South African education of the last century":

Deliberately intended to simultaneously overturn the legacy of apartheid education and catapult South Africa into the 21st Century, it was an innovation both bold and revolutionary in the magnitude of its conception. As the first major curriculum statement of a democratic government, it signaled a dramatic break from the past. No longer would curriculum shape and be shaped by narrow visions, concerns and identities. No longer would it reproduce the limited interest of any one particular grouping at the expense of another. It would bridge all, and encompass all. Education and training, content and skills, values and knowledge: all would find a place in Curriculum 2005.[11]

Like the decision to adopt outcomes-based education as an overarching educational philosophy, the adoption of Curriculum 2005 followed a participatory process involving a wide range of stakeholders, including representatives of national and provincial departments, teachers, school administrators, teacher educators, subject advisers, and researchers. Such an all-inclusive process, which provided opportunities for public responses to draft documents, was new to South Africa and presented a

10. Chisholm (2003).
11. Department of Education (2000, p. 1).

number of practical problems. Levels of expertise among various committees varied widely, and there were problems of continuity and consistency among the various documents produced. A tight timetable left little time for testing and reworking of the new documents, and, as the Curriculum Review Committee that was named to examine their implementation later commented, "The haste to provide a definite break with the past curriculum clearly compromised the quality and coherence of aspects of the C2005 design."[12]

Consistent with the result-oriented nature of OBE, C2005 was structured around a series of general and specific objectives as well as detailed procedures for measuring them. The first building block was a set of twelve "critical outcomes" that broadly defined the educational goals the state education system was setting for South Africa's future workers and citizens. These ranged from the ability to communicate, solve problems, and work effectively with other persons to become "culturally and aesthetically sensitive across a range of social contexts." In order to make these broad goals manageable, the curriculum specified sixty-six "specific outcomes" in eight learning areas: language, mathematics, human and social sciences, natural sciences, arts and culture, economics and management sciences, and life orientation. Finally, each of the sixty-six specific objectives was tied to a number of assessment criteria, which in turn were elaborated by a number of "range statements" and "performance indicators."

Initial Implementation of Curriculum 2005

Despite the fanfare that accompanied its launching in March 1997, the new curriculum got off to a shaky start. The Department of Education had pushed ahead with a January 1, 1998, implementation date even though many officials in the Department of Education argued that it still needed work.[13] The implementation problems encountered by C2005 can be understood in relation to the three basic purposes of OBE discussed earlier.

DEMOCRACY WITH RESPECT TO TEACHERS. Giving teachers considerable latitude in determining the shape and substance of instruction turned out to be problematic in several respects. While Curriculum 2005 specified teaching and learning outcomes, it provided little of the explicit content knowledge that teachers require to achieve these out-

12. Department of Education (2000, pp. 3–6/16).
13. Jansen (1999, p. 154).

comes. In the spirit of democracy and local participation, teachers were expected to generate this content on their own, using not only standard sources such as textbooks but information derived from local sources. They were also given responsibility to determine how to teach the material they created, the pace of instruction, and how much time to allocate to each unit of work.

Our discussions with principals and teachers in a wide variety of schools in Eastern Cape and Western Cape show that such expectations were overambitious. Teachers are typically trained to deliver curriculum, not to write it, and many had neither the skills, the time, nor the inclination to create their own curriculum content. This problem was especially acute among educators in African residential areas who typically had modest training themselves and were already coping with inadequate infrastructures, large classes, and a lack of basic teaching materials such as textbooks and exercise books.

Penny Vinjevold, coauthor of an important early study of the impact of C2005, suggested that the lack of specified content was "a terrible mistake" because it undermined the overall goal of promoting equity within the school system.[14] "Underspecifying turned out to be the exact opposite of an equity model," she commented in an interview. "If you hide the rules of the game from the disadvantaged, you further disadvantage them."[15]

The language of the new curriculum was also a big problem. Curriculum documents introduced more than 100 new terms—"teachers," for example, became "facilitators"—and many educators found them confusing and even gratuitous. Alf Turner, the principal of Pinehurst Primary School in a middle-class section of Cape Town, called the language of C2005 "totally unpractical" for educators whose mother tongue was not English. "The language is difficult to understand as an English speaker," he said. "How do you do it as a Xhosa speaker?"[16]

Perhaps most important, teachers were not given adequate training in either the principles or practical requirements of OBE. Preparing educators to implement a new and radically different instructional model throughout an entire state school system would be daunting under the best of circumstances. In South Africa, the challenge was confounded by

14. Taylor and Vinjevold (1999).
15. Meeting with the authors, February 2002.
16. Unless otherwise indicated, quotations in this chapter are from interviews with the authors between February and July 2002.

the various legacies of apartheid, including shaky administrative structures and a lack of technical expertise, as well as political pressures to move as quickly as possible.

Rather than mount a costly and complex series of professional development courses on its own, the Department of Education introduced a "cascade" model under which educators were trained and in turn passed their knowledge on to colleagues. Teachers frequently complained, though, that district trainers themselves did not always understand C2005, nor did they use it in their own teaching. The result was the "watering down and/or misinterpretation of crucial information."[17] Edwin Philander, principal of the Saambou Primary School, an Afrikaner-medium school in the Manenberg township of Cape Town, told us that he had to send many of his teachers into the classrooms to implement the new curriculum with only two days of training. While he tries to work on OBE at regular Wednesday afternoon staff meetings, he confessed, "Teachers still don't know what is expected of them."

Writing about the implementation process in Gauteng Province, one researcher who was also an insider cited obstacles ranging from the lack of access to photocopying and requirements that training take place after official school hours to a fundamental lack of instructional content. "Training teachers often came to mean little more than bringing a single teacher from a school to a central venue for a dozen hours to give instruction on the philosophy and theory of outcomes-based education, distribute the policy documents and explain how to plan using the new framework," he said. "Other topics, such as how to organize cooperative classrooms and new approaches to assessment, were merely mentioned. Where the district staff worried about the success of the training, they measured it by attendance and what teachers said on evaluation feedback forms. No attempt was made to find out what teachers actually understood about the new curriculum."[18] When Gauteng officials surveyed teachers and principals and published an assessment of the implementation of C2005, their conclusion was blunt: "There is consensus that training was not adequate to successfully initiate C2005 in the classroom."[19]

DEMOCRACY WITH RESPECT TO LEARNERS. While large numbers of South Africans appreciated the new emphasis on learner-centered

17. Department of Education (2000, pp. 1–3).
18. Fleisch (2002a, p. 115).
19. Fleisch (2002a, p. 116).

instruction, the approach ran into practical difficulties here too. OBE called for an elaborate accounting system whereby teachers kept logs that tracked the progress of each student on each learning objective. Teachers complained that such record-keeping was time-consuming and reduced the amount of time they could devote to classroom instruction and curriculum planning.

Some teachers also misinterpreted the notion that students should play a major role in their own learning. Ncumisa Sebola, principal of the Vukany Primary School in a low-income area of Cape Town, told us he liked the idea of learners being active and having an opportunity to explore on their own. "The bad part," he said, "is that some of the teachers say that this means that they themselves don't have to do anything because it is the learners who do the work. OBE should require more work for teachers, not less, but that's not the way many teachers see it."

A related problem arises from the widespread perception that learners who are struggling should not be retained in the same grade at the end of the year. "The idea is that no one fails; everyone carries on," said David de Korte, principal of Windsor High School in Cape Town. "The result, though, was that students come through the system who can't read and write."

EQUAL EXPECTATIONS FOR ALL LEARNERS. The fundamental tenet of OBE and C2005 that schools would have the same goals and expectations for all learners was seen as a way to level the playing field that had been so tilted under apartheid. Unfortunately, some of the central pedagogical principles built into the new approach worked well only under the physical and fiscal conditions found in wealthy schools. Visitors to former Model C schools hear a familiar litany that the schools have been able to handle OBE because "that's what we were doing anyway." Alan Clarke, principal of Westerford High School in Cape Town, a former Model C school that in 2002 charged parental fees of 8,080 rand, commented, "We have the capacity to take what the state says and make it work. We have an ample number of teachers as well as photocopiers and other educational resources."

Educators in schools with fewer resources painted a different picture. Victoria Mabengu, head of department at the Umtata Community School in Umtata in the Eastern Cape, which has twenty-one educators for nearly 1,100 learners, cited the lack of resources in pupils' homes as a major obstacle to implementing the spirit of OBE. "You can't ask them to do something like bring in a magazine," she said. "You need to explain to them what a magazine is, because it's not something that they have in their houses." Karl Williams, a business economics and accounting teacher at Groenvlei High School in the gang-ridden Hanover Park township of Cape Town, echoed this view: "OBE requires constant preparation, and it can only operate well in a well-resourced environment. We have one class with fifty-two children. You can't function under such conditions."

Official documents eventually confirmed the importance of school resources for the success of OBE. In June 2003, Minister of Education Kader Asmal released the results of a baseline study that he had commissioned, the National Report on Systemic Evaluation in the Foundation Phase, which concluded that the resources needed to help pupils cope with the new curriculum were inequitably distributed among schools. Furthermore, learners, on average, had access to only a third of the resources they needed—from books, newspapers, and magazines to radio and television—to handle the learner-centered demands of the new curriculum. "In order for the poor to derive maximum benefits from outcomes-based education, we have to provide minimum library resources in our schools," he said. "This will allow all our students to develop the important skills of processing and analyzing information."[20]

Reconsidering Curriculum 2005

In 1996 Nelson Mandela appealed to the international community to assist South Africa in building up its education system, and nineteen nations came forward to support the President's Education Initiative (PEI) established in November 1998. The initiative was managed by the Joint Education Trust, a nongovernmental organization, on behalf of the Department of Education, and it began its work by commissioning thirty-five research studies on "best practices" in the teaching of core academic subjects and on ways to overcome obstacles such as large classes, among other things. Researchers were given only until the end of 1998 to finish their reports.

In 1999 the PEI unveiled its findings in *Getting Learning Right,* edited by Nick Taylor and Penny Vinjevold. The report characterized

20. Business Day, 2003. See also figure 6-1, which documents the absence of media centers (libraries). As of 2000, only 12 percent of schools throughout the country had computers, and only 20 percent had libraries/media centers.

the overall policy framework developed during the first five years of education under the new democratic government as an "impressive achievement, given the extent to which apartheid education had been entrenched." That said, the authors declared that progress toward the twin goals of educational excellence and expanded educational opportunity "has to date been severely constrained by institutional malfunction in all parts of the system."[21] Their litany of unmet needs ranged from more efficient management systems and a better work ethic among teachers to empirically based research.[22]

Getting Learning Right was particularly harsh in its assessment of the teaching and learning in South African classrooms. The authors found convergence among the thirty-five studies around the notion that teachers had poor conceptual knowledge of their subjects: "Teachers by and large support the intentions of the new curriculum, but lack the knowledge resources to give effect to these in the classroom." Moreover, the notion that teachers should play a leading role in developing content had led many teachers to conclude that textbooks were not important and thus should not be used even when available. "It is important that the value of textbooks be reestablished in the minds of teachers, teacher educators and school managers," they argued.[23]

Taylor and Vinjevold also found fundamental flaws in the design of the curriculum. Specifically, the curriculum's emphasis on teaching from "everyday life" rather than on formal school content was having the opposite effect of what was intended:

The learning programme seems designed to encourage the most superficial approach to hundreds of activities, most of which could be related to the personal experiences of the learners, but few if any of which are likely to result in solid conceptual development .... In the hands of teachers whose own conceptual frames are not strong, the results are likely to be disastrous where school knowledge is totally submerged in an unorganized confusion of contrived realism.[24]

The bottom line of education is, of course, student learning, and on this matter Taylor and Vinjevold were blunt: "Our researchers found

21. Taylor and Vinjevold (1999, p. 227).
22. Taylor and Vinjevold (1999, p. 228).
23. Taylor and Vinjevold (1999, p. 233).
24. Taylor and Vinjevold (1999, p. 121).

that what students know and can do is dismal." On the fundamental
task of reading, for example, they concluded:

At all levels investigated by PEI projects, the conceptual knowledge of students is well below that expected at the respective
grades. Furthermore, because students are infrequently required to
engage with tasks at any but the most elementary cognitive level,
the development of higher order skills is stunted. Books are very
little in evidence and reading is rare. Writing is also infrequent
and, when practiced by students, it hardly ever progresses beyond
single words or short phrases. The single most worrying observation is the evidence suggesting that many teachers are unsure as to
whether reading is specified as an outcome of Curriculum 2005.
Because of this uncertainty and confusion, some teachers are not
teaching reading as an explicit activity.[25]

Taylor and Vinjevold concluded: "The right to learn has to a considerable extent been achieved, and the large majority of South African children now have access to schooling. The immediate priority must be to
get learning right so that the progress of students through the system is
substantially improved."[26]

As discussed in chapter 3, the picture painted by the PEI report was
reinforced by international assessments that appeared in the mid- to
late1990s. The TIMSS-R study, for example, drew attention to the lack
of emphasis on knowing basic science facts and understanding science
concepts. "While most countries placed a major emphasis on this in the
curricula documents," it said, "South Africa did not."[27]

When Kader Asmal became minister of education in 1999, C2005
was in its second year of implementation, and he immediately embarked
on a "listening campaign" to find out how things were going.[28] What he
heard was that "an overwhelming majority of views expressed frustration with the design and implementation of Curriculum 2005."[29] Asmal
wasted little time in dealing with such complaints as well as those documented in *Getting Learning Right*. In February 2000 he announced the
establishment of a six-member Review Committee on Curriculum 2005,

25. Taylor and Vinjevold (1999, p. 231).
26. Taylor and Vinjevold (1999, p. 235).
27. Chisholm (2003, p. 275).
28. Interview with authors.
29. Kader Asmal, Briefing Notes for the Minister's Meeting with Edward B. Fiske
and Helen F. Ladd, July 1, 2002.

headed by Linda Chisholm, to carry out "a substantive review of the new curriculum and its implementation."[30] The committee included persons who had been involved with the development of Curriculum 2005 as well as individuals associated with the PEI Report, but it conspicuously did not include representatives of the South African Democratic Teachers' Union (SADTU). The committee was given until the end of May—not even four months—to investigate these issues by means of document reviews, site visits, and interviews and to issue its report.

Asmal's action was politically courageous. Curriculum 2005 was the first major policy of the new democratic government to come under such harsh scrutiny and, as it turned out, to be publicly reversed. Many in the government were reluctant to make such a public confession of failure. "Asmal's entire bureaucracy was furious with him," recalled Vinjevold in an interview. "We all wanted the new government to work; we wanted our people to show that we could do it. But when we went into the classrooms we saw how the underspecifying of content was hurting. It was painful to have to that say this flagship policy was not working."

Report of the Curriculum Review Committee

Despite its ambitious timetable, the Review Committee was thorough in its investigations. Members examined official and unofficial evaluations, carried out site visits and interviews, and reviewed public submissions. In its report, released on May 31, 2000, the committee reaffirmed the value of outcomes-based education as an educational philosophy and stressed that, for all the problems with implementation, there was strong continuing support for OBE among South African educators. "Many endorse the underlying principles of learner participation, activity-based education, emphasis on relevance, flexibility, anti-bias, inclusion, holistic development, critical thinking and integration," it said. "But equally many are confused about the design and implementation of C2005. It is clear from all the available evidence that although C2005 has generated a new debate on teaching and learning, teachers have a rather shallow understanding of the principles of C2005."[31]

The Review Committee's report accepted all of the major complaints about Curriculum 2005 from educators, including their critique of the underspecification of content. It agreed with those who criticized the

30. Department of Education (2000, Executive Summary).
31. Department of Education (2000, Executive Summary).

complexity of language and administrative structures and the lack of adequate training and support service. It highlighted serious technical problems, including unrealistic time frames for the design and almost instant implementation of Curriculum 2005 and a fundamental "overcrowding" of the curriculum that left too little time for developing basic reading and math skills and core concepts in the sciences. The committee also charged that, in their efforts to avoid prescribing content, curriculum designers had neglected important issues such as "sequence, pace and progression."[32]

The committee recommended that Curriculum 2005 be simplified— among other things, that the number of learning areas be reduced from eight to six and the sixty-six "specific outcomes" scrapped—and that teachers be given more backup in using it. It proposed a National Curriculum Statement that would allocate more time for mathematics and language instruction. It also recommended revised terminology to make documents clear and accessible, and it urged that more attention be paid to teacher orientation, training, and support. It called for more learning support materials, especially textbooks, and for better coordination of national, provincial, and district-level support services. In summary, the committee wrote: "It is vital that Curriculum 2005 in its current form is phased out and a new revised and streamlined curriculum based on the principles that have galvanized educational transformation in South Africa is phased in."[33]

The report of the Review Committee was sharply criticized by the South African Democratic Teachers' Union (SADTU) which, though it had published research of its own echoing many of the committee's findings, portrayed it as a watering down of the principles of OBE, a repudiation of the new government and a return to the past. Eventually, however, SADTU and the minister of education found common ground in the view that OBE should remain the underlying philosophy of education in the post-apartheid era.[34] Kader Asmal accepted the report and appointed a Ministerial Project Committee in November 2000 to manage the streamlining and strengthening of C2005. The time frame called for a draft revised curriculum statement by mid-2001 and public comment by the end of that year, but conservative interest groups concerned with issues of religion and sexuality managed to prolong the discus-

32. Department of Education (2000, Executive Summary).
33. Department of Education (2000, chap. 9).
34. Chisholm (2003).

sions.[35] The new National Curriculum Statement through grade 9—hailed by Asmal as a "clearer and simpler version of Curriculum 2005"—was completed by February 2002 and approved by the cabinet on March 20, 2002.[36] Plans call for implementation of grades R (reception year) through 3 in 2004 and working up to grade 9 by 2008.

Despite the initial reluctance of many in the government to admit that the original C2005 had structural flaws, the revision process went remarkably well. Asmal called this unsurprising. "When Curriculum 2005 was introduced," he said, "key battles with the old order were still being fought, and provincial departments were still in the process of being created. By 2002, key battles had been won and provinces were in place albeit with some misaligned processes and procedures. This meant that the process of curriculum development could be shaped by an emphasis on a curriculum for democracy, citizenship and learner achievement rather than by the need for compromise with an old order."[37]

Not everyone would accept Asmal's judgment that the key battles had been settled. One vocal critic of OBE all along has been Jonathan D. Jansen, dean of the school of education at Pretoria University, who in 1997 wrote a much-quoted article entitled "Why Outcomes-Based Education Will Fail."[38] In a series of books, articles, and speeches, Jansen has lambasted OBE and Curriculum 2005 not only on the usual practical grounds, such as the complexity of its language and inadequate teacher training, but for its basic presuppositions, including the notion of specified "outcomes." There is, he argued, "a fundamental contradiction in insisting that students use knowledge creatively only to inform them that the desired learning outcomes are already specified."[39]

---

35. In a paper on the politics of the curriculum revision process Chisholm (2003) characterizes the unsuccessful efforts of fundamentalist Christians to torpedo the new curriculum as reflective of "the loss of social power of a conservative white minority seeking to reassert itself by ideological means." The net effect was to unify the different strands of the ANC, including the Department of Education and SADTU, around the concept of a "modernizing, liberal humanist, pragmatic approach to reform."

36. Kader Asmal, Briefing Notes for the Minister's Meeting with Edward B. Fiske and Helen F. Ladd, July 1, 2002.

37. Kader Asmal, Briefing Notes for the Minister's Meeting with Edward B. Fiske and Helen F. Ladd, July 1, 2002.

38. Republished in Jansen (1999) as "Why Outcomes-Based Education Will Fail, an Elaboration."

39. Jansen (1999, p. 150).

Most relevant to our focus on equity, Jansen argued that outcomes-based education has been more successful as a political gesture than as genuine educational reform. The goals of OBE are impossible to reach, he said, without commitment to fundamental and systemic reform of the state education system in South Africa, yet the current political and social climate is not conducive to such systemic reforms:

> OBE is primarily an attempt to push forward something innovative into schools at all costs in order to reclaim political credibility for a Ministry of Education which is still charged, within and outside of government, with having delivered little concrete evidence of transformation in the schools. Not a single official interviewed in the national Department of Education believed that OBE should be introduced so soon; yet they all worked feverishly towards implementation at all costs in 1998.[40]

Referring to the launch of the new curriculum in March 1997 along with 2,005 balloons in the colors of the new South African flag, Jansen wrote it was clear that "curriculum and patriotism were firmly linked."[41]

Conclusion

Although the revised Curriculum 2005 is still in the early stages of implementation, some general conclusions can be drawn about the impact of post-1994 curriculum reform on democracy and equity in education in South Africa. Given the political imperatives facing curriculum developers in the mid-1990s, outcomes-based education was a reasonable approach to take. In practice, however, its complexity undermined some of the democratic and egalitarian ideals that it sought to promote.

OBE clearly sent out strong signals that the dawn of democracy in South Africa had ushered in a new educational order. The authoritarian values and top-down pedagogical approaches of apartheid-era education were out—replaced by new values and teaching methods that emphasized democratic participation and the potential of every child to succeed. The power of these signals should not be underestimated, espe-

40. Jansen (1999, p. 154).
41. Jansen and Christie (1999, p. 10).

cially given the fact that the most enthusiastic support for OBE comes from African educators and others who were the most direct victims of the inequities of the old order and who, as a group, faced the most difficulty implementing it in their classrooms.

Some of the practical problems of OBE had to do with its design, notably its complexity and overestimation of the capacity of teachers to develop their own curriculum materials. Others resulted from inadequate implementation, such as inadequate time and resources for training teachers in this new pedagogical approach. Such problems arose in part because curriculum reform was but one of the major issues competing for the attention of educational policymakers and Department of Education managers as they sought to transform the structures they inherited from the apartheid era into a system appropriate to post-1994 South Africa.

Still other problems were more deeply rooted in policy decisions related to resources. As the name implies, outcomes-based education focuses on educational results. In practice, the quality of outcomes in any educational system is heavily dependent on the financial, human, and other resources invested in the system, especially the quality of teachers. Not surprisingly, OBE turned out to work best in privileged schools where teachers enjoyed relatively small classes, had plenty of access to textbooks and other resources, and were already accustomed to group work and the teaching of critical thinking. Such schools typically had built up libraries and supplies of textbooks and other teaching materials over a long period of time.

Conversely, OBE posed difficult, and in some cases insurmountable, challenges for black schools in low-income communities that lacked even the most rudimentary libraries and media centers and where teachers were unsophisticated in using resources such as textbooks even when they did become available. In the absence of substantial investment in the human and physical resources required to implement OBE effectively, it is difficult to envision how this new curricular approach could succeed in furthering the cause of equity in schooling.

The constructivist nature of outcomes-based education also had consequences for equity. The notions of teachers taking the lead in defining the content of curriculum and of students learning from everyday life are appealing alternatives to the rote learning that marked the apartheid era. Likewise, recognizing the value of every learner's experience is a useful corollary to formal school knowledge that sends a powerful message regarding the value of individuals. At some point, however, if they are to be well educated, students need to develop the ability to think in terms of conceptual frameworks. Students in South Africa enter school with widely varying experiences of "everyday life." Middle-class students typically arrive with fairly broad experiences and a foundation for making the leap from personal experiences to formal knowledge. Disadvantaged students, however, arrive with far more limited experiences, and the last thing they need is to be "submerged . . . within their own 'landscapes' and in the process denied access to formal knowledge required for power within society as a whole."[42]

During the apartheid era the Nationalists had no need to provide separate curricula for black schools because such purposes were already achieved by the institutionalized inequality inherent in racially discriminatory funding and the inadequate facilities and unqualified teachers that characterized African schools.[43] The Review Committee drew a parallel conclusion regarding OBE and Curriculum 2005 when it wrote, "The impact of outcomes-based education cannot be equal in unequal conditions."[44] In other words, equal treatment does not translate into equal opportunity when some schools are resource-poor.

42. Fleisch (2002a, p. 137).
43. Jansen (1990, pp. 201–02).
44. Department of Education (2000, pp. 3–9).

nine   **Educational**
         Outcomes

Thus far our analysis of racial equity in South African schools has focused on educational inputs and processes. That is, we have examined the extent to which the new government's policies have succeeded in allocating human, financial, and curricular resources more equitably than in the past. In this chapter we turn to outcomes and educational adequacy.

Outcomes matter in South Africa for several reasons. For one thing, the country is in a hurry to change, and the government is eager to show that it is making progress toward erasing the legacy of apartheid by creating a quality educational system. To measure outcomes, policymakers rely mainly on the proportion of high school students passing their matriculation examinations, an indicator with serious limitations. More generally, outcomes can demonstrate the extent to which the education system is providing adequate education, especially for historically disadvantaged students—meaning the education they need to function in contemporary South Africa.

As noted in chapter 3, South African learners as a whole have performed poorly, both absolutely and in relation to other African countries, on international tests such as the Third International Mathematics and Science Study and the Monitoring Learning Achievement study. Aggregated data and detailed data by race from Eastern Cape and Western Cape shed light on three other outcome measures: progress of students through school, the taking of math courses, and performance on the senior certificate exam. Though our analysis is limited to those two provinces, the basic patterns are indicative of the situation in the other seven.

The racial differences and adverse trends reflected in these measures illustrate the magnitude of South Africa's educational challenges as it seeks to promote educational adequacy for students from disadvantaged racial groups. To be sure, many factors contributing to low achievement and other undesirable outcomes extend well beyond the control of schools, among them poverty, malnutrition, poor employment prospects for secondary school graduates, and the HIV/AIDS pandemic. These broader social problems must be addressed if South Africa is ever to make significant progress toward the goal of providing an adequate education to all students. To assert that schools cannot solve major social problems by themselves, however, does not let the education system off the hook. Further steps could be taken within the system to promote more adequate outcomes for black students as the country moves forward.

In previous chapters we examined steps that the Department of Education has taken in the areas of funding and curriculum. At the end of this chapter we identify three additional policy challenges that affect educational adequacy for black students: language of instruction, quality assurance and support, and the potentially devastating effects of HIV/AIDS.

Progress through School

As indicated in chapter 7, enrollment rates in South Africa are generally high at the primary level but fall off quite significantly at the secondary level. Given that nine years of education are now compulsory, it is reasonable to assert that students who do not complete grade nine have not had an adequate education.

Whether adequacy in South Africa requires all students to continue through grade 12 and to earn a senior certificate is a more complicated issue. At a minimum, the changed environment of post-apartheid South Africa, with its new opportunities and responsibilities for all citizens, would seem to call for more secondary schooling than in the past. One stumbling block here is the "wastage" from having large numbers of students repeat grades and thereby progress at such low rates that they are at risk of dropping out. To explore this issue we examine enrollment patterns and repetition rates across grades by race of the student in Eastern Cape and by former department in Western Cape.

FIGURE 9-1. Learners, by Grade and Race, Eastern Cape, 2001

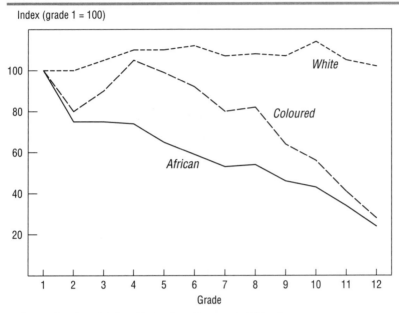

Index (grade 1 = 100)

Grade

Source: Based on data from Eastern Cape Department of Education.

Eastern Cape by Race of Student

Enrollment figures by grade for African, coloured, and white students in Eastern Cape in 2001 (figure 9-1) give some idea of what the progress of a single cohort of students through the education system looks like (except in situations in which the size of cohorts of students vary quite significantly over time or in which repetition rates vary greatly across grades).[1] The enrollment patterns are most striking among Africans. First, there is a substantial drop-off in students between grades 1 and 2, which is not unusual in developing countries in part because repetition rates tend to be high in the first grade.[2] Had we presented comparable figures for an earlier year, the drop-off rate between grades one and two might have been even greater. That is because the national Department of Education, concerned about the large numbers of underage children

1. Although we have comparable data for earlier years we were reluctant to follow groups of students through time because of missing data for some schools in some years.
2. UNESCO (1998).

in grade one and their lack of readiness for school, raised the minimum entry age to first grade from six to seven years for the 2000 school year.

Second, there is a steady decline in the number of students in each successive grade, undoubtedly a sign that some students are dropping out of school, even at the primary level. Third, the probability of Africans getting all the way through grade 12 appears to be very low, on the order of one in four if the probability calculation is based on first-graders and one in three if based on the smaller group of second-graders.

The pattern for coloured students is similar to that for African students, though somewhat less consistent and pronounced. By contrast, white students show consistent enrollment across grades, with some suggestion that the cohorts of white students entering the lower grades in 2001 appear to be somewhat smaller than the cohorts who started three to five years earlier.

Not shown are the repetition rates by race. Such rates appear to be about 10 percent in the primary grades and about 20 percent in the higher grades for both African and coloured students.

Western Cape by Former Department

In the absence of complete breakdowns of students by race in Western Cape, we look instead at students grouped by the schools operated by the former racially defined departments of education. Such an approach is misleading to the extent that students move from one set of schools to another as they progress through school, but we can minimize that problem by looking separately at either primary schools or secondary schools. We do so on the reasonable assumption that most of the students who move, say, from former Department of Education and Training (DET, African) schools to former House of Representatives (HOR, coloured) schools do so at the beginning of the primary school or the secondary school cycles. We do not look at former House of Delegates (Indian) schools because there are so few of them. (See tables 5-1 and 5-2 for racial composition of each type of school.).

As figure 9-2 shows, repetition rates are quite low in the primary grades for all three of these racially delineated groups of schools. The lowest rates of about 2.5 percent are found in the formerly white schools, with rates up to 6.7 percent in the former coloured schools. The reported rates for both the DET and the HOR schools are far lower than those in most primary schools in Eastern Cape.

FIGURE 9-2. Repetition Rates, by Grade by Former Department, Western Cape, 2001

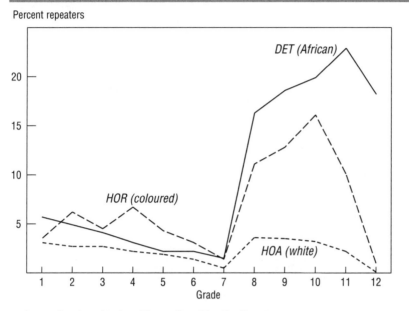

Percent repeaters

DET (African)

HOR (coloured)

HOA (white)

Grade

Source: Based on data from Western Cape Education Department.

The picture changes dramatically at the secondary level in both the DET and HOR schools. For DET schools, the repetition rates are about 20 percent in all five grades, and in the HOR schools they range from 10 to 12.8 percent in grades 8 to 11 before falling sharply to 1 percent in grade 12. One explanation for these patterns may be that students are allowed to progress through primary schools even if they have not mastered the material. Once in secondary school, however, the specter of the matriculation exam in grade 12 induces schools to be tougher on passing students from one grade to another.

Although it is difficult to follow precisely the same group of students over time since some students repeat grades and some new students may enter the system, table 9-1 gives an idea of the progress of boys and girls in grade 8 in 1997 through grade 12 in 2001. Unlike many developing countries, South Africa has more girls than boys in secondary schools. In addition, the ratios suggest that once boys are in the eighth or tenth grade they are less likely than girls to continue on to grade 12.

TABLE 9-1. Progression of Boys and Girls through School, by Year, Western Cape

	Number of students			Ratio of 12th graders to	
Students	1997 (grade 8)	1999 (grade 10)	2001 (grade 12)	8th graders	10th graders
All[a]					
Boys	38,025	30,144	18,296	48.1	60.1
Girls	39,628	34,732	23,613	59.6	69.0
DET (African)					
Boys	4,590	5,681	3,389	73.8	59.7
Girls	5,780	7,679	5,471	94.6	71.2
HOR (coloured)					
Boys	23,039	16,228	7,872	34.2	48.5
Girls	23,537	18,488	10,357	44.0	56.0
HOA (white)					
Boys	7,909	7,367	5,991	75.8	81.3
Girls	7,965	7,645	6,564	82.2	85.9

Source: Based on data from Western Cape Education Department.
a. Includes students in former HOD (Indian) schools as well as in DET, HOR, and HOA schools.

For students in the coloured (HOR) schools, it is reasonable to interpret the ratios as rough estimates of the probability that an eighth-grader in 1997 or a tenth-grader in 1999 would make it to twelfth grade. That interpretation is not possible for the other groups because of the confounding effects of student migration—in-migration to the DET schools as students from Eastern Cape seek better schooling opportunities in Western Cape and out-migration from the HOA schools as students leave to go to private schools or, in some cases, to move to another country. For students in HOR schools, the probability of reaching grade 12 is only about one in three for boys in grade 8 and only one in two for those in grade 10. The estimated probabilities for girls in the HOR schools are somewhat higher than for boys but still well below one out of two students for eighth-grade girls.

Replicating the calculations for HOR schools for students starting in tenth grade each year from 1995 to 1999, we find the probability of making it to twelfth grade falling over time, and hence the dropout rate rising. One possible explanation is the turmoil associated with the massive layoffs of teachers in those schools during that period. Another potential explanation, to which we return later in the chapter, is the possibility that schools responded to the new pressure to demonstrate higher pass rates on the matriculation exam by discouraging students from continuing to grade 12 and thus from taking the exam. In any case, a rising dropout rate is clearly inconsistent with the national goal of improving educational outcomes for black students.

Internal Efficiency Indicators

It is quite common in the international education literature to use enrollment figures of the type depicted in figure 9-1 to calculate the "internal efficiency"of an education system. Such indicators show the effort, as measured in pupil-years of education, needed annually to produce a single enrollee in the final year of the cycle. If all students progress on schedule from grade to grade, the internal efficiency will be 1.0. If some students repeat grades or drop out, the indicator will be higher.

A crude approximation for Eastern Cape puts the internal efficiency for primary school (grades 1 through 7) at 1.35 for Africans and 1.15 for coloured learners.[3] Thus, on average, it takes more than nine pupil-years of schooling to produce one grade 7 African enrollee and about eight pupil-years to produce one grade 7 coloured enrollee. The indicator for Africans is high compared with that for all South African learners and also for other African countries.[4] The efficiency indicators are apparently much closer to 1 for primary schools in Western Cape. Using 2001 enrollment data, we estimate the crude efficiency indicator to be 1.10 for the DET schools and 1.05 for the HOR schools. These figures suggest that total wastage—repetition and dropouts—is far lower for primary schools in Western Cape than in Eastern Cape.[5]

3. The approximation is calculated by expressing the average number of students in grades 1 to 7 as a fraction of the number of students in the final grade of the cycle, in this case grade 7. Ideally, it would be preferable to base the indicator on the progress of a specific cohort of students through school. See UNESCO (1998, pp. 13–14); and Crouch (1999, p. 12).

4. Comparable efficiency indicators from UNESCO data are 1.20 or less in Senegal, Zambia, and Burkina Faso and 1.28 to 1.30 for Kenya, Swaziland, and Guinea, as reported in Crouch (1999, table 7, p. 12).

5. For comparability, these efficiency indicators were estimated using the same method we used for Eastern Cape. We are also able to calculate the indexes by following the cohort of students entering first grade in 1995 through primary school. Using that method, the index for DET schools falls to about 1.05 and for HOR schools it rises to about 1.12.

The term "efficiency indicator"—or even the more precise term "inefficiency indicator"—can be somewhat misleading. It is tempting to interpret it as a measure of the extent to which school resources are being wasted and then to blame the schools for poor management. A more accurate interpretation, however, would focus on what it says about wasted opportunities for students and the magnitude of the educational challenges facing the system. Those challenges will inevitably need to be met through a combination of policies. Some will need to focus on the economic and social problems that contribute to dropout, such as pressures on children to work or to stay at home to take care of ailing parents.[6] Other policies will need to remove the obstacles that keep children from attending school or learning once they get there such as limited transportation and malnutrition. Still others will need to work on improving the quality of schools for disadvantaged children.

Math Enrollments in Western Cape

A second outcome measure has to do with the kind of academic programs that students of various races pursue. Are South African learners enrolling in the kinds of courses that will enable them to function as workers and citizens in the years ahead? To shed light on this issue, we examine patterns of enrollment in math courses in Western Cape, with some attention to physical sciences as well. We chose these subjects because black students were systematically underexposed to technical subjects under apartheid, and they are relevant to employment opportunities in an increasingly knowledge-based and technocratic world economy.

Under apartheid, instruction for Africans was designed to prepare them only for the jobs available to them. Since jobs as laborers required no math, instruction in mathematics was kept to a minimum and taught in an abstract manner. On one of our visits to a rural primary school in Eastern Cape, a regional education official commented on how pleased he was to see on the chalkboard a list of items such as bread, tea, and milk next to their prices in rand. He said that when he had learned math in a similar school many years earlier no effort was ever made to con-

6. Brazil and other countries appear to be having some success in addressing challenges of this type by providing cash payments to low-income families whose children stay in school. See Celia W. Dugger, "To Help Poor Be Pupils, Not Wage Earners, Brazil Pays Parents," *New York Times*, January 3, 2004.

FIGURE 9-3. Math Courses, by Former Department, Western Cape, 2001

Percent of all courses

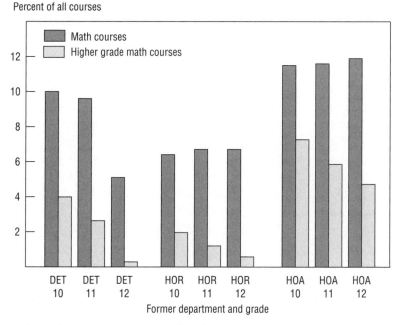

Source: Based on data from Western Cape Education Department.

nect numbers to anything as real as bread, tea, or milk. Math to his generation of Africans came across as an abstract tool that bore little relationship to anything useful. As a result of this legacy, qualified black math teachers remain in short supply and black students tend to perform poorly in math.

For each subject in secondary school, courses are typically offered at either the "standard" or the "higher-grade" level. Students hoping to continue on to university must take the matriculation, or Senior Certificate, exam in a minimum of six subjects, with at least four of them at the higher grade. As shown in figure 9-3, Western Cape black students are still far less likely than whites to take math courses all the way through high school or to choose them as a higher-grade subject. In the former DET (African) schools, math courses accounted for about 10 percent of all courses taken in tenth grade, but this proportion fell by almost half, to 5.1 percent, in grade 12. Between the tenth and twelfth grades, there was an even more precipitous decline in the proportion of math classes taken at the higher rather than the standard level. The combination of students dropping out of school, dropping out of math, and switching from higher-grade to standard-grade courses meant that by grade 12 only 251 African students in the former DET schools throughout Western Cape were enrolled in higher-grade math. Thus, the DET schools are clearly failing to provide an environment conducive to success in math.

The patterns differ somewhat for students in the former coloured (HOR) schools. Only 6.4 percent of tenth-graders (most of whom are coloured) are enrolled in math compared with 10.0 percent of African ones. Also, the percentage of math courses taken at the higher level in HOR schools was lower than in the DET schools in grade 10 but higher in grade 12. This pattern is consistent with the very high dropout rate of students from the HOR schools, most of whom presumably would have been enrolled in the standard-grade courses. The bottom line, however, is the same: a relatively small number of students in the former HOR schools are succeeding in math at the higher grade.

The situation for students of all races in the former white (HOA) schools is quite different. Math courses account for one in eight (almost 12 percent) of the courses that these students were taking in grade 12, and despite some drop-off in the percentage taking math at the higher level, more than 3,500 students were still enrolled in higher-level math in grade 12.

Similar patterns by former departments emerge for enrollments in physical sciences (not shown). Fewer than 200 students were enrolled in higher-grade physical sciences by grade 12 in the former DET schools and only about 650 in the former HOR schools. These numbers are far below the approximately 3,100 students in such classes in the former HOA schools.

Pass Rates on the Senior Certificate Exam over Time

As the one measure of academic outcomes that is readily available, pass rates on the Senior Certificate, or matriculation, examination tend to attract a lot of attention from policymakers. For better or for worse, "matric" results have been used to measure the success of the education reform effort and also to spur effort in individual schools. Since 1999 the national Department of Education has publicly reported pass rates at the school level, thus allowing policymakers to celebrate the success of some schools and to bemoan the mediocrity of others.

The Senior Certificate exam has two levels: "without" and "with" university endorsement.[7] The latter is more difficult because it requires both higher scores and more courses at the higher level. Passing with endorsement is particularly important for students wishing to continue their education because all universities and most technikons in South Africa expect their students to have earned this credential.

Since pass rates on this national exam are published annually and widely reported in newspapers, it is tempting for policymakers and the media to focus on trends in these numbers as a measure of educational progress. One problem is that all of the students who sat for the senior certificate examination in 2001, the last year of our data, began their education under the apartheid system. Thus it is far too early to expect the education reforms to have had much effect on the performance of students in those higher grades. Because a greater portion of their schooling has occurred since the reforms were initiated, a far better indicator would be trends in achievement for students in the lower grades. Unfortunately, no comprehensive data showing such trends are available. Even for these younger students, it would be unreasonable to expect much in the way of achievement gains in such a short time given the time lags in implementing major reforms.

Moreover, trends in matriculation rates are a flawed measure of educational progress because such rates are driven not only by the number of students who pass the exam but also by the number of students who sit for the exam. Thus a rise in the pass rate could simply reflect the fact that fewer students are sitting for the exam. (Figures 9-4 and 9-5 illustrate this observation.)

Both the overall percentage of students passing the exam and the percentage passing with endorsement declined almost continuously from

7. To obtain a pass without endorsement, a student must offer at least six subjects at either the standard- or the higher-grade level and obtain an aggregate mark of 720 on the six best subjects, which is equivalent to a 40 percent score on tests at the standard-grade level. To obtain a Senior Certificate pass with university endorsement, a candidate must offer a minimum of six subjects, at least four of which must be at the higher grade, and obtain a mark of 950, which corresponds to an average mark of 43.2 percent assuming the candidate takes four subjects at the higher-grade level and two at the standard level. The maximum mark for a standard-grade subject is 300 and for a higher-grade subject is 400. Among the courses presented, two must be languages, one of which must be a language of "learning and teaching," namely, English or Afrikaans. A candidate who tries for a Senior Certificate with endorsement but does not meet the requirements is granted a Senior Certificate without endorsement if he or she satisfies the conditions for the latter.

FIGURE 9-4. Senior Certificate Pass Rates, 1979–2001

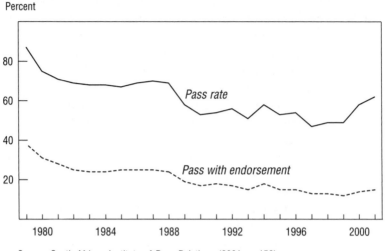

Source: South African Institute of Race Relations (2001, p. 156).

1979 until 1997—at which point the overall pass rate began to rise (figure 9-4). A tempting conclusion might be that the quality of the education system was declining throughout the 1980s and early 1990s and is now finally improving, presumably as a result of new national education policies. Indeed, the rise in the pass rate from 49 percent to 58 percent in 2000 pleased government officials and "exceeded even the minister of education's commitment to a 5 percent improvement in 2000."[8]

But such an interpretation would be hasty. The total number of candidates increased steadily to a peak of 559,000 in 1997 but then declined by about 20 percent (figure 9-5). Meanwhile, the number of students who passed the matriculation exam increased throughout much of the period and then remained essentially constant after 1994. As of 2001, in fact, the number of students passing the exam was about 2,000 lower than the 1994 figure. It thus appears that through the mid-1990s the country's education system was producing increasing numbers of students who were sufficiently well educated to pass the Senior Certificate, but that since then progress has been stagnant. The increase in the matric passing *rates* since 1997 can reasonably be attributed not to the fact that more students are successful—which is not the case—but to the fact that fewer students are sitting for the exam.

8. Jennifer Shindler and Susan Beard, "An Analysis of the 2000 Senior Certificate Examination," *EduSource Data News*, no. 32, March 2001, p. 1.

FIGURE 9-5. Senior Certificate Candidates and Passes, 1979–2001

Number of students (thousands)

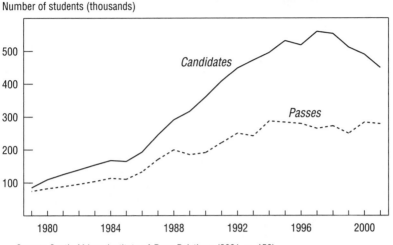

Source: South African Institute of Race Relations (2001, p. 156).

This decline in the number of candidates has not gone unnoticed by policymakers.[9] Among the reasons suggested for the drop-off are changing demographics due to declining birth rates, stricter implementation of the regulations requiring older learners to take alternative education routes, and a variety of responses by individual schools to political pressure to raise their particular pass rates.[10] Such school policies include failing more students in the lower grades and an associated increase in the number of students who drop out of school, discouraging learners who have a poor chance of passing the exam from writing it, and reducing the number of repeaters who are allowed to write the exam.[11] The prevalence of this latter practice is consistent with the fact that the proportion of students taking the exam as repeaters dropped from 12 percent in 1999 to only about 1 percent in 2000.[12]

9. South African Press Association, "High Matric Pass Rate Raises Eyebrows," 2004. See also Prega Govender and Thokazani Mtshali, "Asmal Orders Probe into 'Missing' Matrics," *Sunday Times*, December 30, 2001.

10. The African fertility rate has fallen significantly during the past thirty years. In the early 1970s, the African total fertility rate was more than 5 children per woman, but as of 2000 it was about 2.85 children per woman (Simkins, 2002). This decline accounts for some, but certainly not all, of the drop in the number of candidates.

11. Jennifer Shindler, "An Analysis of the 2001 Senior Certificate Examination," *EduSource Data News*, no. 36, March 2002, pp. 1–2.

12. In 1999 the pass rate was 41 percent for repeaters and 50 percent for nonrepeaters, but in 2000 it was 57 percent for repeaters and 58 percent for first-time can-

TABLE 9-2. Changes in Matriculation Pass Rates and Candidates, by Province, 1996–2001
Percent

	Pass rate		Percent change 1996–2001	
Province[a]	1996	2001	Pass rate	Candidates
Limpopo	39	60	54	−35
Gauteng	58	74	28	−12
Free State	51	59	16	−25
Northern Cape	74	84	14	−7
Western Cape	80	83	4	8
KwaZulu-Natal	62	63	2	8
Mpumalanga	47	47	0	−7
Eastern Cape	49	46	−6	−5
North West	70	63	−10	−21

Source: South African Institute of Race Relations (2001, pp. 264–66), and Department of Education.
a. Ranked by percent change in pass rate.

Further evidence of the inverse relationship between changes in the proportions of candidates and changes in pass rates emerges from provincial data for 1996–2001 (table 9-2). The provinces are ordered by the change in their pass rates between 1996 and 2001. Limpopo's pass rate, for example, increased by more than 50 percent in that period, while the number of candidates sitting for the exam dropped by almost 35 percent. Gauteng, Free State, and Northern Cape experienced similar illusory increases attributable in part to declines in the number of candidates. Free State is particularly striking in that the percentage reduction in the number of candidates far exceeds the change in the province's pass rate. Only two provinces, Western Cape and KwaZulu-Natal, managed to increase their pass rates as well as the number of candidates. Pass rates in Eastern Cape and North West declined despite a falling off in the number of candidates.

Leaving aside the issue of whether schools have manipulated pass rates by limiting the number of candidates, pass rates remain very low in many provinces. In Eastern Cape no more than one out of two students who sat for the exam in any year between 1996 and 2001 passed it, and

---

didates. These patterns suggest reducing the number of repeaters increased the overall pass rates. Jennifer Shindler and Susan Beard, *EduSource Data News*, no. 32. March 2001, p. 2. However, this drop in the proportion of repeaters taking the exam accounts for only a portion of the decline in the number of candidates, and none of the drop between 2000 and 2001.

in 2001 its pass rate of 46 percent was the lowest of all nine provinces. The four provinces of Free Sate, KwaZulu-Natal, Limpopo, and North West had pass rates of about 60 percent. At the high end, three provinces had pass rates above 70 percent in 2001: Gauteng, Western Cape, and Northern Cape.

Also of interest are results on particular exams, such as the more technical subjects of math and physical sciences. Not surprisingly, the results for Eastern Cape, Limpopo, and Mpumalanga fell far short of those for the wealthier provinces of Gauteng, Northern Cape, and Western Cape. The proportion of all candidates (not just those who sat for math) who passed the math exam ranged from a low of 16 percent in Limpopo to a high of 41 percent in Western Cape. The proportion passing at the higher grade ranged from less than 2 percent in Eastern Cape and Limpopo to close to 10 percent in Gauteng. Similar patterns emerge for physical sciences.

Despite the apparently strong showing in Western Cape, closer analysis of exam results over time reveals a less than sanguine picture for African and coloured students in that province. Although reported pass rates appeared to improve in the DET (African) schools, from 38 percent in 1996 to 57 percent in 2001, if the rate is recalculated as the number of passes in any given year as a proportion of the students who were enrolled in grade 10 two years earlier, quite a different picture emerges (figure 9-6). The decline between 1998 and 2001 from 34 percent to 28 in this measure indicates that the DET schools have been doing an increasingly poor job of moving their tenth-graders all the way through to success on the Senior Certificate exam.

Similar patterns are to be found in the schools serving primarily coloured students. Over the four-year period for which we have data, the estimated percentage of tenth-graders succeeding two years later fell from 52 to 45 percent. The 2001 figures suggest that fewer than one in three tenth-graders in the DET schools and fewer than one in two of those in the HOR schools pass the matriculation exam at the end of grade 12. Thus despite its overall success rate on the Senior Certificate, even Western Cape is not doing well by its many African and coloured students in the former DET and HOR schools.

These patterns reinforce our conclusion that many schools are actively discouraging some students who are not likely to pass the exam from continuing in school. That behavior would be a rational response to public pressure from both the national minister of education and

FIGURE 9-6. Pass Rates on Senior Certificate, by Former DET and HOR Departments, Western Cape, 1996–2001[a]

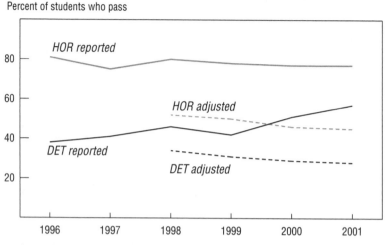

Percent of students who pass

Source: Based on data from Western Cape Education Department.
a. The reported rate is the number of students who passed divided by the number of candidates. The adjusted rate is the number of students who passed divided by the number of students in the tenth grade in those schools two years earlier.

from provincial officials to raise pass rates. Now that pass rates are reported at the school level on an annual basis, such pressures on school principals are especially significant. The mischief caused when policy-makers measure educational success by pass rates on the Senior Certificate exam is further illustrated by a close examination of the schools identified by Western Cape's minister of education in December 2001 and given awards for the impressive improvement of their students between 2000 and 2001 in passing the exam. According to our analysis, five of the seven schools featured large reductions in the number of their candidates during this period, and the reductions were large enough to account for most of the gains in the pass rates.[13]

We cannot, however, rule out the possibility that some students may drop out of school for reasons having little to do with the education sys-

13. This practice of showing improvement by keeping some students from taking the exam is not unique to South Africa. As the United States is now learning, any system that places a high priority on test results will generate that type of response. See, for example, the experience of Houston, Texas, as reported by Schemo, "Questions on Data Cloud Luster of Houston Schools," *New York Times,* July 11, 2003.

tem: they may need to take care of family members who are ill with AIDS, for example, or may be discouraged at the prospects of getting a job even if they pass the exam. Some of the principals of coloured schools whom we interviewed emphasized the poor job outlook. With unemployment rates close to 70 percent for young workers in some of the Western Cape townships, younger students may see no point in continuing in school. Some officials in the Western Cape Education Department argued that perhaps it was appropriate for some students to drop out of school, but such an argument, even at best, would assume that such students have an alternative means to gain the additional skills they need to obtain a good job—opportunities that are not now available.

Additional Challenges

Our analysis of these three outcomes measures—progress through school, course taking, and performance on Senior Certificate examinations—shows that South Africa still faces huge challenges in its efforts to provide black students with an adequate education. Although many black students currently enrolled in formerly white schools clearly have access to better education than was available to them during the apartheid period, their number remains a small proportion of the total. Unfortunately, none of the evidence presented in the previous section indicates much improvement in educational outcomes for the vast majority of previously disadvantaged students. Even in Western Cape, which boasts very high pass rates on the matriculation exam in comparison with other provinces, the students in the former black schools continue to exhibit very poor outcomes, whether measured as progress through school or as success on the matriculation exam.

This outcome is not surprising. Even with the best of policies it would have been difficult to undo the legacy of apartheid in such a short period of time. More relevant at this point is the extent to which the country has been setting a foundation for improved outcomes for black students in the future. We now turn to three aspects of that issue: language in education, quality assurance and support, and the loss of teachers to HIV/AIDS.

Language in Education

A recent summary of the determinants of educational outcomes in South Africa emphasizes "the all-pervasive and extremely powerful influence of language, which stands out as the one factor which is not only unambiguously implicated in learning, but which also offers clear policy lessons."[14] Empirical studies of the Senior Certificate results confirm that African-first-language speakers are at a disadvantage next to native English speakers in that they are studying and being examined in a second or third language. Other studies of targeted groups of students in township or homeland schools also implicate language as an important determinant of performance. They show, for example, that better academic results are obtained when the teacher is instructing in her home language, when the learners are being taught in their home language, and when learners whose home language differs from the medium of instruction in the schools speak that language at home.[15]

As should be clear from previous chapters, however, current language policies are complicated by their political role during South Africa's colonial and apartheid periods. Their earlier use to separate ethnolinguistic groups has had powerful effects on all aspects of life to this day.[16] Afrikaners still use language to preserve their identity and culture, and many African families, seeing English as the language of opportunity, want their children to learn in English.

By the end of the apartheid period, mother-tongue instruction was still the rule for African students but was limited to the first three years of education, at which time learners would switch to one of the two official languages of the country at that time, English or Afrikaans.[17] Such a policy is described as *subtractive/transitional* bilingualism in that the mother tongue is replaced by other languages as the learners progress through school. Such an approach has gained increasing favor among African families who view English as the preferred language for their children. Many language experts, however, believe that three or even four years is simply not sufficient time for children to develop the

14. Taylor, Muller, and Vinjevold (2003, p. 65).

15. Taylor and others (2003, pp. 58–59). These results are based on a baseline study using hierarchical linear modeling of data from 525 schools in four provinces throughout the country. Though the data are imperfect in that much comes from self-reports, Taylor and his colleagues conclude that they are sufficiently clean to generate useful results. One odd result that emerges from the analysis, however, is that learner results in language improve with greater absences of the teacher.

16. Language also played a political role in shaping relations between English and Afrikaners. See chap. 3, n. 13.

17. Initially it was restricted to the first four years of education, but with the introduction of a three-year foundation phase, mother-tongue instruction was limited to the first three grades.

language skills they need in one language before they switch to another. Nor is there sufficient time to expose students to the new language before they are expected to make a complete shift.

To complicate matters further, the 1996 constitution explicitly recognizes eleven official languages—the two white languages along with nine African languages—and promotes the vision of a multilingual and multicultural society. The document grants citizens the right "to use language and participate in the cultural life of one's choice" and the right "to receive education in the language or languages of their choice in public educational institutions where that education is reasonably practicable."[18]

Along with the curriculum reform, but on a completely separate track, the new democratically elected government initiated policy discussions in 1995 related to language and introduced a new language-in-education policy in 1997.[19] Consistent with the ideals expressed in the constitution, that policy called for a shift to an *additive* multilingual model, now preferred by most language experts around the world. Under this approach, children would start learning in their native language and would continue doing so while adding one or more other languages as they progressed through school. Thus they would become fully bilingual or multilingual.

Despite the 1997 policy shift from a subtractive to an additive approach, school practices for Africans have changed little since the 1980s.[20] In a 2002 interview, Theta Suthole, the principal of Nomlinganisela Primary School in the Guguleto township of Cape Town, elaborated on the problem these practices post for young African learners: "In grade 2 they start to learn English words. In grade 3 they learn sentences. In grade 4 all their subjects are taught in English." Not surprisingly, he added, "some of them are not confident about expressing themselves in English."[21] These language obstacles are compounded by the

18. Republic of South Africa (1996, secs. 30, 29).
19. Interestingly, the discussion about curriculum (see chap. 8) also proceeded independently of the language discussion, and the Curriculum 2005 policy was announced before the language policy in 1997. In contrast to the multilingual aspirations for the country embedded in the constitution, Curriculum 2005 appears to assume that only one language has value in South Africa. Heugh (2002, p. 173).
20. That the 1997 national policy has not altered language practices in most schools is evident from our examination of language practices in schools serving Xhosa speakers in Western Cape. In grades 1 to 3 all but 2 to 5 percent of the Xhosa-speaking students are instructed in their mother tongue. The situation changes dramatically after grade 4, when the vast majority of such students are instructed in a language other than Xhosa, usually English.

language limitations of the staff at all grades. In Western Cape secondary schools formerly operated by the DET where almost all the students are Xhosa speakers but are taught mainly in English, only 40 percent of the teachers speak English at home. [22] In other words, instructors for whom English is not the home language are preparing large numbers of African students for matriculation exams to be taken in English.

The delay in implementing the 1997 language-in-education policy calling for an additive approach may be ascribed in part to the common assumption that most African parents want their children to learn in English even if that means undermining their own language and culture. That view is reinforced by many Africans who were in exile during the struggle against apartheid and believe that instruction in English is necessary to prepare Africans for jobs and higher education.[23] It is also shared by many of the middle-class African parents choosing English-medium schools, including those in Eastern Cape discussed in chapter 5. Another possible explanation for the delay relates to the substantial costs involved in producing educational materials in the African languages so students can use them fully. Yet another complication is that not all African children have a clear mother tongue, and in many schools in various parts of South Africa (but less so in the Western and Eastern Cape, where Xhosa is so prevalent), students speak a variety of languages.[24]

Even if most African parents do value English highly and would be willing to have their children do all their learning in English, supporters of the additive model contend that the choice between English and the African languages is not that clear-cut. It is not a matter of choosing one or the other, they argue, but rather of using the additive model both to preserve African language and culture and to promote the deep learning of English that parents want. Various studies make the powerful case that children will do better in English if they have had the opportunity to continue instruction in their mother tongue.[25] Though developing those languages would be costly, supporters of multilingualism empha-

21. Unless otherwise indicated, quotations in this chapter are from interviews with the authors between February and July 2002.
22. Percentages calculated by the authors based on data provided by Western Cape Department of Education.
23. See Heugh (2002, pp. 180–85). See also Mda (1997).
24. See response of Taylor and Vinjevold (1999); and Heugh (2002).
25. For an overview of the effects of bilingual education in the U.S context, see August and Hakuta (1998).

size that the current policy is failing the country's African children because most of their teachers are not very proficient at English.

To some observers, the obvious way to remove the language barrier for African learners is simply to replace the subtractive model with the multilingual additive model called for in the 1997 language-in-education policy.[26] Until that happens, they maintain, African-language speakers will continue to face unfair educational disadvantages. To others, the solution is to accept English as the medium of instruction for most African students and to require classroom teachers to undergo intensive instruction in that language: "There must be both a conscious focus on the importance of language, and explicit policies and programs to develop proficiency among staff, pupils and parents in the official language adopted by the schools," they argue."[27]

In any case, the bottom line is that providing equal opportunity to African learners will require significant commitment and substantial resources in forms such as investing in the development of African languages, providing greater support for language development within the schools, or investing in the English language skills of teachers.[28] South Africa will have difficulty making those large investments, however, until it decides whether the current language practices are to be continued or whether the official 1997 language-in-education policy will be implemented. Until that politically sensitive issue is addressed and sufficient resources are devoted to language development in the schools, language will continue to be a significant barrier to the country's progress toward equal opportunity and adequate outcomes for African students.

Quality Assurance and Support

Somewhat lost amid all the other reforms in the initial drive to promote educational equity in South Africa was the effort to ensure that schools were providing a quality education. Quality assurance has always been on the education policy agenda, but policymakers acknowledge that much more needs to be done to make sure that available resources are used effectively. In practical terms, the challenge is to find ways to link classroom instruction and school management to an external accountability system and then to develop support systems that will enable educators and schools to meet the standards.

26. Heugh (2002).
27. Taylor and others (2003, p. 65).
28. Heugh (2002).

As with so much else in education in South Africa, the issue of quality assurance is complicated by the legacy of apartheid. Though accountability measures are essential to improve processes and outcomes at schools serving mainly black students, lingering resentments against apartheid make them difficult to implement. The authoritarian and heavy-handed nature of Nationalist education fostered a climate of suspicion, much of it focused on the network of school inspectors who kept tabs on what was being taught in classrooms. In the early 1990s outright hostility on the part of students and young teachers led to the collapse of the old inspection system, but memories of that era of abuse and insecurity are hard to overcome.

By the time the new government took over in 1994, state authority had been eroding for well over a decade, and policymakers faced an uphill battle in restoring respect for the school system. An October 1997 analysis of the situation in Eastern Cape, for example, reported that teacher opposition discouraged representatives of the office charged with monitoring schools and appraising teachers from visiting schools: "At present there are no systematic teacher appraisal guidelines in place."[29] Consistent with that conclusion, a 1999 report on Eastern Cape found that nearly three-quarters of teachers surveyed (73 percent) had never been evaluated and that less than 4 percent of them had been appraised during the prior two years.[30]

The fragmented approach to teacher development and school improvement that characterized the apartheid era did not lend itself to extensive accountability. Up through 1995 the major strategy for development was built around in-service training for teachers. Most of this work was carried out by nongovernmental organizations (NGOs) through short-term workshops. Though successful in some ways, they did little to build "the deep knowledge structures and professional ethos required for the long-term qualitative improvement of teaching and learning."[31] The 1997 Eastern Cape report also lamented the lack of coordination between pre-service and in-service training of teachers, a problem that was complicated by the decision to make the training of new teachers a national rather than a provincial task and to shift responsibility from schools of education to universities.[32]

29. Eastern Cape Department of Education (1997, p. 25).
30. Strauss and Burger (2000, p. 20 and table B35).
31. Taylor and others (2003, p. 16).
32. Eastern Cape Department of Education (1997, p. 27).

The South African Schools Act of 1996 required the minister of education to monitor and evaluate standards of education provision, delivery, and performance, and in the late 1990s the Department of Education began to turn its attention to such matters. A Directorate of Quality Assurance was established at the national level, along with comparable structures in the provincial departments and an office to coordinate work at the two levels.[33]

An initial priority was to improve the quality of teachers. Despite significant progress in upgrading the skills of underqualified personnel, as of 2001 more than one in five teachers did not meet even the most minimum qualification level of matriculation plus three years of training (see chapter 6), and many others who technically met the standards had been very poorly trained in low-quality schools of education. Moreover, even teachers with the requisite qualifications required ongoing professional support.

In 1998 the Department of Education launched a development appraisal system for teachers that was hailed as a major step in breaking the long-standing deadlock between teachers and employers over acceptable evaluation procedures.[34] Rather than link evaluations to salary determination or other factors that would affect teachers' careers or working conditions, the idea was to rely heavily on peer evaluation and to focus on professional skill development. But implementation has been slow. Teachers regarded the evaluations as time-consuming and cumbersome, and many of the appraisals were based on casual conversations between teachers rather than classroom observations. Most important, with appraisal decoupled from professional advancement, the system lacked teeth. In some parts of the country teachers did not even allow their school principal to enter their classrooms to observe their performance.[35] Teacher appraisal and support have been complicated further by the limited number of management positions in schools and district offices and thus by a shortage of people available to provide mentoring and support.

33. Seekings (2001, p. 87).
34. This paragraph relies heavily on research by the Center for Education Policy Development as part of a major study of the transformation of the education system, *Education 2000 Plus Project*, funded by the Royal Embassy of the Netherlands. The project consisted of case studies of twenty-seven schools across the country conducted in 1999, 2000, and 2001, analysis of macro data, and analysis of policy and legislation. See also CEPD (2001).
35. Seekings (2001, p. xvi).

At the end of the 1990s, educational officials and the unions agreed to pursue the concept of "whole school" development and to test its effectiveness in one or two provinces. The best-known example is the Education Action Zone (EAZ) project in Gauteng, which was loosely modeled on programs in England and France and aimed at monitoring schools using criteria such as pupil and teacher attendance and curriculum coverage while also providing training and support to educators and learners. Targeted at dysfunctional secondary schools with pass rates on the matriculation exam of less than 20 percent, the program established teams that reported directly to the provincial head office to monitor student and educator discipline and performance in the schools.

This centralized approach to school improvement contrasts with earlier efforts initiated by nongovernmental organizations, the national Department of Education, and various provincial departments of education that took a more grassroots, participatory, and democratic approach. In his evaluation of some of those projects from the perspective of a former insider in the Gauteng Department of Education, Brahm Fleisch concluded that efforts such as the Thousand Schools Project, the Culture of Leaning Program, or the Education Quality Improvement Project that relied on NGOs or democratic processes within the schools were not very successful in improving schools.

Thus the EAZ approach grew out of concern about the limits of the parent participation model and the fact that "most of our school communities appear to be completely unready or uncommitted to take on such a major task unless direct leadership is provided by the state."[36] In place of the early school-by-school improvement strategies, this one articulated clearer standards that were supported by monitoring and inspection systems. EAZ has been credited with improving student success on the matriculation exam, both in terms of rates and absolute numbers, but the jury is still out on its long-term effectiveness as a model for other provinces. It nonetheless represents a significant step in the direction of reasserting state control over the operations of low-performing schools in a constructive and supportive manner.

The Department of Education has also begun to develop alternatives to matric passing rates as a means of assessing student achievement. Under the long-awaited Systemic Evaluation System, begun in pilot

36. Gauteng Department of Education, "Education Action Zones and the Monitoring of Standards in Education: Issues in the Implementation of the Proposed Programmes" (undated), as quoted in Fleisch (2002a, p. 97).

form at grade 3 in 2001, representative samples of students in grades 3, 6, and 9 will be tested to see if they are achieving at appropriate levels. Such data will then be used to evaluate the effectiveness of the system as a whole rather than that of individual students, teachers, or schools. Nevertheless, doubts have been raised about the reliability of tests administered by teachers on their own students as well as the capacity of many schools and district officials to administer the process.[37]

The whole-school improvement and systematic evaluation systems can be viewed as signs that the state education system has at last begun to stabilize following the disruptive restructuring after 1994, and that the foundation has been laid for attention to outcomes and, ultimately, to gains in student performance. Yet the system clearly has a long way to go toward realizing the potential benefits even of these two initiatives. There is little obvious coordination of the two policies, and the absence of any external testing of learner achievement is a serious flaw in the whole-school approach. Moreover, there are few indications that the national and provincial departments of education have the capacity to make use of the information generated by the various quality assurance initiatives.[38]

Hence schools in South Africa remain almost entirely unaccountable for the outcomes of their learners. Training programs and other support measures tend to focus on issues such as institutional vision and pedagogical technicalities and are not linked to defined targets of improved learner performance. As Taylor, Muller, and Vinjevold note, "The South African schooling system is characterized by the absence of accountability measures with 'bite.' This results in a significant diminution of the opportunity to learn, particularly in poorer schools."[39] At the same time, it would be unfair and inappropriate to introduce such accountability measures at the school level without setting up support systems to enable schools and teachers to succeed.

HIV/AIDS and the Supply of Teachers

Looming over all the policy efforts at transforming the education system and improving outcomes for black students is the specter of HIV/AIDS. A 2001 review of change and transformation in the education sector by the Department of Education bluntly asserted: "This is

37. Seekings (2001, p. xvi).
38. Seekings (2001, p. xvii).
39. Taylor and others (2003, p. 16).

the priority that underlies all priorities, for unless we succeed, we face a future full of suffering and loss, with untold consequences for our communities and the education institutions that serve them."[40]

The report goes on to highlight the potential for rising absenteeism among children who are caregivers for sick parents, who have to substitute as heads of households, who must work to supplement family income, or who themselves are ill. In addition, the report raises the possibility that HIV/AIDS could lead to major new demands on the education system in the form of higher demand by sick parents for early childhood education and for second-chance education for learners returning to the education system after an AIDS-related absence from the system. It acknowledges, however, that the full magnitude of the effect on the education system is not yet clear. One of the greatest concerns is how the disease will affect the supply of teachers, a professional group that in South Africa as well as in other African countries has been particularly susceptible to the disease. Even in the absence of the disease, South Africa faces a potentially large shortage of qualified teachers.

The downsizing of teaching staffs at many schools in the mid-1990s dramatically reduced the demand for teacher training programs. At the same time, the supply of spots in such programs dwindled as the teacher training colleges were shut down or incorporated into universities or technikons. As a result, the number of newly qualifying teachers throughout the country fell to about 5,000 in 2001 and was expected to drop to 3,600 in 2004. This number is, among other things, well below the approximately 18,500 teachers expected to leave the profession in that year for reasons unrelated to HIV/AIDS.[41]

Predicted deaths of teachers associated with HIV/AIDS make the looming teacher shortage even more staggering. Assuming the national rate at which teachers are infected with HIV/AIDS is 12.5 percent (slightly above the national average rate) and that the time between infection and death is ten years, about 3,000 HIV/AIDS-related teacher deaths are predicted for 2004, with the number growing exponentially thereafter.[42] Over the ten-year period 2001–10, more than 50,000 teachers are expected to die of HIV/AIDS, with the figure for a province

40. Department of Education (2001, p. section 6).
41. The 2001 estimate is from Vinjevold (2001); 2004 estimates are from Hall (2002, table 3).
42. Hall (2002, table 3).

such as Eastern Cape close to 7,500 and that for Western Cape, where the incidence of HIV/AIDS is far lower, about 1,500.[43] For a country that ended the apartheid period with such a dismally low-quality stock of teachers in the historically black schools, the failure to begin the process of training high-quality teachers for the future represents a serious problem.

HIV/AIDS is clearly a major and potentially devastating issue on the horizon for the South African education system. Not only will AIDS reduce the supply of teachers, but also it will place severe stress on schools facing the additional demands of educating children who are orphaned by the disease. The reason we have devoted so little attention to the challenge of HIV/AIDS in this book is simply that so few hard data are yet available and that so few of the people we talked to in the schools were willing to identify it as a problem.[44] As the deaths mount during the next decade from South Africa's high infection rates during the 1990s, however, the country's failure to address the problem could well end up being a significant obstacle to educational equity in the future.

Conclusion

Using the criteria of progress through school, nature of courses taken, and success on the matric exam, we find black students on average continue to perform at low levels. Thus South Africa appears to have made little progress toward racial equity defined by the concept of educational adequacy.

Educational adequacy for blacks remains under the powerful shadow of South Africa's past. Colonial history and apartheid's influence on language policy and quality assurance magnify the challenges the country faces as it tries to grapple with policy issues that are clearly not unique to South Africa. The task of combating the negative effects of these legacies is now being complicated by a new threat, the HIV/AIDS pandemic.

To say that the goal of racial equity measured by the standard of educational adequacy has been—and is likely to continue to be—elu-

43. Hall (2002, table 2).
44. We do not mean to imply that the Department of Education is unaware of the problem. Among other actions, it commissioned a major study of the problem of teacher supply and demand in the age of HIV/AIDS (Crouch 2001). That report estimates that 30,000 new teachers per year will need to be educated.

sive, however, is not to deny its strategic importance. As we noted in chapter 5, most black South African learners still attend schools that formerly served only black students, and that will always be the case given the raw numbers and the geographic distribution of black students throughout the country. To ensure that black South Africans receive an adequate education, there is no substitute for enhancing the quality of those schools.

ten   Equity in
Higher Education

Few institutions of higher education have a more illustrious history than University College of Fort Hare. Founded by Scottish missionaries in 1916 as the first college to educate Africans, it boasts an alumni roll that reads like a Who's Who of southern African leaders: Nelson Mandela, Govan Mbeki, Robert Sobukwe, Mangosuthu Buthelezi, and Robert Mugabe among them. Located in the rural town of Alice in the impoverished Eastern Cape, Fort Hare evolved over the years from a teacher training institution into a university with strengths in agriculture and rural development, but in 1982 its academic evolution abruptly stopped. The Nationalist government placed it under the control of the government of the newly established "independent" homeland of Ciskei, and its faculty and administrative ranks became a repository for mediocre Afrikaner academics and unemployed civil servants.

Like other black universities, Fort Hare was a center of agitation against apartheid in the 1980s and early 1990s, and the advent of a new democratic government in 1994 brought hope of a better future but little substantive change. Idealistic academics, both black and white, returned from exile elsewhere in Africa eager to rekindle the image of Fort Hare as a training ground for African leaders, but most were disillusioned with what they found and soon departed. The university continued to struggle with inadequate facilities and poor management, and enrollments dropped, in part because many of the most talented African students were availing themselves of their new opportunities to attend historically white institutions from which members of their race were previously barred.

What to do about Fort Hare has been the most visible of a complex set of questions for policymakers in the post-apartheid effort to build an effective and equitable system of higher education. Should the government make the significant investments that would be required to turn Fort Hare and other admittedly mediocre African universities and technikons into viable academic institutions? Or should such institutions be seen as vestiges of the hated apartheid system and be closed down or merged? The all-important priority has been how best to serve African students. Are such students better off in "historically black" universities and technikons that, for all their academic weaknesses, know something about how to deal with academically underprepared students? Or are they better off trying to make their way in the academically superior, but often intimidating, environment of "historically white" institutions?

The problems facing higher education in post-apartheid South Africa were similar in important respects to those at the primary and secondary level. In both cases the government inherited networks of educational institutions defined by the race of the students they served and governed through a convoluted, even bizarre, set of structures designed to bolster the system of apartheid. At both levels the first steps were to unify state-run educational institutions under the umbrella of a single national system and thereby to send out a powerful signal that students of all races were welcome in any institution.

Like the primary and secondary levels, higher education faced enormous problems related to the legacy of apartheid, including limited resources, financial mismanagement, poor teaching, and low achievement in institutions serving black students. Here, too, reform in the post-1994 period was shaped by the terms of the political compromises that facilitated the transition from apartheid to a new democratic social and political order. Just as the formerly white Model C schools retained considerable control over their admissions policies and exercised the right to generate substantial revenues from fees, the historically white universities and technikons enjoyed operational independence and access to private resources that allowed them to become stronger than ever, sometimes at the expense of their historically black counterparts. The assertion by Minister of Education Kader Asmal, quoted in chapter 4, that "reform must proceed with inherited assets and liabilities" applies as much to higher education as to the schooling sector.

In other important respects, however, the challenges related to universities and technikons differed substantially from those at the primary and secondary level. For one thing, higher education is not compulsory, so policymakers were dealing with a smaller proportion of the relevant age cohorts. Because black students at the tertiary level are potentially more mobile than younger students and because black students accounted for a far smaller proportion of overall enrollment than was the case at the primary and secondary level, there was greater leeway at the tertiary level for providing opportunities to black students through the racial transformation of the historically white universities and technikons. In addition, the national government had direct responsibility for the public universities and technikons and thus was not constrained by the need to work through provincial governments.

At the same time, the government was burdened by an enormous range of issues, from macroeconomic policy to health and public safety. The restructuring of higher education was clearly a far less urgent political issue than putting primary and secondary schools on a sound footing. Moreover, policymakers at the higher education level faced the special challenge of what to do with Fort Hare and the other sixteen historically black institutions whose financial and academic viability— and, indeed, whose continuing raison d'être—was in question. In this chapter we examine the new government's responses to these issues, particularly as they relate to the equitable treatment of historically disadvantaged students and institutions.

Higher Education on the Eve of Democracy

The new black-run government that came to power after the elections of 1994 inherited a higher education system consisting of thirty-six universities and technikons, some of which were historically white and some historically black (table 10-1).[1] The white universities were among the best in Africa and included both English-medium and Afrikaans-medium institutions. During the colonial period, the British had established the University of Cape Town, founded in 1918, and subsequently

1. The terms "historically white" and "historically advantaged" are generally used interchangeably, as are the terms "historically black" and "historically disadvantaged." We will generally employ "historically white" and "historically black," or sometimes simply "black" or "white," to denote the nature of the institution during the apartheid period.

TABLE 10-1. Universities and Technikons, by Date Founded and Sector

Universities			Technikons		
Historically white					
Cape Town	1918	English	Cape	1967	White
Natal	1949	English	Free State	1981	White
Rhodes	1951	English	Natal	1967	White
Witwatersrand	1922	English	Port Elizabeth	1967	White
Free State	1950	Afrikaans	Pretoria	1967	White
Port Elizabeth	1964	Afrikaans	Vaal Triangle	1967	White
Potchefstroom	1951	Afrikaans	Witswatersrand	1967	White
Pretoria	1930	Afrikaans			
Rand	1966	Afrikaans			
Stellenbosch	1918	Afrikaans			
Historically black					
Fort Hare	1959	African	Border	1988	African
North	1960	African	Eastern Cape	1987	African
North West	1980	African	Mangosuthu	1979	African
Transkei (Unitra)	1977	African	Northern Gauteng	1980	African
Venda	1982	African	North West	1976	African
Zululand	1960	African			
Durban-Westville	1960	Indian	ML Sultan	1969	Indian
Western Cape	1960	Coloured	Peninsula	1972	Coloured
Medunsa	1976	Special purpose	Vista	1982	Special purpose
Distance learning					
Unisa	1946	Mixed	Technikon SA	1980	Mixed

Source: Based on Cooper and Subotsky (2001, table 1.1).

the Universities of Witwatersrand, Natal, and Rhodes. These institutions were "liberal" in the sense that they dissociated themselves from the interests of the state and viewed themselves as members of an international community of scholars. The English-medium universities used their connections with the business community to raise substantial private funds and thus minimize their dependence on the government. The Afrikaans-medium universities, starting with Stellenbosch (1918) and the University of Pretoria (1930), dedicated themselves to promoting the language and culture of Afrikaners prior to apartheid. After the Nationalists took power in 1948 they established four new Afrikaans-medium universities to further this work and to train administrators of the apartheid system. Isolated by language and politics from the international community, these universities were run in authoritarian fashion and were almost totally dependent on the government for financial support and the funding of research.[2]

Black universities fell into two categories as well: those in the Republic of South Africa and those in the self-governing territories and "independent" homelands. With the exception of Fort Hare, which predated apartheid and assumed university status in 1959, all were set up after 1960 to train needed African workers, especially teachers and civil servants. These institutions were managed by Afrikaners loyal to the Nationalist government, and decisions on matters ranging from curriculum to clerical appointments had to be approved either by the racially appropriate department of education or by the relevant homeland authority. The academic programs of these universities mirrored those of Afrikaans-medium universities, albeit at far less ambitious levels. Two were set up for non-African blacks: Durban-Westville for Indians and the University of Western Cape for coloureds.

In the late 1970s, the Nationalist government began establishing both white and black technikons to provide technical and vocational programs, with both types run by administrators sympathetic to the goals of apartheid. In addition, the government operated two distance learning institutions: the University of South Africa (Unisa) and Technikon South Africa. Though ostensibly white institutions, they were not subject to racial quotas and thus enrolled many black students.

Needless to say, access to higher education under apartheid was grossly inequitable, with the racial mix of students in tertiary education bearing little resemblance to their proportions in the population. As late as 1992, white students, though they made up only 12 percent of the school population, accounted for 60 percent of enrollment in technikons and 50 percent of that in universities.[3]

There was also an enormous difference in the relative academic quality of historically advantaged and disadvantaged institutions. The historically white institutions were by and large well funded and boasted well-qualified faculty and students and adequate facilities. By contrast, most black institutions were located in remote areas, isolated from the academic mainstream. They were systematically underfunded, their curricular offerings were limited, and their administrative and faculty ranks were weak. Many, if not most, of their students were ill-prepared for

2. For a description of the evolution of the various types of universities and technikons, see Cooper and Subotzky (2001, chap. 1).
3. Bunting (1994, p. 10, table 3).

college-level work, and the academic programs were "dumbed down" to accommodate both the level of preparedness of many entering students and the limited career options open to black graduates. During the apartheid era some of the institutions serving black students were the beneficiaries of donor funds from outside South Africa that provided needed supplements to government funds, but these funds dried up after 1994 when donors turned their attention to supporting government initiatives.

When the English and the Afrikaners led the government, they had invested heavily in the higher education institutions that served their respective ethnic group, and it was widely assumed that the black-majority government after 1994 would follow in this tradition and lavish resources on black universities and technikons. But the question of what to do about the black institutions was a vexing one. Encouraged by some of the powerful white institutions, many government officials opposed the building up of the historically black sector on the grounds that its institutions were inefficient and costly, that turning them into respectable academic centers would require huge investments, and that, since most of them were creatures of apartheid, such investments would, in effect, perpetuate vestiges of that hated system.

Other political and educational leaders, including many of their prominent alumni, rallied to the cause of the historically black institutions. They urged significant investment in the sector on the ground that, for all their academic and financial problems, these places had honorable traditions of serving disadvantaged students and remained the only realistic options for large numbers of South Africans. The quality problems of these institutions, they noted, were partly a reflection of the fact that they were scenes of conflict during the anti-apartheid movement—a role for which they should be rewarded rather than punished—and they dismissed the argument that to support them would be to perpetuate a structure of apartheid. As Brian Figaji, principal and vice chancellor of Peninsula Technikon in Cape Town, commented in an interview, "Is the University of Stellenbosch any less an apartheid institution than Fort Hare? Wasn't Stellenbosch a 'homeland' of a different sort?"[4] Some black leaders also supported investing new resources into the black institutions as a form of institutional redress for the way in which they and their constituents suffered under apartheid. Because of

4. Unless otherwise indicated, quotations in this chapter are from interviews with the authors between February and July 2002.

its distinguished history and the fact that it was founded long before the apartheid era, Fort Hare was seen by both sides as a special case that would need to be supported no matter what happened to other historically black institutions.

To the surprise of many in South Africa—and for reasons discussed in the next section—the new black-run government chose not to take up the cause of the historically black institutions. This decision had profound consequences for higher education in South Africa.

Government Policies toward Higher Education

In July 1997 the government issued a policy paper laying out a set of goals regarding the size, structure, governance, funding, and other aspects of post-apartheid higher education in South Africa. The document, entitled *Education White Paper 3: A Programme for the Transformation of Higher Education,* began: "Higher education plays a central role in the social, cultural and economic development of modern societies. In South Africa today, the challenge is to redress past inequalities and to transform the higher education system to serve a new social order, to meet pressing national needs, and to respond to new realities and opportunities."[5]

The policy paper was the culmination of a series of discussions dating to the late 1980s. As the grip of the apartheid system weakened and pressure mounted to produce more highly trained workers for the South African economy, the race-based approach to organizing tertiary institutions fashioned by the National government during the early years of apartheid began to unravel. The number of black students attending universities and technikons increased, and African, coloured, and Indian students began enrolling in significant numbers in institutions from which they had previously been barred. Gradually a new vision began to emerge of a post-apartheid system of higher education that would not only serve the developmental needs of a democratic South Africa but also promote the equity that had been so conspicuously lacking in the past.

On the eve of South Africa's first truly democratic elections, the African National Congress had circulated *A Policy Framework for Education and Training,* laying out its agenda for education reform at all levels (see chapter 4). It envisioned an expanded system of tertiary edu-

5. Department of Education (1997a, p. 7).

cation that would be driven by "the democratic values of representivity, accountability, transparency, freedom of association and academic freedom" and that would make a priority of "the redressing of historical imbalances."[6] Six months after the 1994 elections, President Nelson Mandela established the National Commission on Higher Education (NCHE), a diverse group of thirteen persons, including nine blacks and four women, to suggest ways to rid higher education of the aberrations of apartheid and to restructure the system around the needs and values of the new democracy. The NCHE issued its report in September 1996, and its analysis and recommendations were echoed in the July 1997 government policy paper. It described the existing system of higher education as marked by "fragmentation, inefficiency and ineffectiveness, with too little co-ordination, few common goals and negligible systemic planning." With regard to equity, it faulted the system for, among other things, "gross discrepancies in the participation rates of students from different population groups, indefensible imbalances in the ratios of black and female staff compared to whites, and equally untenable disparities between historically black and historically white institutions in terms of facilities and capacities."[7]

The policy paper went on to lay out a set of strategic principles for a new national higher education plan that not only repudiated the race-based foundations of apartheid-era tertiary education but sought to rectify past injustices. As a starting point, it called for a single unified system of higher education, run by the national government, that would be committed to serving students of all races.[8] In a significant departure from the ANC's call for substantial expansion of the tertiary system as a prerequisite for equitable access, however, the government document, which was written after the introduction of the restrictive macroeconomic policy known as GEAR (see chapter 4), took an equivocal position. While declaring that the "Ministry of Education is committed to the planned expansion of the system," it added the qualification, "What is not clear, however, is what increases in participation rates for black students, and overall, are possible within the foreseeable future in the context of the government's macro-economic framework and fiscal policies."[9]

Finally, and perhaps most important from the perspective of equity, the 1997 policy paper strongly endorsed the concepts of providing dis-

6. African National Congress (1994, p. 79).
7. Department of Education (1997a, p. 1.4).
8. Department of Education (1997a, p. 2.1).
9. Department of Education (1997a, pp. 24, 23).

advantaged individuals with financial support and of providing redress to historically disadvantaged institutions. The document called for "a flexible, responsive and sustainable National Student Financial Aid Scheme (NSFAS)" that would allow poor students to aspire to higher education. Such a system, it asserted, is "not an optional extra" but rather "an essential condition of a transformed, equitable higher education system." Given that free higher education was not a viable possibility, it reasoned, the costs of higher education should be shared equitably by public and private beneficiaries. Direct costs to students should be proportionate to their ability to pay, and "financial need should not be an insuperable barrier to access and success in higher education."[10] Thus the policy paper committed the Ministry of Education to "targeted redistribution of the public subsidy to higher education" and flatly asserted, "The relative proportion of public funding used to support academically able but disadvantaged students must be increased."[11]

The policy paper also strongly endorsed the concept of redress with respect to institutions:

Institutional redress will play an important role in the planning process to ensure that inherited inequalities between the historically black and historically white institutions are not intensified, but diminished. This will require the Department of Education and the [Council on Higher Education] proactively assisting institutions to develop planning capacity and appropriate institutional missions, as well as ensuring that new programs are appropriately located within the existing institutional landscape. In this respect, redress funding will be allocated where needed to enable institutions to offer the agreed program mix in an effective manner.[12]

It then added that targeted funding for purposes of institutional redress was a temporary strategy.[13] The recommendations from the policy paper subsequently became the basis for the Higher Education Act of 1997.

Racial Equity in Higher Education

In 1994, heartened by growth in the tertiary sector that took place in the waning years of apartheid, policymakers and educators were opti-

10. Department of Education (1997a, pp. 4.39, 4.7, 4.8).
11. Department of Education (1997a, p. 2.26).
12. Department of Education. (1997a, p. 2.19).
13. Department of Education (1997a, p. 4.34).

mistic that student enrollment in universities and technikons would continue to follow a steep upward trend. Given that most of the new entrants to the higher education system would be black students, such an expansion would accomplish two important equity-related purposes. First, it would allow historically white institutions to transform themselves into integrated institutions without curtailing the number of white students they served. Second, expansion would facilitate an increase in both overall enrollment levels and the participation rate of black students, defined as the ratio of the number of black students enrolled in higher education to the age-appropriate black population.

The crystal balls used to predict continued rapid expansion of the system, however, turned out to be cloudy. The National Commission on Higher Education projected that overall enrollment in universities and technikons would increase steadily, from 570,000 in 1995 to 710,000 in 2000—an increase of 25 percent—and that it would continue to climb in subsequent years. Instead, total enrollments rose only modestly during this period, from 570,900 in 1995 to 586,100 in 1999, before falling back to 581,100 students in 2000. Thus the net gain in enrollment was less than 2 percent.[14]

Why were the NCHE projections too high? One reason is that they did not take into account problems in the primary and secondary schools serving blacks. As discussed in chapter 9, the number of students emerging from secondary schools with the matriculation examination credentials that qualified them for enrollment in higher education not only failed to increase as expected but actually declined. But this explanation can be carried only so far. Ian Bunting of the University of Cape Town estimates that in 2000, despite the declining matric passing rate, there were about 40,000 school-leavers with full matric endorsements and 190,000 with a school-leaving certificate (without the "endorsement" that would qualify them for university admission) who did not enter the public higher education system the year after they completed school. In Bunting's view, such students represent "a considerable pool of potential entrants into the higher education system" that could, if tapped, raise participation rates to levels close to the NCHE's target of 30 percent. Clearly, other forces were at work as well.

A second reason for the failure of the system to expand as projected was the sharp plunge in the number of white students attending institu-

14. Enrollment projections from Bunting and Cloete (2000, p. 12). Actual enrollments provided to the authors by Ian Bunting.

FIGURE 10-1. University Enrollments, by Race, 1993–2000[a]

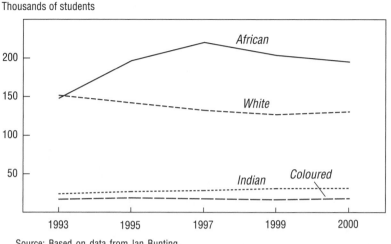

Thousands of students

Source: Based on data from Ian Bunting.
a. Figures include both contact and distance students.

tions of higher education. As shown in figures 10-1 and 10-2, white enrollment declined by 14 percent in universities and by a substantial 52 percent in technikons. During this period the absolute number of white students in universities dropped from 151,800 to 130,400, while their proportion of total enrollments fell from 45 percent in 1993 to 34 percent in 2000.

No one seems to have a firm fix on the causes of this white flight. Various theories hold that white students who in the past would have enrolled in higher education either entered the work force, left the country, or enrolled in the growing private higher education sector. Whatever the explanation for the disappearing whites, the phenomenon was neither planned, expected, nor sought by the architects of South Africa's higher education policy.

Finally, there is the all-important matter of financial aid to students. Before 1994 black students had access to a substantial number of bursaries, some from the government and some from sources outside South Africa. At the University of the Western Cape, for example, a predominantly coloured institution, students who qualified for admission, especially prospective teachers, were offered bursaries. All of the major documents relating to post-1994 policy in higher education acknowledged that financial assistance was the necessary lubricant if black students

FIGURE 10-2. Technikon Enrollments, by Race, 1993–1999[a]

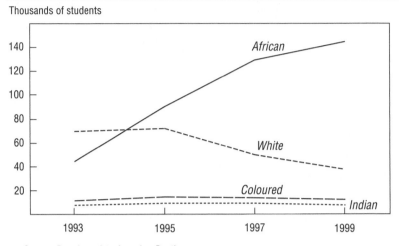

Thousands of students

Source: Based on data from Ian Bunting.
a. Figures include both contact and distance students.

were to take advantage of the new race-blind admissions, and, as just noted, the 1997 policy paper was clear in its insistence that a well-funded and consistent student aid scheme was a prerequisite for providing equal opportunity to all students.

The National Student Financial Aid Scheme (NSFAS) was put in place with a funding formula that applied to all thirty-six universities and technikons. These bursaries were never funded adequately, however, and their effectiveness varied widely across institutions. At best, financial aid covered only 60 to 70 percent of the total costs of education, so substantial numbers of black students who were unable to come up with the remaining funds were forced to drop out of higher education unless they were able to obtain supplementary bursaries from universities or technikons. White institutions were often able to supplement government funds with additional bursaries to cover residential costs and other expenses for black students, but more impoverished black institutions were forced to spread available funds across large numbers of students.[15]

The inadequate funding of NSFAS became critical in 1997, when the government began to lean on universities and technikons to collect unpaid tuition and fees from students and to suspend those who did not

15. Bunting (2002b, p. 175).

pay. At the beginning of 1998, students owed universities and technikons in South Africa a total of 500 million rand, with 370 million rand of this total owed to historically black universities.[16] University and technikon administrators adopted a variety of policies to collect the unpaid fees, including requirements for minimum payments at the time of registration and the withholding of academic results or degrees from delinquent students.

Students protested such policies vigorously through demonstrations, boycotts, and even the burning of buildings in February 1998 at several black campuses, among them Western Cape, Fort Hare, Unitra, Venda, Technikon Free State, and Technikon Natal. Some even closed down for brief periods.[17] In the end, however, the government stuck by its insistence that fees be paid. Large numbers of students were forced to abandon their studies, while still others were discouraged from embarking on postsecondary education in the first place. Amanda Manyatshe, an undergraduate at the University of Cape Town, complained that the government financial aid scheme was inadequate and that "a lot of my friends last year did not have enough money to pay their fees and were excluded." It is no coincidence that African enrollment in universities declined after 1997 (figure 10-1).

Transformation across the System

Although the overall size of the tertiary education system did not increase as expected, major changes occurred in the distribution of students within it. The new democratic government had moved quickly to organize the country's universities and technikons into a single multiracial system under the authority of the national Department of Education, thereby removing any remaining vestiges of race-based admissions policies at individual institutions and sending out a strong signal about the values that would henceforth guide tertiary education in South Africa. The impact of these changes was significant in two respects.

First, the number of blacks enrolled in higher education institutions increased significantly, as did the black proportion of overall enrollment in higher education. The total number of African, coloured, and Indian students in universities rose from 188,600 in 1993 to 266,500 in 1997 before declining to 245,100 in 2000 (figure 10-1)—for a net gain of

16. Monica Bot, "A Tertiary Update: October 1997–July 1998," *EduSource Data News*, no. 22, October 1998, p. 6.

17. Monica Bot, "A Tertiary Update: October 1997–July 1998," *EduSource Data News*, no. 22, October 1998, p. 7.

about one-third. Similarly, black students as a proportion of all students rose during this period, from 55 to 65 percent. As already noted, though, part of the explanation for the increased proportion of blacks in universities was a significant fall in white enrollment.

Parallel trends occurred in technikons. As shown in figure 10-2, the number of black students in technikons more than doubled during this period, from 62,800 (47 percent) of total enrollment in 1993 to 164,900 (82 percent) of all students in 1999, the latest year for which data are available. White enrollment in technikons dropped dramatically, from 70,000 to 37,700, and the white proportion of all students fell from about 53 to 19 percent during this period.

Second, as already noted, blacks had begun moving into previously white institutions in the late 1980s and early 1990s, and the dropping of all racial barriers for admission after 1994 intensified this trend, shown in table 10-2. It is important to distinguish here between contact students (those who attend classes on the university campus) and distance learning students. Afrikaans universities, in particular, greatly expanded their distance programs as a way of serving black students. As a result of these programs, by 2000 blacks accounted for 58 percent of students at Afrikaans-medium universities. Unfortunately, we are not able to determine the percentage of contact students who are black, but it is presumably far below 58 percent. In contrast, the English universities did not set up distance programs but nevertheless managed to increase the percentage of black students to 62 percent. By 2000 at the prestigious University of Cape Town just over 50 percent of the 11,500 undergraduate students and about 42 percent of the 5,500 postgraduate students were black.

Table 10-2 also shows that far more black students were enrolled in the former Afrikaans and English universities than in the historically black ones. Transformation in the sense of racial integration was even more dramatic in the historically white technikons. In 2000 black students accounted for 77 percent of students in those technikons.

The major reason for the growing black presence in historically white institutions was that, for understandable reasons, academically talented black students were quick to take advantage of their new right to enroll in high-quality universities and technikons from which they would have been excluded in the past. As Lebo Digoamaje, a twenty-one-year old Tswana-speaking student at the University of Cape Town (UCT), told one of us, "We want to take advantage of access to the best resources."

TABLE 10-2. Distribution of All Students and Black Students, by Type of Institution, 2000

	Students (thousands)			Black students		
					Percent	Percent of
		Distance		Number	of all	all black
Institution	Contact	learning	Total	(thousands)	students	students
Universities						
Historically black	61.7	9.6	71.3	69.9	98.0	16.0
Afrikaans	92.2	58.5	150.7	87.4	58.0	20.0
English	64.1	0	64.1	39.7	62.0	9.1
Unisa (distance learning)	0.1	115.2	115.3	71.5	62.0	16.4
Technikons						
Historically black	46.0	0	46.0	46.0	100.0	10.4
Historically white	83.7	11.6	95.3	73.4	77.0	16.8
Technikon SA (distance learning)	0	60.1	60.1	49.2	82.0	11.3
Total	347.8	255.0	602.8	436.6	72.0	100.0

Source: Based on data from Ian Bunting.

The downside of this is that many students now view black institutions as inherently inferior. "Where there are black people, it won't be the best," said Teboho Wessie, a twenty-year-old business science major at UCT. "It's like going to an all-black high school. You know that somehow the resources and education are not good."

The racial transformation of several historically white universities was also intensified by expansion policies that included aggressive recruiting of black students. This gave them an advantage over historically black universities because they had the financial resources to supplement government financial aid with local bursaries to cover living and other expenses. UCT, for example, offers aid packages covering fees, room and board, and a travel allowance to 2,000 students a year from homes where the gross annual income is no more than 100,000 rand. Students contribute on a sliding scale from 3,000 to 10,000 rand toward the total cost of 28,000 rand for those who are residential and 14,000 rand for commuters.

The availability of financial aid is crucial to black students in particular. Martin Hall, the deputy vice chancellor at UCT, agreed on the need for a strong government financial aid scheme. He noted that while the number of black students at his institution is growing, most of them come from middle-class families. "People call them 'Model Cs' because of the high schools they attended," he commented. "They wear designer clothes and have cell phones."

Low Participation Rates of Black Students

Despite enhanced racial diversity at historically white South African universities and technikons, data on gross participation rates of blacks—defined as the number of black students enrolled in higher education divided by the age-appropriate black population—show that blacks are still substantially underrepresented in higher education. Although the absolute numbers of Africans and coloureds showed some gains between 1993 and 2000, the participation rates of both groups remained low throughout this period. Whereas the African rate increased by nearly half, from 9 to 13 percent (figure 10-3), the rates for coloured and Indian persons actually declined during these years. Consistent with our earlier data on the decline in white enrollments, the most striking change in participation rates occurred among whites, whose gross enrollment rate plunged from 70 to 47 percent during a period when the overall participation rate was dropping only slightly, from 17 to 16 percent. The 1997 government policy paper had lamented the fact that the percentages of the twenty to twenty-four-year-old cohort enrolled in higher education differed greatly by the race of the student.[18] Three years later these inequalities persisted.

Effectiveness of Universities and Technikons

Achieving racial equity in higher education is only partly a matter of ensuring that more blacks gain access to the system. Equally important is the proportion of those who, once admitted, persist in their studies and end up graduating with a useful credential. By this measure, South Africa has a long way to go. Ian Bunting calculated the average rates at which students from the four racial groups succeeded in passing undergraduate contact courses at universities and technikons in 2000. The average for all students was 77 percent at universities and 67 percent at technikons, but these rates varied substantially across the racial groups. At the university level, the passing rates were 84 percent for whites, 80 percent for Indians, and 72 percent for African and coloured students.

---

18. Department of Education. (1997a, p. 2.22).

FIGURE 10-3. Gross Participation Rates in Higher Education, by Race, 1993 and 2000

Percent of 20- to 24-year-olds enrolled

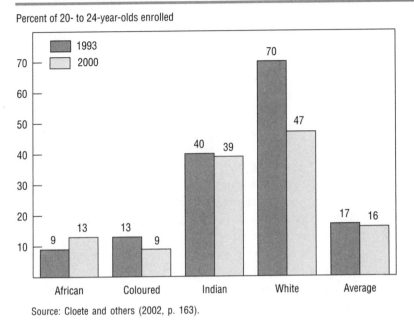

Source: Cloete and others (2002, p. 163).

At the technikon level, whites also had the highest rate: 79 percent. This compared with 72 percent for coloured and Indian students and 64 percent for Africans.[19]

The most striking aspect of these data would seem to be that no particular sector of either universities or technikons serves black students well. As Derrick Swartz, the vice chancellor of Fort Hare, commented, "No institution has lived up to the ideal of coping with the needs of our disadvantaged students." At the university level, historically black institutions show success rates in contact courses of 71 percent for African students and only 65 percent for coloured students. The lowest success rate of any institution was found at Fort Hare, where only 56 percent of its almost exclusively African students succeeded in contact courses. Both Afrikaans- and English-medium historically white universities show somewhat higher success rates for such students than historically

19. Ian Bunting calculated these success rates as the weighted average across courses of the number of students who pass each course divided by the number of students officially enrolled, where the weights are the numbers of fulltime equivalent students in each course.

black ones, but the differences are not large. Among technikons, it appears that historically black institutions do a substantially better job than historically white units in educating coloured students, whereas the historically white technikons do somewhat better with African and Indian students.

The question of where black students are best served is complex and controversial. As already seen, many of the most academically talented black students have opted to enroll in the historically white institutions because they regard them as stronger academically, but many of them struggle once they are there. Monwabisi Danstile, a business student at the University of Cape Town from Transkei, said that he initially had difficulty in math because of poor secondary school preparation and that he found it difficult to communicate with some of the lecturers. Although he said that racial tension was not a problem, he spent most of his time among Xhosa-speaking friends. Teboho Wessie, another UCT student, also spoke of de facto social segregation on campus. "Late in my first year I realized that I was not interacting with whites," she commented. "There are black tables and white tables in the dining hall. Whites don't think we are on the same wavelength or know as much as they do. They probably think we won't pull our own weight."

For such reasons many educators argue that many black students are better served at historically black institutions. Professor S. U. S. Ngubentombi, the dean of education at Unitra, argued that whereas institutions associated with apartheid "still have a stigma of inferiority," they offer support systems that are unavailable in the white universities. "This university has been here since the mid-1970s," he pointed out. "The staff here have learned to deal with disadvantage. They are willing to improvise and to take whatever time students need. Other institutions put up high standards and only accept the most talented students. We develop materials to teach all students, and we offer them role models as well."

It should be noted that systemic inefficiency in the sense of low graduation rates is not limited to black students but extends to the system as a whole. Bunting's data show that graduation rates in the university plus technikon sectors fell far short of levels predicted by policymakers. In 1993 only 17 percent of all students registered at universities and only 10 percent of those in technikons completed their degrees or diplomas in that year, and in 2000 these figures were still only 16 percent and 9 percent respectively. "To satisfy the efficiency requirements set out in the

White Paper, the system's average should have reached at least 20 per-cent by 2000," he wrote. "This implies that the system produced nearly 30,000 fewer graduates than it should have in 2000."[20]

Other Inequities

Overall enrollment figures mask continuing racial inequities of other sorts as well, such as the fact that black students were disproportion-ately enrolled in distance education rather than contact programs. Simi-larly, black students who do make it to university tend to study in lower-level rather than upper-level tracks at both the undergraduate and graduate levels, and they are likely to enroll in the humanities and the social sciences, not in math, science, and technology.[21] Black students also tend to be under more pressure than whites to complete their edu-cation quickly by taking three-year rather than four-year courses of study.

In summary, race-blind admissions policies adopted after 1994 had mixed results. The removal of legal restrictions made a strong symbolic statement about the values of the new South Africa, and even in the absence of a major expansion of the system the number of blacks enrolled in universities and technikons increased. So did the black pro-portion of all students, though this was partly a result of vanishing whites. Further, a substantial number of black students enrolled in the historically white institutions from which black students had been barred in the past.

Nevertheless, race-blind government policies failed to deal with important obstacles that many blacks faced in seeking to avail them-selves of their new options and in succeeding in those new opportuni-ties. The most glaring was the failure to provide adequate financial aid. In the absence of sufficient aid, low-income black students were at a serious disadvantage and subject to the availability of supplemental aid at particular universities. Given that the historically black universities did not have the resources to assist impoverished students, the system clearly favored middle-class black students with the wherewithal and the credentials to attend the historically white universities. Black stu-dents who could not get into the historically white institutions or who could not afford to go to a university far from home faced a difficult sit-

20. Bunting (2002b, p. 167).
21. Bunting (2002b, p. 171).

uation. For reasons discussed in the next section, the quality of the historically black universities deteriorated during the late 1990s. Thus race-blind policies did little to promote equal educational opportunity for all but the students from middle-class black families.

Equity and the Funding of Institutions

Having applied race-blind principles to the admission of students to higher education, policymakers in the post-1994 period adopted a similar approach to the distribution of public funds to universities and technikons. They used what was known as the South African Post-Secondary Education (SAPSE) formula, which had been developed by the National government in the early 1980s for funding white universities. In 1988 it was extended to black institutions in the Republic of South Africa and in 1994 to those in the territories and homelands. The new democratic government continued to use the formula after it came to power in 1994. The two basic elements of the formula were the number of enrolled students in the particular institution and the number of successful students, but additional funds were given for heavy enrollments in certain curricular areas (notably the natural sciences) and in advanced courses.[22] In other words, institutions with similar numbers of students pursuing similar courses of studies were eligible for similar amounts of funding.[23]

As a result of the differential rates of enrollment growth in the various sectors, the Afrikaans universities, which had been so aggressive in establishing distance education programs, experienced a much larger growth in government appropriations than did the English or the historically black universities. Between 1995 and 2001, government appropriations rose by 40.5 percent at Afrikaans universities but by only 12.5 and 5.0 percent at English and black universities, respectively. Government appropriations at historically black technikons rose by 58.4 percent, well above the 42.9 percent rate for white technikons.[24]

While the SAPSE formula was blind to the type of institution, its impact was by no means neutral with respect to historically black and

22. Bunting (2002a, p. 118–19).
23. Wildeman (2003) argues that SAPSE was consistently underfunded between 1998 and 2002. His data show that appropriation levels were less than 80 percent of the needs of universities as determined by the funding formula and that during the period the state's contribution decreased by 15 percent.
24. Data modified by the authors from Bunting (2002a, fig. 7, p. 138).

white institutions. It worked against black institutions experiencing enrollment declines and in favor of white institutions, which tended to have relatively higher enrollments in the programs rewarded with extra funds. The situation bears striking parallels to that of the former Model C schools at the primary/secondary level, which qualified for additional funding and teacher slots because they were more likely than their less advantaged counterparts to offer specialized courses.

The formula had other differential impacts. Drawn up as it was by the apartheid government for the purpose of funding white universities, the formula took what was essentially a hands-off approach to the management of higher education. Institutions exercised considerable discretion in determining the shape of their programs and how they would spend their allotments, and it was assumed that this flexibility, combined with the newfound ability of students of all races to move about the system, would be sufficient to ensure a viable higher education marketplace. However, the formula took no heed of historical factors that made it difficult for black institutions to compete in this market, notably their inadequate facilities, poorly trained teachers, and the needs of large numbers of their students for remedial assistance. Another complication for black institutions was that government appropriations for higher education did not keep pace with enrollment growth, and institutions became increasingly reliant on private funds raised either through student fees or research activities. Once again, black institutions found themselves at a relative disadvantage because rules were set up under the implicit but unwarranted assumption that the playing field would be level.

Recognizing the inadequacy of the SAPSE formula for black institutions, the 1997 government policy paper called for a new funding framework as well as funds for redress.[25] Because of their years of systematic deprivation under apartheid, South Africa's historically disadvantaged universities and technikons clearly needed more funds than advantaged ones if they were to successfully compete for students. Thus equal treatment, or race-blindness, in the funding of institutions of higher education was not sufficient. Redress and adequacy would require that the historically black institutions be treated differently than the historically white universities.

Derrick Swartz, the vice chancellor of Fort Hare, estimated that his institution was underfunded by as much as 1 billion rand in terms of

---

25. For a comprehensive discussion of the evolution of funding patterns, see Bunting (2002a, 2002b).

physical plant and human capital on both the professional and administrative sides. "We're losing out to the historically white universities as well as to UNISA and, to a lesser extent, technikons," he said. "The government assumed that there was a level playing field, but that's not the case. Well-endowed institutions are better able to capitalize on new technologies, but black ones do not have the financial resources to invest. The irony is that black institutions did better under the previous white government than under a supposedly black one." Brian Figaji, the rector and vice chancellor of Peninsula Technikon in Cape Town, suggested that black institutions are still paying for the role they played in the fight against apartheid. "Black institutions were sites of struggle and were used as institutions to bring about change," he commented. "Their students were encouraged to protest, and campuses would be closed down. In the process these institutions were destabilized and left with the most angry and least academically and financially strong students. But no one said: let's repair the damage done through destabilization."

Moreover, the inadequacies of the student financial aid scheme discussed in the previous section had serious implications for the historically black institutions. Because high proportions of their student bodies qualified for financial assistance, these universities and technikons were disproportionately affected by government requirements that they drop from their rolls students who were unable to pay their fees. Meanwhile, their white counterparts, especially Afrikaans-medium universities, were enrolling black students through financial incentives and innovative delivery mechanisms such as distance learning and satellite campuses. As a result, virtually all of the historically disadvantaged institutions faced severe financial problems.

Historically black institutions were particularly hard-hit by the collapse of bursaries for teachers. Such bursaries had been established in the 1980s as a means of providing teachers for the expanding primary and secondary school sector, and they were important to the financial success of universities that offered teacher training programs, such as Western Cape and Fort Hare. Brian O'Connell, vice chancellor of the University of the Western Cape, noted that at one point his institution had more than 1,000 students registered for teaching. With the rationalization of the teaching force in the mid-1990s, however, this source of student support dried up, and the student numbers declined dramatically.

In practice, virtually no attention was paid to *redress*. Recognizing that government student aid formulas were detrimental to the black universities, the 1997 policy paper had explicitly called for "targeted funding to redress inequalities and deficiencies experienced in particular by historically disadvantaged institutions."[26] Leaders of the black institutions had counted on receiving such funding for institutional redress, especially since they understood that it would be virtually impossible to collect substantial fees from their impoverished students. An allocation of 27 million rand was distributed to black institutions in 1997 using an established formula, and this process could have been continued by the Department of Education. The Treasury, however, would have regarded such a program as rewarding inefficiency, and the initiative died.[27]

The concept of redress turned out to be tenuous for reasons that went beyond funding. Under apartheid, historically disadvantaged institutions had a built-in raison d'être. They were the only option available for most blacks seeking an education beyond the secondary level, and they were needed by the apartheid regime to turn out teachers and government workers. In the new democratic South Africa, the need for these institutions was less clear. Since members of their previously captive audience now had access to a broad spectrum of institutions, they could no longer justify their existence as the only option for a particular racial group. In any case, such a racially defined mission was inconsistent with the values of the post-apartheid period, and it was undermined by the reality that thousands of black students were voluntarily abandoning them for places in white institutions to which they now had access. "Fort Hare cannot survive on sentiment," observed John Hendericks, executive dean at Fort Hare. "It has to sustain itself on excellence."

True, historically black institutions remained the only practical option for thousands of other black students, but on what basis did they warrant the kind of investments that would be required to overcome the legacies of apartheid and serve these students well? Were the black institutions creatures of apartheid that had outlived their relevance? Or were they troubled academic institutions that—with a proper infusion of resources—could be turned into first-rate institutions dedicated to educating underserved populations? This debate has never been resolved, but over the years, as concerns for cost control triumphed over equity concerns, the concept of redress became increasingly irrelevant to the debate.

The National Plan for Higher Education, issued in 2001, emphasized the distinction between "social (i.e. individual) redress and institutional redress" and then pointed out that since many black students now

26. Department of Education (1997a, p. 4.34).
27. Cloete and Maassen (2002, p. 456).

attend previously white institutions, "the former is not reducible to the latter." The plan affirmed the continuing relevance of the concept but added that the focus must move beyond "current notions of redress, which are narrowly focused on the leveling of the playing fields between the historically black and historically white institutions." While the negative impact of apartheid on historically black institutions cannot be ignored, the document added, the fact remains that "some of the affected institutions have been able to turn around and achieve stability." Rather than continue to allocate redress funds to a few institutions with serious financial difficulties, emphasis in the future should focus on the identification of new institutional missions for the historically black institutions supported by "business plans with clearly identified needs linked to performance improvement and efficiency measures."[28]

Thus for a variety of reasons attributable largely to the financing strategies of the government, the initial years of the new democratic South Africa turned out to be disastrous for historically black universities. Enrollment at such universities remained virtually stable at about 75,000 students between 1990 and 2000, while the historically white universities enjoyed a substantial increase of 62 percent, from 120,000 to 194,000. Among the historically black institutions that lost students were the University of Transkei in Eastern Cape, which experienced a 33 percent drop in enrollments, and the University of Western Cape, which lost close to 23 percent of its students. Among white universities, Stellenbosch gained 38 percent and Cape Town 25 percent.[29]

The particular problems facing historically black universities varied by region and by institution. The University of Transkei, or Unitra, in Eastern Cape is a good example of an institution that got into serious trouble over the issue of redress. Its leaders took to heart the talk of redress funding in the mid-1990s and went ahead with an aggressive building plan that included a new library, an administration building, and residence halls. Peggy Luswazi, the university registrar, remarked: "It was assumed that these would be paid for. That was a mistake." The campus now has the physical air of a modern university, but one that serves only a fraction of the students it was built to accommodate and has had a running crisis of governance to which the minister of education has responded by sending in a series of temporary administrators. In response to the low quality of the primary and secondary education

28. Ministry of Education (2001, pp. 10–11).
29. Calculated by the authors from data provided by Ian Bunting.

in the Transkei region, Unitra has set up bridging courses aimed at students who passed matric but did not qualify for exemptions. "We think it is one of the best development programs in the country," said the registrar. "The problem is that we have to fund it out of our regular budget, and we have trouble collecting fees from our students. There is financial aid, but it's not enough. It only covers about 50 to 60 percent of students' expenses." In the absence of job opportunities in the area, students have difficulty finding work to pay off their loans.

Not surprisingly, many of the students at Unitra are there because they had no other options. Siyabulela Tshangela, whose mother was a domestic worker and whose father died when he was young, wanted to go to the University of Cape Town but was unable to obtain a bursary. So he enrolled in Unitra in the hope that political leaders would find a way to keep it going. "Closing Unitra would be a disaster," he said, "because it would deny the majority of students in this region access to education at the university level."

Historically black institutions in the Western Cape faced different issues. The University of the Western Cape had prospered over the years as an institution serving coloured students in a "coloured labor preference" area. Politically, Western Cape was known as a bastion of the political left, and it was particularly strong in fields such as history, biblical studies, psychology, and Afrikaans. Enrollment dropped considerably after 1994, however, mainly because of the loss of many coloured students, and the university had to lower its admissions standards. At one point Africans accounted for two-thirds of the enrollment, but that proportion has now dropped to about half because many of the Africans have not been able to pay the fees.

As already noted, enrollments in the technikons increased at a far faster rate than did enrollments in universities. While that growth occurred in both the historically white and the historically black technikons, one of the more striking trends has been the movement of black students into the historically white technikons. Cape Technikon in Cape Town was a predominantly white institution and remained so well into the early 1990s. By 2000 black students were in the majority. Marcus Malusi Balintulo, the rector and vice chancellor, said that the technikon has made a conscious effort both to retain white students and to bring in more nonwhites through expansion. Cape Technikon is notable for the fact that only 13 percent of its students come from outside the Western Cape, but it recently built a new 864-bed dormitory in order to broaden its draw.

Various theories have been advanced for why the government broke with political tradition, pursued by the English and Afrikaners before them, of investing heavily in universities serving their own ethnic group. Many believe that because the new black-dominated government was operating within the context of a government of "national unity" it took seriously its responsibilities to govern on behalf of all South African institutions. "The government did not position itself as a black government," commented Derrick Swartz of Fort Hare. "It positioned itself as a rational government that was nonracial."

Another important, and probably decisive, factor was the shift in 1997 to a macroeconomic policy of fiscal restraint (see chapter 4). An important signal was sent out in July 2000 when the Council on Higher Education, which had been set up in May 1998 to provide advice to the minister of education on higher education policy, issued a report entitled *Towards a New Higher Education Landscape* that revisited many of the issues of the 1997 policy paper. It did so through the lens of efficiency, however, rather than of equity. The council defined the critical problems facing the system as fragmentation of institutions, a disconnect between the labor market and what students were studying, and poor persistence and graduation rates as well as inequities relating to the distribution of students and staff by race, gender, and social class. Among other things, the report called for the closing of institutions with fewer than 4,000 fulltime equivalent students, and it offered some examples of how institutions could be merged to make the system more efficient—a detail that drew considerable opposition not only from institutions that would be affected but also from within the government. Controversy over the details of mergers aside, the fundamental message was clear: cost control and efficiency, not equity, were now at the top of the policy agenda.

In the absence of interventions specifically designed to strengthen them, the historically black institutions had little choice but to watch many of their traditional students move into white universities and technikons. The middle-class black students who could take advantage of those new opportunities clearly benefited. For many other black students, the net effect has undoubtedly been negative in that the education they receive at the historically black institutions has deteriorated.

A Restructured System of Higher Education

After the passage of the Higher Education Act of 1997, discussions continued both within and outside the government over how higher education should best be structured so as to achieve the goals laid out in the 1997 policy paper, including enhanced access and increased quality within a context of fiscal restraint. Implementation came slowly, though, in part because higher education was only one of numerous sectors competing for the attention of the new government and because much of the time of administrators was devoted to dealing with immediate financial and other crises at the historically black institutions.

In February 2001 the cabinet approved the National Plan for Higher Education, which was intended to implement the goals of the 1997 legislation. Confirming the policy shift away from access and equity toward efficiency, the plan asserted that the "main focus over the next five years will therefore be on improving the efficiency of the higher education system through increasing graduate outputs."[30] Further, the document established a national working group (NWG) to make concrete proposals for consolidating institutions. The NWG was dominated by financial heavyweights—it was chaired by financier Saki Macozoma—rather than experts in higher education. Not surprisingly, its report, released in January 2002, placed substantial emphasis on the financial viability of universities and technikons and endorsed some controversial mergers, including the union of the University of the Western Cape with Peninsula Technikon and the merging of Fort Hare with historically white Rhodes University.

The specific merger proposals produced another storm of criticism, especially from the vice chancellors of institutions slated to lose their independence and from leaders of the historically black institutions, who claimed that the interests of these institutions and the students they served were being sacrificed for the good of their white counterparts. The politician in the middle of the firestorm, Minister of Education Kader Asmal, took note of the various concerns and came up with his own proposal.

In May 2002, on Asmal's recommendation, the cabinet approved a revised national plan that embraced most of the recommendations of the NWG but backed away from some of the more controversial mergers. It called for the consolidation of thirty-six existing institutions into a restructured system of twenty-one institutions, consisting of eleven universities, six technikons, and four "comprehensive universities" offering both university and technikon programs. Largely for political reasons, Fort Hare and the University of Western Cape both survived as indepen-

---

30. Ministry of Education (2001, p. 1).

dent universities. The University of Transkei fared less well in that it was to be closed, with its campus to be used for an expanded technikon.

The so-called Asmal Plan represented an effort to make South Africa's higher education system more financially and administratively efficient while addressing concerns about racial equity. In doing so, Asmal walked some fine lines. He argued that South Africa has neither the need for, nor the managerial talent to sustain and manage, thirty-six universities and technikons. The new plan called for a reduction, but, presumably with racial considerations in mind, it did not envision closing down any existing teaching sites. Instead, some current sites would be put under new management and in some cases given new academic missions. Whether the new plan would in fact reduce costs or reduce the demands on administrators, however, is far from clear. The idea that one could fix dysfunctional institutions by merging them seems a bit optimistic.

Conspicuously, the Asmal plan for the most part leaves historically white universities untouched. The only exception is the East London campus of Rhodes University, which is to become part of Fort Hare. Such a move should strengthen Fort Hare by giving it an urban campus to complement its traditional strengths in agriculture on its campus in Alice. Thus just as the formerly all-white Model C primary and secondary schools were protected by the political compromise that led to the post-1994 social order, so, too, were the historically white universities. The major gesture toward equity comes in the form of the setting of new transformational targets for each of them. In addition, Afrikaans-medium universities such as Stellenbosch would be required to offer more English-medium instruction in order to make them more accessible to Africans.

To some people, the failure of Asmal's plan to force more change in the historically white universities is a major flaw. To others, the much more salient feature is that it includes no significant investments in historically disadvantaged institutions for purposes of institutional redress. While it does call for the creation of several "centers of excellence" consisting of one or more of these institutions, those centers are not developed in the plan and, according to some of the vice chancellors we interviewed, were added almost as an afterthought in order to rationalize a political decision.

Although some of the trade-offs built into the Asmal plan seem reasonable enough on the surface, there are some lingering oddities. For example, the plan calls for the merging of two technikons in Western Cape, one (Peninsula) that has traditionally served coloured students and one (Cape) that has traditionally served white students. The only justification for the consolidation appears to be the political necessity of forcing some sort of institutional shake-up in the Western Cape province. Once the merger of Western Cape and Peninsula Technikon was taken off the table as too controversial, there were no other reasonable alternatives.

A more serious limitation is that the plan will leave Transkei's 4 million people with technikons but no university. The government argues that students from this area can enroll in universities elsewhere or in distance learning through the University of South Africa (Unisa), but this argument is flawed. As Derrick Swartz, the vice chancellor of Fort Hare, observed, "Despite what is said about the mobility of the student market, it is really only the black middle class that can move. The poor won't have the resources and will need to study at a local university." Many students can afford to attend a university only if they can live with relatives, and most students in Transkei are much more likely to have relatives in the city of Umtata, where the University of Transkei is located, than in other provinces.

The new National Plan for Higher Education still faces major obstacles. It is not yet clear how the mergers will be financed, and critics continue to argue that it fails to address the needs of large numbers of black students, especially those in the former homelands. The inadequacy of the student aid scheme also remains a major unresolved issue.

Conclusions

The story of equity and higher education in South Africa can be seen as one of high hopes but modest progress. Public policy initially focused on providing equal educational opportunity for individuals through expansion of the system and on institutional redress but then switched to cost control and managerial efficiency. In the meantime, in the absence of redress for the historically black universities, middle-class black students voted with their feet and chose the better-endowed historically white institutions over the poorer historically black ones. After watching the educational marketplace evolve for several years, the government in 2001 finally moved toward a more interventionist approach with the goal of doing something about the dysfunctional institutions.

So what can be said about South Africa's efforts to build a more equitable higher education system after 1994? Like the primary and secondary schools, South Africa's system of higher education was deracialized. In sharp contrast to practices under apartheid, students of all races are now eligible to attend any university or technikon for which they qualify on academic grounds and can muster the necessary finances. Likewise, allocations of government funds to institutions no longer take the racial makeup of their students into account. Higher education in South Africa can now be accurately described as operating on the principle of equal treatment.

However, there are serious limitations to equal treatment in and of itself. Certain policies may be race-blind but have differential effects on persons of different races. The most obvious example is student aid. Black students can now enroll at universities and technikons from which they were previously excluded, but many are unable to persist because of inadequate financial assistance. Their new right of access has thus become a hollow privilege.

Likewise, evenhanded funding formulas for all institutions did not take into account the fact that historically black institutions faced problems that their more privileged counterparts did not and thus needed additional funds in order to compete on a level playing field. In the absence of institutional redress, the historically black universities floundered. The problem of whether to invest in historically disadvantaged universities and technikons, especially those in the homelands that were creatures of apartheid and, as such, not intended to meet the standards of modern tertiary institutions, remains a troubling one for which there are no clear answers.

It is thus fair to say that South African higher education made only modest progress as measured by the criterion of equal educational opportunity, which requires that policymakers take into account the racial legacies of the apartheid system in order to promote more equal outcomes by race. On one level, the changes in higher education in the immediate post-1994 period can be seen as another example of equitable ideals foundering on the rocks of fiscal realities. In this respect, higher education in South Africa has much in common with social programs in other developing nations caught up in neoliberal economic policies that mandate austere fiscal budgets. Events in South Africa can also be viewed as illustrative of the difficult challenges facing the new democratic government in the immediate post-apartheid period. Higher education was only one area in which new procedures and structures had to be created quickly and simultaneously. Moreover, an important reason that black participation in higher education failed to rise at the same pace as in the early 1990s had to do with the inadequacies of the primary and secondary school systems.

Thus it is hardly surprising that the policies laid out in the 1997 policy paper took so long to implement. Nor is it surprising that the decisive government action of 2002 focused on the relatively manageable—albeit controversial—issues relating to the size and organization of the higher institutions. By doing so it avoided taking on the more difficult task of ensuring high-quality educational opportunities for low-income black students throughout the country.

eleven Conclusion

The story of South Africa's efforts to promote racial equity in the post-apartheid period is inherently compelling. Few countries have ever had the need—much less the political opportunity—to engage in such far-reaching social, political, philosophical, and structural changes on a national scale. The racial inequities of the apartheid system were so egregious and the struggle against that system so intense that South Africa entered its new democratic era with a deep commitment to a multiracial and egalitarian society and with one of the most progressive constitutions of any country in the world.

As part of that commitment, the country embarked on a major overhaul of its state education system. Leaders of the democratically elected government fully understood that South Africa had to create and maintain a quality state education system accessible to everyone if it were going to produce the skilled workers it needed to rejoin the global economy that had shunned it during the later apartheid years. Such a system would also be central to building and maintaining democratic institutions and to fostering the social stability that had eluded South Africa for so many decades and caused so much suffering.

South Africa thus provides a fascinating case study of a country whose education reforms were driven largely by an equity imperative. After examining the policies designed to promote equity through access to education, school finance, curriculum, and higher education, we conclude that South Africa has made great progress along some dimensions.

Along other dimensions, however, equity has remained elusive for reasons largely related to the country's historical legacy and the pressures it faced as a result of the new global economic environment.

Progress toward Equity

South Africa has made significant progress toward racial equity conceived as *equal treatment* of persons of all races. The racially defined state education system inherited from the Nationalists has been replaced with one that is race-blind with respect to student access to particular schools, universities, and technikons and where race no longer plays a role in how public resources are distributed among schools. Further, the Department of Education sent out powerful signals through a new "outcomes-based" curriculum that South Africa is now a multiracial democracy. For those accomplishments the country deserves great praise.

The country been less successful, however, in promoting equity defined as *equal educational opportunity* for students of all races. Though in principle race-blindness means that black learners now have access to any school they choose to attend, including high-quality ones that formerly served only white students, such opportunities are in practice limited to black families in urban areas with the resources to pay substantial school fees, transportation, and other costs. Most black families continue to reside in township and rural areas that were part of the apartheid system, and the overwhelming majority of black learners still attend schools with inferior facilities, poorly trained teachers, and inadequate supplies of textbooks and other teaching resources. Despite the laudable democratic aims of the new Curriculum 2005, the hasty manner in which it was initially implemented did a disservice to the disadvantaged students whom it was intended to help. While the new emphasis on equality of treatment in higher education has helped to transform the previously white universities and technikons, these policies have nearly devastated many of the historically black institutions. In short, South Africa has done little since 1994 to "level the playing field" for all students through redress of the many legacies of apartheid.

Finally, the country has not made much progress toward equity conceived of as *educational adequacy*. South African learners perform abysmally on international comparisons. Repetition and dropout rates among black students are high and matriculation pass rates low, with little evidence of improvement. An adequacy measure of equity need not require that whites and blacks exhibit similar outcomes. What it does require, though, is that outcomes for black students be raised to a minimum threshold that will equip them to function as workers and citizens in the new democratic era. Despite the initial aspirations of the African National Congress (ANC), South Africa has not yet made either the social or educational investments that this standard would require. Overall, then, racial equity in education remains elusive in South Africa.

Why Equity Has Been Elusive

The reasons for this state of affairs fall into three general categories. The first is the powerful legacy of apartheid that both created the political pressure for a more equitable education system and constrained efforts to achieve it. The second is the limited availability of financial and human resources, while the third relates to certain elements of the power-sharing arrangements that emerged from the negotiated settlement.

The Legacy of Apartheid

The long period of colonialism followed by four decades of apartheid hugely complicated South Africa's move to a more racially equitable education system. As shown in chapters 2 and 3, apartheid was ruthlessly effective in separating the races geographically and in privileging the interests of white South Africans. Though the homelands in theory provided a place for Africans to pursue their own aspirations, in practice they served to impoverish much of the African population and to subject them to dysfunctional systems of government, poor schools, and few opportunities for employment. Though a black middle class developed during the apartheid period, the vast majority of Africans emerged from apartheid with low educational attainment, low income, and a scarcity of job opportunities.

The apartheid education system for Africans underinvested in school facilities, provided poor training for teachers and school principals, and followed an impoverished curriculum. Despite some significant investments in that system during the waning years of apartheid, the quality of education provided to most black students in the country as of 1994 was far below the quality that they needed to function in the new era. Moreover, the long struggle against apartheid, much of which was played out in the schools, engendered a destructive distrust of authority within the black schools. In terms of higher education, the placement of universities for blacks in remote locations as well as the staffing of them with second-rate Afrikaans academics and managers produced a set of inferior institutions that could not compete with the more richly endowed former white universities once the latter opened their doors to black students.

The importance of this legacy of inequity for the reform of the education system cannot be overstated. Policymakers did not have the option of simply installing a new breed of managers and teachers imbued with the values of the new era. Rather, they had to work with existing educators who had been trained under the former system, who in many cases were underqualified, and who had worked within the system at a time of great stress and turmoil. Though many of these schools were clearly disorganized and inefficient, changes had to be made with sensitivity to the deeply embedded negative attitudes of teachers toward authority. Efforts to keep children in school and to succeed on the matriculation exam were complicated by extensive family poverty, child malnutrition, undereducated parents, and, increasingly, the devastation of families caused by HIV/AIDS.

Investments to address the language challenges faced by African pupils have been stymied in part by the country's long history of using language policy for political purposes. Moreover, to cost-conscious national policymakers, the managerial inefficiency and low quality of the apartheid-era black universities provided an appealing, though not necessarily correct, rationale for not investing in them. All in all, the challenges involved in fashioning a more equitable system were huge, and even in the best of circumstances reform efforts would have had to play out over an extended period of time.

Limited Financial and Human Capacity

In fact, circumstances were far from ideal for equity-oriented reforms. In chapter 4 we identified three specific constraints within which the education reforms had to be developed and implemented: the sharing of power that emerged from the negotiated settlement, the lack of new resources for education, and the limitations of managerial capacity. Though all three clearly affected the nature of the education reforms, it is the latter two—limitations of financial and human resources—that emerged as the restrictive factors insofar as equal educational opportunity and educational adequacy are concerned.

Under the constraint of constant funding, education policymakers in South Africa were unable to move very far beyond equal treatment toward the more expensive goals of equal opportunity and adequacy. In particular, the country has not come close to marshaling the investments in basic school infrastructure—including facilities, electricity, sanitation, and media centers—needed to meet its obligation to provide basic facilities to all children. Although it made some early progress in building new schools in poor provinces, the program lagged. Capital spending slowed way down during the late 1990s and only now is beginning to rise again. Similarly, the lack of resources has made it difficult to raise the qualifications of large numbers of teachers to the prescribed minimum level, or to provide the professional development needed by all teachers on an ongoing basis. While the norms and standards program for nonpersonnel spending was a valiant effort to help poor schools, its impact to date has been limited, mainly because of the lack of funds in most provinces.

South Africa was not able to raise its spending on education in part because policymakers thought education spending was already too high in comparison with that in other countries. A second factor was the government's decision to adopt an austere growth, employment, and redistribution program (GEAR), the negative effects of which were exacerbated by a slowdown in the world economy (see chapter 4). In hindsight, it is tempting to criticize South Africa for adopting GEAR rather than pursuing a more Keynesian economic strategy to reduce unemployment. Though successful in reducing the deficit, the GEAR approach was singularly unsuccessful in attracting foreign investment and in generating jobs. Further, the resulting rate of economic growth was far below that needed to finance the types of investments proposed under the ANC's Reconstruction and Development Program.

Despite GEAR's limitations, it is not appropriate to second-guess South African policymakers from this later vantage point. Though many people around the world clearly wanted the new government of South Africa to succeed, the political shift from white to black power made many investors nervous and left South Africa fragile and vulnerable. Given the neoliberal economic wisdom prevailing in the international investment community and strongly promoted by international organizations such as the World Bank and the International Monetary Fund, the large debts that the new government inherited from the apartheid government, and the obvious economic failures of other developing countries that had tried to pursue expansionary populist policies, it is easy to understand why the new government in South Africa concluded it had little choice other than to pursue an austere macro policy.

One interpretation of that decision is that the new government opted for short-run austerity in the hopes of establishing a firm foundation for longer-run prosperity, and perhaps this strategy will indeed serve the country well in the future. In the meantime, there is little doubt that the decision to constrain spending, however necessary it was perceived to be at the time, hindered South Africa's efforts during the late 1990s to promote its progressive social agenda. One can only wonder how things might have been different had the prevailing international economic climate at the time been less neoliberal and more accepting of an old-fashioned Keynesian approach to public spending and economic growth.

Even if more public money had been available for education, however, the country's efforts to promote equity would still have been seriously constrained by the limitations of human capacity. There was a clear lack of managerial capacity at all levels of the education system. Inadequate staffing at the national Department of Education contributed to the inferior training and other difficulties encountered in the implementation of Curriculum 2005. Capacity problems are apparent in all provinces, but are especially acute in poor ones such as Eastern Cape. The inability to fill top managerial slots in that provincial department of education undermined its ability to deliver services and left the competent managers overworked. Within provinces, efforts to move in the direction of quality assurance are severely hampered by a shortage of managers to provide the necessary support to struggling schools. At the school level, the carryover of unqualified principals and teachers from the apartheid era impedes progress toward quality education. Finally, the lack of sufficient managerial capacity in universities and technikons has been cited as a main reason for the need to consolidate institutions.

In the absence of personnel and structures capable of assuming financial and programmatic responsibility for new initiatives, it proved difficult for policymakers to design methods of promoting racial equity in the form of equal opportunity and adequacy. To some, the lesson might be that it would have been undesirable to invest additional money in the system until that capacity could be developed. We believe, however, that more funding was necessary precisely in order to develop capacity. Thus the two constraints—limited funding and limited human capacity—interacted with each other to limit the country's success in promoting equity.

Nowhere are the negative effects of this symbiosis more obvious than in the reform of the curriculum. As an intentionally radical departure from the pedagogical and curricular approaches of the apartheid era, outcomes-based education and its embodiment in Curriculum 2005 required extensive training of teachers. Largely because of cost considerations, the national Department of Education adopted a "cascade" approach whereby limited numbers of educators were trained in the new methods and then charged with training others. All too often, it became a case of "the blind leading the blind," and many teachers were left unprepared to deal with the challenges presented by the new curriculum. Similarly, the lack of funds available for textbooks caused education officials to argue—incorrectly—that textbooks were not really necessary for the implementation of Curriculum 2005. Neither of these problems proved to be serious in historically white schools with competent faculties and adequate libraries, but they clearly undermined teaching and learning in schools serving disadvantaged African and coloured learners. Thus constraints on funding and human capacity have sharply limited the ability of the new curricular approach, one that enjoys wide support among educators and the public at large, to fulfill its potential to promote equity in South African schools.

School Governing Bodies and the Use of School Fees

Another obstacle to the pursuit of equal educational opportunity was the decision to allow significant self-governance of schools in the form of school governing bodies and to encourage such bodies to levy school fees. At the same time that public funds were being distributed more equally across schools, those serving affluent communities were able to enhance the quality of the education they provided by the use of school fees. In addition, through their fee, language, and other policies, such schools were able to influence the mix of students they served. As a result, economic class appears to be replacing race as the determinant of who has access to the former model C schools.

The Outlook for the Future

It is important to keep in mind that education reform in South Africa is still very much a work in progress. As of this writing, the process had been under way for less than a decade. Though equity in the sense of equal educational opportunity or educational adequacy has to date proved to be an elusive goal, some of the basic structures or conditions are in place to generate a more equitable system in the future. By far the most important of these structures is the new federal system itself. Another is the fact that most families still have their children in the public schools. Still other potentially important programs and policies for enhanced equity are in their infancy and will require significantly more attention in the future. Included in this category are systems of quality assurance and support, investments in the human capacity of the education system, and investments in the capacity of children to learn.

A Well-Designed Federal Structure

Although the new federal system is less centralized than the African National Congress would have preferred, it generally does a good job of balancing the political imperative of distributing power to the nine new provinces with equity objectives. Not only did the South African version of federalism give policymakers sufficient immediate authority to pursue educational equity in the sense of equal treatment, but it also established structures that can be used in the future to distribute disproportionately more funds to poorer provinces and schools, and hence to promote equal educational opportunity and educational adequacy, should policymakers have the funds and choose to use them in that way.

A key feature of the federal system is that while the provinces are responsible for delivering social services, including education, the national government still raises and distributes the requisite revenue. As a result, South Africa has avoided one of the major dangers to equity from having education delivered at the provincial level. Because of their historical patterns of economic development, some provinces would inevitably have had much greater revenue-raising capacity, and hence capacity to spend, than others. Instead, the funds raised at the national level are distributed among the provinces in a race-blind and equalizing manner. Though some disparities in education spending across provinces remain, the disparities are far smaller than they would have been had the provinces been empowered to raise their own revenue. Moreover, they are also less than the existing disparities in income and wealth across the provinces.

Though to date this funding structure for education (and other social services) has been used primarily to promote equity in the form of equal treatment, it is sufficiently flexible to be used to pursue equity in its other forms of equal opportunity and educational adequacy. In particular, the formula for distributing the equitable share grants to each province could readily be altered to incorporate factors reflecting the higher costs of educating students in some provinces than in others, as was recommended by the Finance and Fiscal Commission for the 2001–04 budget cycle. In addition, the tool of conditional grants to provinces for specific purposes is available to further specific national equity goals. Conditional grants for education have not been used more extensively to date because a major priority of national policymakers was to give the new provincial legislatures the prerogative of making their own budgetary decisions. As the federal system matures, however, the basic structure is clearly in place to promote equity goals beyond equal treatment.

In addition, the new federal system assigns to the national government, in consultation with the provinces, the responsibility for setting national educational norms and standards. As we explained in chapter 6, the existence of the federal system means that national norms, such as those relating to the allocation of teaching slots or to the distribution of funds for nonpersonnel spending (the so-called norms and standards program), cannot be implemented across the country as a whole but rather only across schools within provinces. Nonetheless, the power to set those national norms has had the desired effects of equalizing the ratio of learners to educators across schools within each province and of forcing the provincial departments of education to distribute nonpersonnel funding in a progressive manner in favor of poor schools. Though the redistributive effects have been limited to date because of tight provincial budgets, the structure is clearly available for national norms that would do more to promote equal educational opportunity and educational adequacy. Recent decisions by the South African cabinet suggest the country is beginning to move in that direction.[1]

Commitment to the Public System and the Role of School Fees

The fact that most learners in South Africa are still in the public schools represents a significant success for education policymakers and bodes well for an equity agenda—but only if pressure is maintained to

1. In a press statement on June 16, 2003, the twenty-seventh anniversary of the Soweto uprising, Education Minister Kader Asmal announced that he was asking the Department of Education to significantly raise the amount of money allocated per learner for nonpersonnel spending for poor learners and to make it uniform throughout the country, presumably with the support of additional national funding.

enhance funding for these schools. That will require new attention to the broad question of the proper balance between reliance on public and private resources for funding schools and, specifically, to policies regarding school fees.

There are some difficult trade-offs here. It is vitally important for South Africa to continue to give most voters a stake in the public school system. Allowing school governing boards to charge fees initially served this purpose by giving middle-class parents of all races strong incentives to keep their children in the state system. As reliance on fees has increased, however, the stake that parents in wealthy schools have in the level of public funding has decreased. At the same time, fees have done little to improve the quality of schools in disadvantaged areas where revenue from fees is low and the opportunity costs of trying to collect them high.

Without disagreeing that school fees were important initially, we believe it may well be time to reexamine fee policies now that the post-apartheid state education system has demonstrated its viability. The challenge is to find politically acceptable ways to preserve the benefits of allowing fees in middle-class schools where parents are willing to pay them, though possibly with some form of limitation, while at the same time providing a base payment in lieu of fees for schools where fees are of little help in improving education quality (see chapter 7).

Quality Assurance and Support Systems

Central to the willingness of the public to support funding for public education, and ultimately to the educational adequacy of the system, is the development of quality assurance and support systems. Quality assurance systems are currently in their infancy in South Africa, with their development to date having been hindered both by the legacy of apartheid and the absence of the financial and human capacity. Capacity is needed not only to develop the tests or whatever other measures that will be used for quality assurance, but also to provide support to ill-trained teachers and failing schools. Given the history of underinvestment in black schools, it would clearly be inappropriate at this point to impose tough accountability provisions designed to be punitive. Instead, accountability needs to be introduced in a constructive and positive manner.

Such an approach would ideally include national testing of a random sample of students in selected primary grades as a way of marking progress of the system over time and providing realistic assessments of where students are and where they need to be in relation to international norms. Test results of this type for primary school students would be far superior to the current reliance on matriculation pass rates as a measure of the progress of the country toward educational adequacy. In addition, accountability would require appraisal systems for teachers that combined evaluation with opportunities for professional development, as well as programs for whole school reform, possibly along the lines of the Education Action Zone program in Gauteng.

Given the legacy of apartheid and the antipathy of educators to external evaluation, such systems will not be easy to introduce and will take time to implement. They will also cost money. Thus quality assurance and accountability should not be viewed as a substitute for more resources, but rather as part of an integrated package of what is needed to promote educational adequacy. On the one hand, more resources are needed to implement such systems and to provide the additional managerial and technical support to educators and schools that are determined to be failing. On the other, attention to quality assurance is necessary to maintain the public's confidence that additional funding for education will be used in a productive way to increase academic quality.

Investments in Human Capacity

Additional investments in physical facilities, especially in historically disadvantaged areas, are undoubtedly a necessary part of a strategy to promote equal educational opportunity. Even more important, however, is the need for additional investments in people, including not only the educators in schools but also managers—from the district level through the provincial level to the national Department of Education.

Every study we have seen forecasts a significant shortage of teachers, particularly, but not limited to, math and science teachers, even in the absence of the effects of HIV/AIDS. Once the adverse effects of HIV/AIDS on the existing stock of teachers are included, the predicted shortfalls are even greater (see chapter 9). Moreover, as of 2000 more than one in five teachers was deemed underqualified despite the relatively low standard of three years of schooling after matriculation. Finally, all teachers are in dire need of ongoing professional development, not only because of the new curriculum but also because new quality assurance systems may be in store.

Educating teachers at either the initial stage or through in-service programs is made difficult by the absence of qualified staff and programs for such training. When the government closed the old colleges of education as part of its restructuring program and moved education training programs to universities and technikons, large numbers of staff from the former teacher colleges left the profession. With the shortage of expertise in teacher education at these institutions, many simply replicated inherited programs, even though they were of low quality and could not provide the skills required under the new more ambitious standards for educators. Further, the geographic distribution of the programs for teacher training in the universities is not well matched to the geographic distribution of the needs for new teachers. For example, Western Cape had five institutions of higher education offering initial teacher education in 2001, whereas Limpopo, with double the number of learners, had only two.[2] The lack of a national plan for teacher development represents a serious obstacle to the development of an equitable education system.

Investments in the Capacity of Children to Learn

The promotion of educational adequacy in South Africa is clearly hampered by powerful social and economic forces over which schools have little control. High unemployment rates in black residential areas lead many students to ask why they should make the effort to persist and succeed in school, and pervasive poverty affects virtually every aspect of school life, from physical security to the ability of parents to support their children's learning. While the education system cannot be expected to solve such problems single-handedly, there are ways in which it can address their impact on the educational process by investing in the capacity of children to learn.

Neither family poverty nor malnutrition are conducive to adequate educational outcomes. Yet large proportions of African families, particularly those in rural areas and ones headed by women, are currently living below any reasonable poverty standard, and many of their children are malnourished. Exacerbating the poverty problem has been a significant increase in unemployment starting in the 1990s and the devastation of HIV/AIDs. Not only will AIDS-related illness reduce the supply of teachers, but it will place severe stress on the system as schools face the additional demands of educating children who are orphaned by the disease. The HIV/AIDS problem swamps all others and will require a

2. Vinjevold (2001a).

major concerted effort by the Departments of Health and Education to address it.

In addition, if South Africa is serious about ensuring adequate educational outcomes for black children, it will need to improve and enhance its school feeding programs and undertake other efforts to enable children to come to school ready to learn. Though school feeding programs run by the Department of Health have been in place for several years, they have not been free from controversy. In Eastern Cape, for example, where the feeding needs are huge, concerns about fraud, corruption, and contaminated peanut butter forced the province to suspend that program in 2002. With the recent transfer of the school feeding program from the national Department of Health to the Department of Education, the latter is now in a stronger position to harness school feeding programs to the goal of educational adequacy and must do so if progress toward that goal is to be made.

Similarly, South Africa will need to pay more attention to early childhood education. The combination of few good preschool programs for black and rural children and the (cost-saving) decision to raise the school-entering age from six to seven means that many black children enter grade 1 not ready to learn. The ANC has long understood this need, as is evident from its 1994 call for a reception year for all students. Although the national Department of Education has instituted a conditional grant for Early Childhood Development, that grant is woefully inadequate, and much more will need to be done to promote educational adequacy for poor black children.[3]

Finally, language policy is central to building pupils' capacity to learn. South Africa has done a disservice to African learners by not making the necessary investments to address the language challenges faced by students who speak one of the African languages at home but who need English to function in the world economy. The language issue is complex and understandably controversial, but it must be resolved in ways that allow learners of all linguistic backgrounds to succeed in school.

Overall Outlook

Unfortunately for South Africa, much of what is needed to further the cause of educational equity defined as equal opportunity or ade-

---

3. Wildeman (2003) illustrates this point with reference to Free State, which has an estimated 80,000 learners eligible for ECD services, only 10 percent of whom would be funded under the national policy finalized in 2001.

quacy will cost money. In addition, the payoffs from some of the required investments could take years to emerge. Though some of them, such as a more robust school feeding program, could generate immediate benefits, the benefits from others—such as investments in the infrastructure for quality assurance and support or for adequate training of teachers and other personnel—will be realized only over a longer period of time, a fact that may make them hard to sell politically.

Consequently, it is difficult to predict how much additional progress South Africa is likely to be able to make in the near future. Much will depend, first, on the growth rate of the economy and the rate of job creation and, second, on how policymakers weigh additional investments in education in relation to those in other areas of pressing need, including health care and programs to provide a social safety net. In retrospect, it appears that South Africa may have lost an important window of opportunity. There was considerable support for educational redress right after the election when the legacy of apartheid was clear and on everyone's mind. The introduction of GEAR and the slowdown of the economy, however, interfered with that progress. As time goes by, and the black middle class becomes increasingly comfortable in its situation, support for additional spending that has a strong redistributive component may be harder to gain.

One thing that is clear about South Africa's future efforts to promote equity in education is that such efforts cannot be based on race alone. Black South Africans emerged from the apartheid era with a strong commitment to the establishment of a nonracial society. This conviction underlay the new government's immediate moves to create a single educational system for all South Africans and to apply race-blind principles to policy areas such as access to education and teacher pay scales. Black members of the Government of National Unity were sensitive to the fact that they were now stewards of a government for *all* South Africans, not merely for blacks who had suffered so mightily under apartheid. Such thinking was one of the reasons that the new government did not rush to the aid of historically black universities and technikons as a sector.

Nevertheless, the need for redress to assist schools that were systematically deprived during more than four decades of apartheid is clear, and the overlap between race and disadvantage is substantial. Ample opportunity exists for programs of redress defined in socioeconomic terms for both schools and institutions of higher education provided such programs are linked to measures of quality assurance.

General Insights from South Africa's Experience

Despite the unique features of South Africa's transition from apartheid to democracy, this country's efforts to promote a racially equitable education system still offer some general insights for education reform in other countries. Though none of these insights is novel, their power comes from the clarity with which they emerge from the South African experience.

One observation is so obvious that it is almost not worth mentioning: *history matters*. It mattered in South Africa not only because apartheid left the new democratic South Africa with the legacy of a grossly uneven playing field but also because—for better or for worse—it strongly influenced subsequent possibilities for leveling the field. In a positive vein, the particular character of the struggle against apartheid, including what many outsiders view as a surprising willingness of Nelson Mandela and other Africans to put past evils behind them, shaped the progressive values that underlay the new constitution and generated support for a multiracial society and commitment to a racially equitable education system.

In a more negative vein, the terms of the negotiated settlement, such as the sharing of power among provinces, directly affected how far and how fast the national government could move toward equalizing resources across the country. Various elements of the struggle against apartheid made it difficult for the country to introduce accountability and quality assurance and to address the complex and politically charged issue of language in schools. Popular resentment of the authoritarian style of apartheid-era pedagogy drove the decision to adopt outcomes-based education and Curriculum 2005, and it can also be seen as contributing to the haste with which these were implemented. Insofar as history matters, policy ideas that work well in one country may not be appropriate for another country or may at a minimum require significant adaptation. That insight is important both to reformers within a country, who need to be cautious in importing apparently successful ideas from other countries, and to external consultants, who need to have a rich and deep understanding of the country's history if their advice is to be useful.

A second insight is that, starting from an inequitable education system, it is difficult if not impossible to promote equity in the sense of equal educational opportunity or educational adequacy without additional public resources. In a word, *resources matter*. Some policymakers may think that equity can be promoted simply by taking resources from the wealthy jurisdictions and schools and giving them to poor jurisdictions and schools. Others might argue that any resources necessary for an equity agenda can be obtained by making schools more efficient or by relying on the private sector to provide school fees. The South African experience illustrates the difficulty with such reasoning. Here we have a country that was far more committed to equity than any other developing country, yet even it could go only so far with limited resources. To be sure, it did succeed in redistributing significant resources away from the rich provinces and schools toward the poor schools. Nevertheless, in the absence of additional public resources, it was unable to take the all-important step of giving poor provinces and poor schools the wherewithal to provide equal educational opportunity or to promote educational adequacy. However, the conclusion that money matters does not imply that it is the only thing that matters.

A third insight is that *implementation matters*. Although some policy initiatives, such as quality assurance and support programs, are still in their infancy, South Africa indisputably has a number of well-designed policies on the books now. What has been lacking in many cases has been the capacity to implement those programs in an efficient, noncorrupt, and effective manner.

Managerial capacity was most clearly lacking within the new provincial governments and education departments of provinces formed out of the former homelands. Likewise, years of authoritarian rule and the struggle against it left a legacy of poor management in many of the township schools. But the capacity problems of the system were by no means limited to the poor provinces. They also undermined many initiatives of the wealthier provinces and of the National Department itself, as we saw in discussions of the initial implementation of Curriculum 2005. Other examples include the department's effort to rationalize the teaching force, which ended up costing the government billions of rand in voluntary severance packages, and the decision to move forward with the restructuring of the higher education system without adequate attention to the costs of implementing the plan. The lesson here is clear: in addition to good intentions and policies, serious reform requires both the managerial capacity to implement programs successfully and close attention to the design of effective implementation strategies.

A final observation is one to which we have repeatedly returned in our discussion: *equal treatment is not sufficient as a guiding principle of equity.* South Africa's experience is particularly interesting because the causes of its unlevel playing field are so clear and so recent. This situation contrasts with that in other countries such as the United States, where substantial time has elapsed since the periods of explicit discrimination in the form of slavery and Jim Crow policies. Hence it is difficult to make a clear link between the injustices of the past and the current situation. In addition, it leaves open the plausible story that the victims of past injustices have in more recent years engaged in behaviors that have contributed to their current plight. By contrast, no one in the South African context could reasonably dismiss the educational plight of the blacks as the result of their own actions. They were clearly the victims of an egregiously unfair system.

South Africa has shown that equity requires aggressive actions to off-set the legacies of the past. Simply moving away from a system in which schools were treated differently because of the race of the students they served to a system in which all schools are treated the same may be a crucial first step. But it is far from sufficient.

Appendix Tables

APPENDIX TABLE A. Estimates of National Enrollment Rates[a]

Source	Proportion of 7- to 13-year-olds enrolled	Gross (by grade)	Net (age appropriate by grade)
EMIS/DIB95	0.998		
OHS95	0.962		
SALDRU	0.953[b]		
EFA 1997			
Grades 1–7		0.965[c]	0.871[c]
EMIS 1999			
Grades 1–7		1.06	0.933
Grades 8-12		0.89	0.614

a. Entries in the first two rows were calculated from data reported by age of student in Luis Crouch and Thaba Mabogoane, "Aspects of Internal Efficiency Indicators in South African Schools: Analysis of Historical and Current Data," *EduSource Data News*, no. 19, December 1997, table 1.

In row 1, the figure is based on enrollment data from the education management information system (EMIS) and on population data from the Demographic Information Bureau (DIB) data set.

In row 2, the figure is from Enrollment and Population: Central Statistical Services, 1995 October Housing Survey (OHS).

The SALDRU estimate was reported in Luis Crouch, "Education Data and the 1996 Census: Some Crucial Apparent Problems & Possible Strategies for Resolution," *EduSource Data News*, no. 24, March 1999, table 6.

EFA 1997 data were reported in Ministry of Education (2000, table 4).

EMIS 1999 gross enrollment figures were reported in *EduSource Data News*, no. 33, June 2001, table 3; net figures were estimated from information in table 2 on appropriately aged learners as a percent of total enrollment for the year 1998. The percentages are 88 percent for primary school students and 69 percent for secondary school students. The gross enrollment rate is defined as the total number of students enrolled in the specified grades divided by the estimated number of children in the appropriate age range for those grades. The net enrollment rate is the number of children of the appropriate age enrolled in the specified grades divided by the estimated number of children in the appropriate age range.

b. Seven- to fifteen-year-olds.

c. Excludes students in independent schools.

APPENDIX TABLE B. Determinants of Matriculation Pass Rates, Western Cape, 2001[a]

Determinant	Basic I	With former department II
Teacher variables		
Learner to educator ratio	−0.0097**	−0.005**
	(6.00)	(2.56)
Average qualification of teachers[b]	0.122**	0.095**
	(3.04)	(2.49)
Percent of teachers underqualified[c]	−0.016**	−0.0065
	(3.10)	(1.30)
School governing body teachers (share)[d]	0.258**	0.181*
Family income		
Community poverty	−0.528**	−0.285**
	(6.59)	(3.25)
Annual school fee	0.000013**	0.000014**
	(2.12)	(2.25)
Other control variables		
Poverty of school conditions	−0.161	−0.138
	(0.96)	(0.88)
Former HOA (white)	. . .	Base
Former DET (black)	. . .	−0.285**
		(5.52)
Former HOR (coloured)	. . .	−0.121**
		(3.14)
Former HOD (Indian)	. . .	−0.011
		(0.08)
Constant	−0.308	−0.089
	(0.59)	(0.16)
Number of observations	277	277
Adjusted R^2	0.62	0.67

**Significant at the 5 percent level.
*Significant at the 10 percent level.

a. Dependent variable is the number of students who passed the matriculation exam as a fraction of all students who took the exam, with those who received endorsements for university entrance weighted at 1.33 an ordinary pass. Equations were estimated by ordinary least squares; t statistics are in parentheses.

b. Based on the teacher qualification scale that runs from 10 to 17.

c. Full qualification is matriculation plus three years, which translates to 13 on the teacher qualification scale.

d. School governing body teachers as a fraction of government-funded teachers.

References

African National Congress. 1994. *A Policy Framework for Education and Training.* Johannesburg.

Ajam, Tania. 2001. "Intergovernmental Fiscal Relations in South Africa." In *Intergovernmental Relations in South Africa: The Challenges of Co-Operative Government,* edited by Norman Levy and Chris Tapscott. Cape Town: Institute for Democracy in South Africa (IDASA).

Aliber, Michael. 2003. "Chronic Poverty in South Africa: Incidence, Causes and Policies." *World Development* 31(3): 473–90.

Anderson, Kermyt J., Anne Case, and David Lam. 2001. "Causes and Consequences of Schooling Outcomes in South Africa: Evidence from Survey Data." *Social Dynamics* 27(1): 37–59.

Appiah, Elizabeth N., and Walter W. McMahon. 2002. "The Social Outcomes of Education and Feedbacks on Growth in Africa." *Journal of Development Studies* 38(4): 27–68.

Asmal, Kader, and Wilmot James. 2001. "Education and Democracy in South Africa Today." In *Why South Africa Matters,* special issue of *Daedalus* 130 (1): 185–204.

August, Diane, and Kenji Hakuta. 1998. *Educating Language Minority Children.* Washington: National Academy Press.

Beinart, William. 2001. *Twentieth-Century South Africa.* Oxford University Press.

Beinart, William, and Saul Dubow. 1995. *Segregation and Apartheid in Twentieth-Century South Africa.* London: Routledge.

Buckland, Peter, and John Fielden. 1994. *Public Expenditure on Education in South Africa, 1987/8 to 1991/92: An Analysis of the Data.* Washington: World Bank.

Bunting, Ian. 2002a. "Funding." In *Transformation in Higher Education: Global Pressures and Local Realities in South Africa,* edited by Nico Cloete and others, 115–46. Cape Town: Juta.

———. 2002b. "Students." In *Transformation in Higher Education: Global Pressures and Local Realities in South Africa,* edited by Nico Cloete and others, 147–80. Cape Town: Juta.

Bunting, Ian, ed. 1994. *A Legacy of Inequality—Higher Education in South Africa.* Rondebosch, South Africa: University of Cape Town Press.

Bunting, Ian, and Nico Cloete. 2000. *Higher Education Transformation: Assessing Performance in South Africa.* Pretoria: Center for Higher Education Transformation.

Burnett, Nicholas, and Raja Bentaouet-Kattan. 2002. *User Fees in Primary Education.* Washington: World Bank.

Carnoy, Martin. 1995. "Structural Adjustment and the Changing Face of Education." *International Labour Review* 134(6): 653–73.

Case, Anne, and Angus Deaton. 1999. "School Inputs and Educational Outcomes in South Africa." *Quarterly Journal of Economics* 114(3): 1047–84.

Center for Education Policy Development (CEPD). 2001. *Transformation of the South African Schooling System: A Report of the Second Year of Education Plus.* Johannesburg.

Chisholm, Linda. 1997. "The Restructuring of South African Education and Training in Comparative Context." In *Education after Apartheid,* edited by Peter Kallaway, Glenda Kruss, Aslam Fataar, and Gari Donn. Cape Town: UCT Press.

———. 2001. "Values, Multiculturalism and Human Rights in Apartheid and Post-Apartheid South African Curriculum." Paper delivered at Conference on Values, Education and Democracy, Cape Town, January.

———. 2002. "Continuity and Change in Education Policy Research." In *The History of Education under Apartheid 1948–1994,* edited by Peter Kallaway. Pinelands, South Africa: Pearson Education South Africa.

———. 2003. "The Politics of Curriculum Review and Revision in South Africa." Paper presented at Seventh Oxford International Conference on Education and Development, September 11. Convened by the U.K. Forum for International Education and Training.

——— 2003. "The State of Curriculum Reform in South Africa: The Issue of Curriculum 2005." In *State of the Nation: South Africa 2003–4,* edited by John Daniel, Adam Habib, and Roger Southall. Cape Town: HSRC Press.

———. 2004. "Introduction." In *Changing Class: Education and Social Change in Post-Apartheid South Africa,* edited by Linda Chisholm. Cape Town: HSRC Press.

Chisholm, Linda, Crain Soudien, Salim Vally, and Dave Gilmore. 1999. "Teachers and Structural Adjustment in South Africa." *Educational Policy* 13(3): 386–401.

Cloete, Nico, and Peter Maassen. 2002. "The Limits of Policy." In *Transformation in Higher Education: Global Pressures and Local Realities in South Africa,* edited by Nico Cloete, Richard Fehnel, Peter Maassen, Teboho Moja, Helence Perold, and Trish Gibbon, 447–90. Cape Town: Juta.

Cloete, Nico, and others, eds. 2002. *Transformation in Higher Education: Global Pressures and Local Realities in South Africa.* Lansdowne, South Africa: Juta.

Colclough, Christopher. 1995. "Report to the Department of Education." Pretoria, South Africa, November.

———. N.d. "Notes on a Scheme for Schools Fees, to be Introduced Voluntarily by Schools." Processed.

Cooper, David, and George Subotzky. 2001. *The Skewed Revolution: Trends in South African Higher Education, 1988–1998.* Bellville: University of the Western Cape, Education Policy Unit.

Crouch, Luis. 1995. *School Funding Options and Medium-Term Budgeting for Education in South Africa.* Consultant's Report prepared for the Department of Education, South Africa.

———. 1999. "Will South Africa Be Able to Afford to Educate Her Children into the 21st Century?" Processed.

———. 2001. *"Turbulence or Orderly Change? Teacher Supply and Demand in the Age of AIDS."* An occasional paper sponsored by the Department of Education, Pretoria.

Crouch, Luis, and Thaba Mabogoane. 2001. "No Magic Bullets, Just Tracer Bullets: The Role of Learning Resources, Social Advantage, and Education Management in Improving the Performance of South African Schools." *Social Dynamics* 27(1): 60–78.

Davenport, T. R. H. 1998. *The Transfer of Power in South Africa.* Cape Town: David Philip.

de Clercq, Francine. 1997. "Effective Policies and the Reform Process: An Evaluation of the New Development and Education Macro Policies." In *Education after Apartheid: South African Education in Transition,* edited by Peter Kallaway, Glenda Kruss, Aslam Fataar, and Gari Donn. Cape Town: UCT Press.

de Klerk, Vivian. 2002. "Language Issues in Our Schools: Whose Voice Counts? Part I: The Parents Speak and Part II: The Teachers Speak." In *Perspectives in Education,* edited by Kathleen Heugh, 20(1): 1–27.

Department of Education. 1995. *White Paper on Education and Training,* Notice 196 of 1995. Pretoria.

———. 1997a. *Education White Paper 3: A Programme for the Transformation of Higher Education.* Pretoria: Republic of South Africa Government Gazette, no. 386 (18207).

———. 1997b. *Committee of Principals: Requirements and Conditions of Matriculation Endorsement and the Issuing of Certificates of Exemption.*

Higher Education Act 101. Government Notice 1226. Pretoria: Republic of South Africa Government Gazette, no. 21805.

———. 1998a. *National Norms and Standards for School Funding.* Pretoria: Republic of South Africa Government Gazette, no. 1934.

———. 1998b. *Regulations for the Creation of Educator Posts in a Provincial Department of Education and the Distribution of Such Posts to the Educational Institutions of Such a Department.* Pretoria: Republic of South Africa Government Gazette, no. 19627.

———. 1999. *Terms and Conditions of Employment of Educators Determined in Terms of Section 4 of the Employment of Educators Act, 1998.* Pretoria: Republic of South Africa Government Gazette, no. 19767.

———. 2000. *South African Curriculum for the Twenty-First Century: Report of the Curriculum 2005 Review Committee.* Presented to the Minister of Education on May 31. Pretoria.

———. 2001. *Education Change and Transformation in South Africa: A Review 1994–2001.* Pretoria.

———. 2003. *Report to the Minister: A Review of the Financing, Resourcing and Costs of Education in Public Schools.* Pretoria.

Donaldson, Andrew. 1992. "Financing Education." In *McGregor's Education Alternatives,* edited by Robin and Anne McGregor. Cape Town: Juta.

Eastern Cape Department of Education. 1997. "Teacher Supply, Utilisation and Development: Existing Realities in the Eastern Cape Province" (October). East London.

———. N.d. *Review of Education Indicators 1995–2000.* East London.

Evans, W. N., S. E. Murray, and R. M. Schwab. 1999. "The Impact of Court-Mandated School Finance Reform." In *Equity and Adequacy in Education Finance: Issues and Perspectives,* edited by Helen F. Ladd, Rosemary Chalk, and Janet Hansen. Committee on Education Finance, National Research Council Report. Washington: National Academy Press.

Financial and Fiscal Commission. 1995. *The Financial and Fiscal Commission's Recommendations for the Allocation of Financial Resources to the National and Provincial Governments for the 1996/97 Fiscal Year.* Pretoria.

———. 1998a. *Public Expenditure on Basic Social Services in South Africa: An FFC Report for UNICEF and UNDP.* Pretoria.

———. 1998b. *The Financial and Fiscal Commission's Recommendations for the Allocation of Financial Resources to the National and Provincial Governments for the 1999/2000 Fiscal Year.* Pretoria.

———. 2000. *Recommendations for 2001–2004 MTEF Cycle.* Pretoria.

Fiske, Edward B., and Helen F. Ladd. 2000. *When Schools Compete: A Cautionary Tale.* Brookings.

———. 2002. "Financing Schools in Post-Apartheid South Africa: Initial Steps toward Fiscal Equity." Paper prepared for International Conference on Education and Decentralisation: African Experiences and Comparative Analysis, Johannesburg, June 10–14.

———. 2004. "Balancing Public and Private Resources for Basic Education: School Fees in Post-Apartheid South Africa." In *Changing Class: Education and Social Change in Post-Apartheid South Africa*, edited by Linda Chisholm. Cape Town: HSRC Press and London: Zed Press.

Fleisch, Brahm. 2002a. *Managing Educational Change: The State and School Reform in South Africa.* Sandton: Heineman.

———. 2002b. "State Formation and the Origins of Bantu Education." In *The History of Education under Apartheid, 1994–98*, edited by Peter Kallaway, 39–52. Pinelands, South Africa: Pearson Education South Africa.

Fuller, Bruce. 1987. "What School Factors Raise Achievement in the Third World?" *Review of Educational Research* 57(3): 255–92.

Gutmann, Amy. 1987. *Democratic Education.* Princeton University Press.

Hall, Graham. 2002. "The Impact of the AIDS Pandemic on Teacher Supply and Demand in South Africa 2001–2010." Paper presented at the HIV/AIDS and the Education Sector Conference, May 31. Pretoria.

Hannum, Emily, and Claudia Buchman. 2003. *The Consequences of Global Educational Expansion: Social Science Perspectives.* Cambridge, Mass.: American Academy of Arts and Sciences.

Hanushek, Eric. 1986. "The Economics of Schooling: Production and Efficiency in Public Schools." *Journal of Economic Literature* 24(13): 1141–77.

———. 1997. "Assessing the Effects of School Resources on Student Performance: An Update." *Educational Evaluation and Policy Analysis* 19(2): 141–64.

Haysom, Nicholas. 2001. "The Origins of Co-Operative Governance: The Federal Debates in the Constitution-Making Process." In *Intergovernmental Relations in South Africa: The Challenges of Co-Operative Government*, edited by Norman Levy and Chris Tapscott. Cape Town: IDASA.

Hedges, Larry V., Richard D. Laine, and Rob Greenwald. 1994. "Does Money Matter? A Meta-Analysis of Studies of the Effects of Differential School Inputs on Student Outcomes." *Educational Researcher* 23(3): 5–14.

Heugh, Kathleen. 1995. "From Unequal Education to the Real Thing." In *Multilingual Education for South Africa*, edited by Kathleen Heugh, Amanda Siegrühn, and Peter Plüddemann, 42–52. Johannesburg: Heinemann.

———. 2002. "The Case against Bilingual and Multilingual Education in South Africa: Laying Bare the Myths." In *Perspectives in Education* 20(1): 171–96. Special issue edited by Kathleen Heugh.

Hillman, Arye L., and Eva Jenkner. 2002. *"User Payments for Basic Education in Low-Income Countries."* International Monetary Fund Working Paper. Washington.

Howie, Sarah J., ed. 1997. *Mathematics and Science Performance in the Middle-School Years in South Africa: A Summary Report of South African Students in the Third International Mathematics and Science Study.* Pretoria: Human Sciences Research Council.

Hunter Report. 1995. *Report of the Committee to Review the Organization, Governance and Funding of Schools.* First Text Copy Edition. Pretoria: Department of Education.

International Monetary Fund. 1997. *IMF Concludes Article IV Consultation with South Africa.* Public Information Notice 97/20. August 25. Washington.

Jansen, Jonathan D. 1990. "Curriculum as a Political Phenomenon: Historical Reflections on Black South African Education." *Journal of Negro Education* 59(2): 195–206.

———. 1999. "Why Outcomes-Based Education Will Fail: An Elaboration." In *Changing Curriculum: Studies on Outcomes-Based Education in South Africa*, edited by Jonathan Jansen and Pam Christie, 145–56. Kenwyn: Juta.

Jansen, Jonathan, and Pam Christie, eds. 1999. *Changing Curriculum: Studies on Outcomes-Based Education in South Africa.* Kenwyn: Juta.

Jimenez, Emmanuel, and Vincent Paqueo. 1996. "Do Local Contributions Affect the Efficiency of Public Primary Schools?" *Economics of Education Review* 15(4).

Kadzamira, Esme, and Pauline Rose. 2001. "Educational Policy Choice and Policy Practice in Malawi: Dilemmas and Disjunctures." Working Paper 124. Institute of Development Studies, Brighton, U.K.

Kallaway, Peter. 2002. "Introduction." In *The History of Education under Apartheid, 1994–98*, edited by Peter Kallaway, 39–52. Pinelands, South Africa: Pearson Education South Africa.

Karlsson, Jenni, Gregory McPherson, and John Pampallis. 2001. "A Critical Examination of the Development of School Governance Policy and Its Implications for Achieving Equity." In *Education and Equity: The Impact of State Policies on South African Education*, edited by Enver Motala and John Pampallis. Cape Town: Heinemann.

Kros, Cynthia. 2002. "W. W. M. Eiselen: Architect of Apartheid Education." In *The History of Education under Apartheid, 1994–98*, edited by Peter Kallaway, 53–73. Pinelands, South Africa: Pearson Education South Africa.

Krueger, Alan B., and Michael Lindahl. 2001. "Education for Growth: Why and for Whom?" *Journal of Economic Literature* 39(4): 1101–36.

Kruss, Glenda 1997. "Educational Restructuring in South Africa at Provincial Level: The Case of the Western Cape." In *Education after Apartheid: South African Education in Transition,* edited by Peter Kallaway, Glenda Kruss, Aslam Fataar, and Gari Donn. Cape Town: UCT Press.

Ladd, Helen F., Rosemary Chalk, and Janet Hansen, eds. 1999. *Equity and Adequacy in Education Finance: Issues and Perspectives.* Committee on Education Finance, National Research Council Report. Washington: National Academy Press.

Ladd, Helen F., and Janet Hansen, eds. 1999. *Making Money Matter: Financing America's Schools.* Washington: National Academy Press.

Liebbrandt, Murray, and Ingrid Woolard. 2001. "The Labour Market and Household Income Inequality in South Africa: Existing Evidence and New Panel Data." *Journal of International Development* 13: 671–89.

Lodge, Tom. 1983. *Black Politics in South Africa since 1945.* London: Longman.

Lodge, Tom, Bill Nasson, Steven Mufson, Hkehla Shubane, and Nokwanda Sithole. 1991. *All, Here, and Now: Black Politics in South Africa in the 1980s.* New York: Ford Foundation; Foreign Policy Association.

Loeb, Susanna. 2001. "Estimating the Effects of School Finance Reform: A Framework for a Federalist System." *Journal of Public Economics* 80:225–47.

Loury, Glenn C. 2002. *The Anatomy of Racial Inequality.* Harvard University Press.

Mandela, Nelson. 1994. *Long Walk to Freedom.* Boston: Little, Brown.

Maylam, Paul. 2001. *South Africa's Racial Past: The History and Historiography of Racism, Segregation, and Apartheid.* Aldershot: Ashgate.

Mda, Thobeka V. 1997. "Issues in the Making of South Africa's Language in Education Policy." *Journal of Negro Education* 66(4): 366–76.

Michie, Jonathon, and Vishnu Padayachee. 1998. "Three Years after Apartheid: Growth, Employment and Redistribution?" *Cambridge Journal of Economics* 22: 623–635.

Ministry of Education. 2000. *Education for All: The South African Assessment Report.* Pretoria.

———. 2001. *National Plan for Higher Education.* Pretoria.

Minorini, Paul, and Stephen D. Sugarman. 1999. "Educational Adequacy and the Courts: The Promise and the Problems of Moving to a New Paradigm." In *Equity and Adequacy in Education Finance: Issues and Perspectives,* edited by Helen F. Ladd, Rosemary Chalk, and Janet Hansen. Washington: National Academy Press.

Moll, Peter G. 1998. "Primary Schooling, Cognitive Skills and Wages in South Africa." *Economica* 65: 263–84.

Motala, Shireen, and Salim Vally. 2002. "People's Education: From People's Power to Tirisano." In *The History of Education under Apartheid, 1994–98,* edited by Peter Kallaway, 174–94. Pinelands, South Africa: Pearson Education South Africa.

Narsee, Hersheela. 2002. *Teacher Development and Support.* Johannesburg: Centre for Education Policy Development, Evaluation and Management.

Nicolaou, Katerina. 2001. "The Link between Macroeconomic Policies, Education Policies and the Education Budget." In *Education and Equity: The Impact of State Policies on South African Education,* edited by Enver Motala and John Pampallis. Sandown, South Africa: Heinemann.

Oxfam. 2001. "Education Charges: A Tax on Human Development." Briefing paper (November 12). Oxford, England.

Pampallis, John. 1991. *Foundations of the New South Africa*. Cape Town: Maskew Miller Longman.

———. 1998. "Decentralization in the New Education System: Governance and Funding of Schooling in South Africa 1992–1997." In *Democratic Governance of Public Schooling in South Africa*, 164–70. Durban: Education Policy Unit (Natal).

———. 2003. "Education Reform and School Choice in South Africa." In *Choosing Choice: School Choice in International Perspective*, edited by David Plank and Gary Sykes, 143–63. New York: Teachers' College Press.

Perry, Helen. 2000. "Is the Education System Delivering to Children?" In *Are Poor Children Being Put First? Child Poverty and the Budget,* edited by Shaamela Cassiem, Helen Perry, Mastoera Sadan, and Judith Streak. Cape Town: IDASA.

Plank, David N., and Gary Sykes. 2003. *Choosing Choice: School Choice in International Perspective*. New York: Teachers' College Press.

Price, Robert M. 1991. *The Apartheid State in Crisis: Political Transformation in South Africa, 1975–1990*. Oxford University Press.

Rawls, John. 2001. *Justice as Fairness: A Restatement,* edited by Erin Kelly. Belknap Press.

Reagan, Timothy G. 1987. "The Politics of Linguistic Apartheid: Language Policies in Black Education in South Africa." *Journal of Negro Education* 56(3): 299–312.

Republic of South Africa. 1994. *White Paper on Reconstruction and Development*. Government Gazette no. 353(16085). Cape Town: Ministry in the Office of the President for General Information.

———. 2001a. *Budget Review*, Appendix E (Explanation Memorandum on the Division of Revenue). February. Pretoria: National Treasury.

———. 2001b. *Intergovernmental Fiscal Review, 2001*. Pretoria: National Treasury.

Reschovsky, Andrew, and Howard Chernick. 2001. *Financing Health, Education, and Welfare in the New South Africa*. La Follette School of Public Affairs Policy Report 12(1). Madison, Wis.

Robbins, David. 2001. *Education Pathfinders: A Short History of the Joint Education Trust*. Braamfontein, South Africa: Joint Education Trust.

Sampson, Anthony. 1999. *Mandela: The Authorized Biography*. Alfred A. Knopf.

Seekings, Jeremy. 2000. *The UDF: A History of the United Democratic Front in South Africa 1983–1991*. Cape Town: David Philip.

———. 2001. *Making an Informed Investment: Improving the Value of Public Expenditure in Primary and Secondary Schooling in South Africa*. Report for the Parliament of South Africa, commissioned by the Standing Committee on Public Accounts.

Simkins, Charles. 2002. "The Jagged Tear: Human Capital, Education, and AIDS in South Africa, 2002–2010." *CDE Focus*. Occasional Paper 7 (March).

Soobrayan, Bobby. 1998. "People's Education for People's Power" (originally published in 1990). In *Democratic Governance of Public Schooling in South Africa: A Record of Research and Advocacy from the Education Policy Unit (Natal)*, 30–36. Durban, South Africa: Education Policy Unit.

South African Institute of Race Relations. 2001. *South Africa Survey 2001/2002*. Johannesburg.

———. 1997. *South Africa Survey 1997/1998*. Johannesburg.

Sparks, Allister. 1990. *The Mind of South Africa*. Boston: Little, Brown.

———. 1996. *Tomorrow Is Another Country: The Inside Story of South Africa's Road to Change*. University of Chicago Press.

Spitz, Richard, with Matthew Chaskalson. 2000. *The Politics of Transition: A Hidden History of South Africa's Negotiated Settlement*. Johannesburg: Witwatersrand University Press.

Statistics South Africa. 2000. *Measuring Poverty in South Africa*. Pretoria.

Strauss, J. P., and M. A. Burger. 2000. *Monitoring Learning Achievement Project, Eastern Cape*. Pretoria: Department of Education.

Swilling, Mark, and Bev Russell. 2002. *The Size and Scope of the Non-Profit Sector in South Africa*. Co-published by Graduate School of Public and Development Management (University of Witwatersrand) and the Centre for Civil Society (University of Natal).

Taylor, Nick, Johan Muller, and Penny Vinjevold. 2003. *Getting Schools Working: Research and Systemic School Reform in South Africa*. Cape Town: Pearson Education South Africa.

Taylor, Nick, and Penny Vinjevold. 1999. *Getting Learning Right*. Report of the President's Education Initiative Research Project. Johannesburg: Joint Education Trust.

United Nations Development Program (UNDP). 2001. *Commitment to Education: Public Spending*. Human Development Report.

United Nations Educational, Scientific, and Cultural Organization (UNESCO). 1998. *Wasted Opportunities: When Schools Fail*. Paris.

———. 2000a. *Final Report of the World Education Forum*. Paris.

———. 2000b. *Dakar Framework for Action*. Paris.

Vally, Salim, and Console Tleane. 2001. "The Rationalisation of Teachers and the Quest for Social Justice in Education in an Age of Fical Austerity." In *Education and Equity: The Impact of State Policies on South African Education*, edited by Enver Motala and John Pampallis. Sandown, South Africa: Heinemann.

Vally, Salim, and Yolisa Dalamba. 1999. *Racism, "Racial Integration" and Desegregation in South African Public Secondary Schools*. Johannesburg: South African Human Rights Commission.

van der Berg, Servaas. 2001. "An Analysis of the Impact of Resource Inputs and Socio-Economic Status on South African Education Using Multiple Data

Sets." Paper to the Bi-Annual Conference of the Economic Society of South Africa, Johannesburg, September 13–14.

———. 2001. "Resource Shifts in South African Schools after the Political Transition." *Development Southern Africa* 18(4): 309–25.

van der Berg, Servaas, and Ronelle Burger. 2002. "Education and Socio-Economic Differentials: A Study of School Performance in the Western Cape." Conference on Labour Markets and Poverty in South Africa, Muldersdrift Lodge, Johannesburg, South Africa.

Vinjevold, Penny. 2001. "Provision of Initial Teacher Education in 2001: Institutions, Student Numbers and Types of Programmes." Paper prepared to inform the national Department of Education's National Teacher Education Plan. Johannesburg: Joint Education Trust.

Weber, Keith Everard. 1992. *Learning through Experience: An Analysis of Student Leaders' Reflections on the 1985–86 Revolt in Western Cape Schools.* Master of philosophy thesis, University of Cape Town.

Weeks, John. 1999. "Stuck in Low Gear? Macroeconomic Policy in South Africa, 1996–98." *Cambridge Journal of Economics* 23(6): 795–811.

Whiteford Andrew, and Dirk Ernst Van Seventer. 2000. "South Africa's Income Distribution in the 1990s." *Studies in Economics and Econometrics* 24(3): 7–30.

Wieder, Alan. 2002. "Informed Apartheid: Mini-Oral Histories of Two Cape Town Teachers." In *The History of Education under Apartheid, 1994–98*, edited by Peter Kallaway, 197–210. Pinelands, South Africa: Pearson Education South Africa.

Wildeman, Russell. 2001a. "A Progress Report on the Implementation of the Norms and Standards for School Funding 2000." Brief no. 76. IDASA Budget Information Service. Cape Town: IDASA.

———. 2001b. "School Funding Norms 2001: Are More Poor Learners Benefiting?" Brief no. 79. IDASA Budget Information Service. Cape Town: IDASA.

———. 2003. "Public Expenditure in Education." In *Human Resources Development Review 2003: Education, Employment, and Skills in South Africa*, edited by A. Kraak and H. Perold. Cape Town: HSRC Press and Michigan State University Press.

Wilson, Francis. 2001. "Employment, Education, and the Economy." In *South Africa Survey 2001/2002*, 3–32. Johannesburg: South African Institute of Race Relations.

Wolpe, Harold. 1995. "Capitalism and Cheap Labour Power in South Africa: From Segregation to Apartheid." In *Segregation and Apartheid in Twentieth Century South Africa*, edited by William Beinart and Saul DuBow. New York: Routledge.

Woods, Donald, and Mike Bostock. 1986. *Apartheid: A Graphic Guide.* London: Camden Press.

Index

Abrahams, Shafiek, 47–48
Accountability, 193–97, 242
Active learning, 155, 163
Additive multilingual instruction
    model, 191, 192–93
Adequacy approach. *See* Educational
    adequacy
Administration and management,
    school system: authority, 67–69, 84,
    238; authorization for fees, 131–32;
    challenges for post-apartheid
    reform, 75–77, 237, 247–48;
    financial control, 85; higher educa-
    tion institutions, 203; legacy of
    apartheid system, 235; school
    autonomy, 83, 85–86, 238; school
    governing bodies, 84–85; structure,
    63, 83–84
Admissions: discrimination in, 85,
    99–100, 142–43; fee policy and,
    142–43; language and, 94–95; poli-
    cymaking authority, 85. *See also*
    Enrollment patterns
Adult education and training, 13, 61
Affirmative action. *See* Redress
African National Congress, 17, 28–30,
    42; in Eastern Cape province, 79;
    transition planning, 61–69, 71, 73,
    135; in Western Cape province, 79

Africans, 4; apartheid educational
    system for, 43, 44; educational
    attainment and literacy, 56–57;
    higher education enrollment and
    graduation, 213–19; historically
    black colleges, 46, 201, 205–06;
    household income, 53–54; language
    of instruction, 191–93, 244; math
    instruction, 180–82; native peoples
    of South Africa, 18; origins and
    development of South Africa, 18,
    19; racial distribution in school sys-
    tem, 86–92; socioeconomic status at
    transition, 11
Afrikaans language, 18, 19, 43–44, 190
Afrikaners, 18, 19, 21–24, 69, 204–05
Angola, 30, 35
Apartheid system: demise of, 2–3, 17,
    27–39; educational reforms in
    1990s, 50–51; educational system
    resistance to, 47–50; educational
    system under, 3, 9, 41–47; enforce-
    ment, 27–28, 32–33; higher educa-
    tion, 203–06; inequities of, 2; lan-
    guage policies, 43–44; legacy of,
    6–7, 52–59, 102, 194, 202, 234–35,
    246; origins of, 1, 17, 23–24; politi-
    cal enfranchisement, 9; principles of,
    24–25; racial classifications in, 4–5;

Mack

Mock